AUTHOR'S NOTE

Focus: The Future of Your Company [...] book written with the help of my dau[...]

In the ten years since our partnersh[...] into a first-class marketing strategist. She has been widely quoted in media like the *Wall Street Journal* and the *New York Times*.

In October 2002, *Business 2.0* magazine named Laura as a "management guru" of the year alongside such high-profile authors as Larry Bossidy, Noel Tichy, and C.K. Prahalad.

She has also become a full partner in our publishing endeavors. Since *Focus* was first published, Laura and I have written four other books: *The 22 Immutable Laws of Branding, The 11 Immutable Laws of Internet Branding, The Fall of Advertising & the Rise of PR,* and our latest *The Origin of Brands*.

But *Focus* remains our most basic book. Many people have told us that of all the "Ries" books they have read, *Focus* is their favorite because it's the one book that distills all of our marketing concepts in a simple and unified way.

Focus is also the one book that has had the most effect on our own business which is consulting with large corporations, primarily Fortune 500 firms. We have taken our own advice and focused our business. Our letterheads, our business cards, our brochures and our Web site say: "Ries & Ries, *Focusing Consultants.*"

I wish I could also report that since the 1996 publication of *Focus,* companies in general have become more focused. But it's not true. Corporate America rarely runs out of reasons to reach out into new directions, to get into new businesses, to get into new markets, to get into new territories.

To our loyal readers it should come as no surprise that the Four Horsemen of the Apocalypse are named Diversification, Line Extension, Synergy, and Convergence. And they continue to wreak havoc in the corridors of Corporate America.

• Diversification is the first horseman. The late Coca-Cola chairman Roberto Goizueta was criticized for not taking his company into other businesses, like PepsiCo did with its acquisitions of Pizza Hut, Taco Bell, and Kentucky Fried Chicken.

"There's a perception in this country," replied Goizueta, that you're better off if you're in two lousy businesses than if you're in one good one—that you're spreading your risk. It's crazy." We agree.

See Chapter 6, A Tale of Two Colas, in which we recommend that PepsiCo spin off its restaurant chains. That's exactly what they did, a year after the *Focus* book was published.

• Line Extension is the second horseman. Under the general approach of "taking advantage of the equity we have in our brands," many companies spend endless hours trying to figure out how to take their brand names and use them in other categories. It's usually an exercise in frustration.

IBM, for example, put its mainframe name on personal computers (the IBM PC). In the twenty-three years that IBM marketed personal computers, they reportedly lost $15 billion. This year they finally threw in the towel and sold the business to Lenovo, a Chinese company, for the bargain price of $1.5 billion. If IBM can't make line extension work, why should you expect your company to do so?

What should IBM have done? The obvious answer was to give its personal computer brand a different name. See Chapter 12, Building a Multistep Focus.

Also you might want to check Chapter 13, Disciplining a Dinosaur, which recommends that IBM focus on "open" operating system software, which they finally did several years ago. According to press reports, IBM is spending a reported one billion dollars a year developing and promoting its Linux strategy. Good for them.

• Synergy is the third horseman. If diversification and line extension fail to justify a company's expansion, there's always the excuse of "synergy." One plus one equals three. (Except that one plus one normally works out to one-and-a-half.)

Take Hewlett-Packard's merger with Compaq, spearheaded by HP's former CEO Carly Fiorina. According to *The Economist*, "Ms. Fiorina laboured on through the criticisms, doggedly defending her merger with Compaq and insisting that 'synergies' would eventually make HP a leader in all of its businesses."

Synergy strikes out again. If you try to stand for everything, you lose focus. With the Compaq merger, the new bulked-up Hewlett-

Packard tried to stand for everything from enterprise storage and servers to consulting and outsourcing services. Not to mention printers and personal computers.

Compare Hewlett-Packard before and after the Compaq merger. In the seven years before the merger, HP had sales of $296.3 billion and net profits after taxes of $18.7 billion, or a net profit margin of 6.3 percent.

What happened after the merger? Their net profit margin dropped to 2.4 percent.

No wonder Carly Fiorina was fired.

• Convergence is the latest and greatest horseman and the one likely to cause the most trouble. See Chapter 3, The Driving Force of Division. (Today we call the driving force "divergence" to contrast its difference with "convergence.")

Nobody has bought the convergence line like the consumer electronics industry. Almost every major company in the field has publicly endorsed the concept.

Headline of a recent Sony advertisement: "Convergence: An empowering blend of audio, video, and information technologies." When you make everything, as Sony does, convergence can seem like an answer to your prayer.

Unfortunately, Sony makes everything except money. In the last decade Sony's net profits after taxes were just 9/10th of one percent of sales.

There's one focused company in the consumer electronics field, Nintendo. The company makes only videogames and videogame players.

Compare a focused company (Nintendo) with an unfocused company (Sony). Even though Nintendo is 1/13th the size of Sony, Nintendo made more money in the last decade than Sony. On average, Nintendo makes a net profit of 13.9 percent after taxes.

As a matter of fact, Nintendo made more money in the past decade than the six largest Japanese consumer electronics companies combined, even though they were (in terms of revenues) 70 times Nintendo's size.

That's the power of focus.

—Al Ries
Atlanta, Georgia, 2005

Also by Al Ries

The 22 Immutable Laws of Marketing

Positioning: The Battle for Your Mind

Marketing Warfare

Horse Sense: The Key to Success Is Finding a Horse to Ride

Bottom-Up Marketing

FOCUS

THE FUTURE OF YOUR COMPANY DEPENDS ON IT

AL RIES

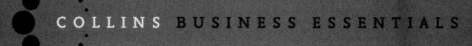

COLLINS BUSINESS ESSENTIALS

*Dedicated to Jack Trout, the best business partner
any person could have*

A hardcover edition of this book was published in 1996 by HarperBusiness, an imprint of HarperCollins Publishers.

FOCUS. Copyright © 1996, 2005 by Al Ries. All rights reserved. Printed in the United States of America. No part of this book may be used or reproduced in any manner whatsoever without written permission except in the case of brief quotations embodied in critical articles and reviews. For information address HarperCollins Publishers, 10 East 53rd Street, New York, NY 10022.

HarperCollins books may be purchased for educational, business, or sales promotional use. For information please write: Special Markets Department, HarperCollins Publishers, 10 East 53rd Street, New York, NY 10022.

First paperback edition published 1997

Designed by Caitlin Daniels

The Library of Congress has catalogued the hardcover edition as follows:

Ries, Al.
    Focus: the future of your company depends on it / Al Ries. — 1st ed.
      p. cm.
    ISBN 0-88730-764-7
    1. Marketing—Management. 2. Success in business. I. Title.
  HF5415.R5438   1996
  658.8—dc20   95-53946

ISBN-10: 0-06-079990-0
ISBN-13: 978-0-06-079990-8

07 08 09 ❖ / RRD(H) 10 9 8 7 6 5 4 3 2

CONTENTS

PREFACE

After spending most of my adult life working in marketing and studying the practice of marketing, I've written a book on how to focus a corporation.

The book is devoted to the real objective of the marketing process, which is not just selling a product or service. It's finding the future.

The primary job of corporate management is to find the future. Not just the future in general, but specific futures for the corporations under their care. A focus is the future in the sense that it makes a prediction about where the future lies and then takes specific steps to make that future happen.

That's where the subject of marketing comes in.

"Any business enterprise has two, and only two, basic functions," writes Peter Drucker, "marketing and innovation."

"Marketing is the distinguishing, the unique function of the business," continues Mr. Drucker. "A business is set apart from all other human organizations by the fact that it markets a product or a service. Neither Church, nor Army, nor School, nor State does that. Any organization that fulfills itself through marketing a product or a service is a business. Any organization in which marketing is either absent or incidental is not a business and should never be run as if it were one."

It's about time that marketing received the recognition it deserves. Except that Peter Drucker wrote these words in *The Practice of Management,* a book first published in 1954. It's taken quite a while for Mr. Drucker's concept to reach the boardrooms of Corporate America.

But then again, a corporation changes its emphasis very slowly.

After World War I, the emphasis was on manufacturing. The art of management was embodied in the time-and-motion studies of Frederick Taylor. Business success went to those companies that could get their products out the door faster and cheaper than the competition.

After World War II, the emphasis gradually shifted to finance. The art of management was embodied in the "portfolio" concept. Business success went to those corporations that did the best job of buying and selling companies in order to put together a high-yielding portfolio.

Where are we today? Both the manufacturing and the financial aspects of management seem to have run their course. Today the emphasis is on marketing.

What do Bill Gates (Microsoft), Bert Roberts (MCI), Ross Perot (Perot Systems), Sam Walton (Wal-Mart), Mike Harper (ConAgra), Fred Turner (McDonald's), Michael Eisner (Walt Disney), John Smale (Procter & Gamble), Robert Goizueta (Coca-Cola), and Roger Smith (General Motors) have in common?

You might recognize these men as some of the most celebrated chief executives of the past decade. Actually, they are that and also, according to *Advertising Age* magazine, "Marketers of the Year" from 1985 to 1994. (Michael Eisner repeated in 1995.)

Advertising Age recognizes the reality of business today. The chief executive is also the chief marketing executive. "Marketing," Hewlett-Packard cofounder David Packard once said, "is too important for the marketing department."

Arguably the most successful company of the past decade is Microsoft. Here's what Lou Gerstner of IBM has to say about Bill Gates and his company, "Our biggest competitor in software is not a very good technical company. But it's one of the best marketing companies I've ever seen, and I've spent twenty years in marketing."

What's a marketing person doing writing a management book, you might be thinking? Good question.

An even better question: What's a management person anyway?

Answer: A marketing person who can read a balance sheet and a profit-and-loss statement.

INTRODUCTION
To the Collins Business Essentials Edition 2005

By Laura Ries, President, Ries & Ries, Atlanta Georgia

It was an exciting time back in 1994 when I first started working with my dad.

The Internet was just getting off the ground so we rushed to be among the first to stake out a "name" claim. Luckily we were able to latch onto "www.ries.com." (Thank goodness, our name wasn't Smith or Jones.)

The Internet was important for another reason. My dad had put me in charge of research for the *Focus* book he was working on. In those days, research usually meant many long and arduous trips to the library, a chore I distinctly disliked during my days at Northwestern. The Internet changed all that.

Now, with a few mouse clicks, you could assemble an enormous array of information which is exactly what I did to supply much of the data for the first edition of *Focus,* which came out in 1996.

Unlike the five previous books by Al Ries, *Focus* is different. It's longer and more detailed. It also contains many more facts, figures, and case histories than his other books, again thanks to the Internet.

Since then, we have continued the same pattern in our books (*The 22 Immutable Laws of Branding, The 11 Immutable Laws of Internet Branding, The Fall of Advertising & the Rise of PR* and *The Origin of Brands*). In our opinion, it's not enough to state a marketing concept or principle, supported by a case history or two. To demonstrate the validity of the principle, you must dissect the numbers.

In other words, you must look at profit and loss, not just positioning and strategy. An idea or concept may sound good, may even get some favorable write-ups in the media, but does it work financially?

After all, the bottom line is the bottom line. That's where success or failure is measured. If an idea doesn't make money, it doesn't work, no matter what the critics might say.

But that's not enough. In addition to analyzing the financial performance of many different companies, we also try to consider two other factors: time and competition.

Take time. What works in the short term doesn't always work in the long term. Sometimes it take decades for an unfocused company to become unraveled.

Take competition. What works in the absence of competition doesn't always work in the presence of focused competitors.

The airline industry is a good example of these two forces at work. Once upon a time, the industry was flying high. In 1975, the ten biggest airlines in America were: United, Eastern, Delta, American, TWA, Allegheny, Northwest, Braniff, Western, and Pan American. Total revenues for the scheduled U.S. airline industry for the previous decade was $102.1 billion and net profits after taxes were $1.6 billion, or 1.6 percent.

Today, Eastern, TWA, Braniff, and Pan American are gone. Allegheny is now USA Airways and Western was bought by Delta. And the airline industry is in deep trouble thanks to loss of focus and the arrival of focused competition.

Take American, for example. In the last 10 years, American Airlines took in $180 billion in revenues and managed to lose almost a billion dollars.

This is the airline that is widely admired for a number of marketing innovations including the launch of the first frequent flyer program.

It's not only American that has crashed financially. In the last 10 years, the five largest U.S. airlines (American, United, Delta, Northwest, and Continental) rang up $657 billion in revenues and racked up $646 million in losses.

What's wrong with the airline industry is also what's wrong with many companies in Corporate America. Management makes decisions that are right in the short term and wrong in the long term. As a result, they lose focus on their core business.

Go back in history. Whenever an airline came to a fork in the sky, they took both forks. One of the first decisions that had to be made was, Should we carry passengers or should we carry cargo?

"Let's take both forks," was the almost unanimous reply. "We have extra space under the passenger compartments, so it's a no-brainer." So every major airline in America carries both passengers and cargo.

Not very much cargo, though. American Airlines' cargo revenue last year was only $558 million, or three percent of revenues. In comparison, cargo revenue last year at FedEx was $24.7 billion. And they managed to make $838 million in profits instead of losing a billion like American did.

Both forks thinking is very pervasive, however. At one point in time, United Parcel Service had the dumb idea of putting seats on its planes on the weekends and flying charter passengers.

The next fork in the sky for the airline industry was passenger destinations. Should we fly to business or should we fly to vacation destinations?

"Let's take both forks," was the almost unanimous reply. "Why should we limit ourselves to one type of destination? Houston or Hawaii? We can do both."

The next fork in the sky was the scope of operations. Should we fly domestic or should we fly international?

"Let's take both forks," was the almost unanimous reply. So every major U.S. airline flies passengers to both domestic and international cities.

The next fork in the sky was class of service. Should we offer first class, business class or coach service?

"Let's take all three forks," was the almost unanimous reply. So every major airline has multiple classes of service.

In retrospect, it's easy to see the fallacy of an all-forks strategy. But in the short term, many of these marketing moves increased revenues and profits. It's only in the long term, and in the presence of narrowly-focused competition, does an all-forks strategy fall apart.

Competition is the killer. In the airline industry it was the arrival of Southwest, the one-fork airline. Business destinations only, no vacation locations. Coach class only, no first or business class service. Domestic flights only, no international service.

No forks on Southwest flights either. The airline serves no food. Won't carry pets. Doesn't allow advance seating reservations or inter-airline baggage exchange.

As a result of its one-fork strategy, Southwest Airlines can operate its system with only one type of aircraft, the Boeing 737. Delta, for example, operates six types of aircraft, not including aircraft operated by Delta Connection subsidiaries ComAir and Atlantic Southeast Airlines.

A narrow focus can greatly improve operations. In Southwest's case, scheduling and maintenance is much easier to manage. If your mechanics are servicing only one type of aircraft, they can do a better job. (In 31 years of operation, Southwest Airlines has never had a passenger fatality.)

A narrow focus can greatly improve profits. In the last 10 years, Southwest Airlines took in $44.3 billion in revenues and had net income after taxes of $3.6 billion, or an astounding net profit margin of 8.1 percent. (Even in its best years, the U.S. airline industry never reached this level of profitability.)

On the stock market, Southwest Airlines is currently worth $12.4 billion, or more than three times as much as American, United, Delta, Northwest, and Continental . . . combined.

So what are America's all-forks airlines doing to counter the Southwest threat? Do you suppose they are getting the message that the road to success is "narrowing the focus?"

Not at all. They are meeting the threat posed by Southwest (along with JetBlue and AirTran) with their usual strategy. When you reach a fork in the sky, take both forks.

Should we run a full-service airline or a no-frills airline?

"Let's take both forks," is the usual approach. So Delta Air Lines launches Song. And United Airlines launches Ted.

And what can you say about United's idea of launching a premium service (p.s.) on its transcontinental flights? So now in addition to first, business and coach fares, United will now have first p.s., business p.s., and coach p.s. fares.

P.S. to United: This isn't going to work.

You'll find "all forks" thinking in almost every company, in almost every industry. Since the original *Focus* book was published, the problem has not gone away. It may be even worse today as companies strive to meet short-term financial goals.

That's why we believe the *Focus* book will continue to have relevance for today's managers in today's competitive environment.

INTRODUCTION

The sun is a powerful source of energy. Every hour the sun washes the earth with billions of kilowatts of energy. Yet with a hat and some sunscreen you can bathe in the light of the sun for hours at a time with few ill effects.

A laser is a weak source of energy. A laser takes a few watts of energy and focuses them in a coherent stream of light. But with a laser you can drill a hole in a diamond or wipe out a cancer.

When you focus a company, you create the same effect. You create a powerful, laserlike ability to dominate a market. That's what focusing is all about.

When a company becomes unfocused, it loses its power. It becomes a sun that dissipates its energy over too many products and too many markets.

Whither Corporate America? Are companies focusing themselves to develop the power of a laser or are they trying to outshine the sun?

The sun seems to be winning.

In the past few decades an explosion of new goods and services has hit the marketplace. The combination of rapid technological development and less costly production techniques has led to a massive increase in the number and variety of products available to consumers everywhere.

Computers, copiers, color television, video cameras and recorders, cellular phones, facsimile equipment, the list is endless.

Existing companies responded by expanding their product lines. General Electric, a manufacturer of electrical equipment, got into television sets, jet engines, computers, plastics, financial services, and a host of other products and services unrelated to their core electrical lines. And so did virtually every company in the world from American Express to Zenith.

Today the bloom is off the rose. It should have been obvious that a company cannot keep expanding its product line forever. You reach a point of diminishing returns. You lose your efficiency, your competitiveness, and most ominous of all, your ability to manage a diverse collection of unrelated products and services.

You become a red giant, a burned-out hulk of a star hundreds of times larger than the sun, but with a surface temperature half as hot. Red giants have included companies like General Motors; IBM; and Sears, Roebuck.

Stars can't be focused, but companies can. That is the message of this book. The time has come to develop a company's power by narrowing its focus.

Fortunately some chief executives have already gotten the message. Recently, the media has reported many examples of companies that have focused or refocused their operations.

Even mighty General Electric is no longer expanding; it's contracting. In the past decade, the company has sold hundreds of businesses and cut its workforce almost in half. General Electric has sold off major businesses like computers, television equipment, and small appliances.

Mathematically, of course, annual growth rates of 10, 15, or 20 percent are impossible to sustain over an extended period of time. Last year General Motors had revenues of $155 billion. If the company grew at an annual rate of 20 percent, in twenty-one years GM would be a $7.1 trillion Red Giant, larger than the current gross domestic product.

What you are seeing today is the beginning of a reaction to this overexpansion. Instead of expanding, some companies are going in the opposite direction. They are getting back to basics. They are learning the lesson of the laser. How to focus.

And so should you. The future of your company depends on it.

THE UNFOCUSING OF CORPORATE AMERICA

What's the driving force in Corporate America? In a word, growth.

Management demands substantial increases in annual sales and profits, even when companies are in markets that show no overall growth.

Predictably, in order to meet these targets, companies offer more varieties and flavors. Or they branch out into other markets. Or they acquire other firms or products. Or they set up joint ventures.

Whether you call this expansion process "line extension" or "diversification" or "synergy," it's the process itself, the urge to grow, that causes companies to become unfocused.

That's why a company like IBM can have $63 billion in revenues and still lose $8 billion. And General Motors can have $133 billion in revenues and still lose $23 billion.

While growth might be an admirable result of other initiatives, the pursuit of growth for its own sake is a serious strategic error. It's the major reason why so many American corporations have become unfocused.

Chief executive officers have been paying the price for their strategic mistakes. There's no question that many CEOs have made strategic errors that have unfocused their companies. Never in history have so many chief executives been handed their hat and told to go home by their own boards of directors.

To name a few: James Robinson at American Express, John Sculley at Apple, Anthony D'Amato and Ervin Shames at Borden, Barry

Gibbons at Burger King, Rod Canion at Compaq, Ken Olsen at Digital Equipment, Kay Whitmore at Eastman Kodak, Robert Stempel at General Motors, Tom Barrett at Goodyear, John Akers at IBM, Joseph Antonini at Kmart, William Agee at Morrison Knudsen, and Paul Lego at Westinghouse.

It's not just the pursuit of growth that causes unfocusing problems. Unfocusing itself seems to be a natural phenomenon that occurs without any conscious effort on a company's part.

A successful company usually starts out highly focused on an individual product, service, or market. Over time, the company becomes unfocused. It offers too many products and services for too many markets at too many different price levels. It loses its sense of direction. It doesn't know where it's going or why. Its mission statement loses its meaning.

You've probably worked for a company like that. Most people have. At first, everything seems to be going well. The initial product or service turns out to be a big winner. The company has momentum and great expectations. The stock is taking off like a rocket.

But success creates something else: the opportunity to branch out in many different directions. The halls are filled with anticipation and excitement. Most often heard comment in the corridors: "We're going to rule the world."

Such a scenario could describe General Motors in the sixties. Sears in the seventies. IBM in the eighties. And Microsoft in the nineties.

It never happens. After a while things start to go wrong. What seemed like a world of opportunity turns into a world of problems. Objectives unmet. Sales flattening. Profits declining. The press unflattering.

"I sometimes wonder if the people at the top of most big U.S. corporations are afflicted with attention deficit disorder," says consultant Barry Spiker. "They don't stay focused." This is what happened at General Motors, Sears, and IBM. But the jury is still out on Microsoft. If history repeats itself, as it generally does, Microsoft is the next IBM, the next company to become unfocused.

In the physical world, unfocusing is called entropy, or disorder. And Rudolf Clausius's law of entropy states that over time, the entropy of any closed system increases. Let's say you straighten out your clothes closet. A month later, the closet is a mess. You have witnessed the effects of entropy, one of the fundamental laws of nature.

Corporations are no different from clothes closets. Over time, every company tends to become unfocused.

Also garages. Let's say you take a Saturday afternoon in April to straighten out your garage. It's hard work, but at the end of the day you're pleased with yourself because everything looks great. You have a place for everything and everything's in its place. You make yourself a promise: From now on you're going to put everything back where it belongs and keep the garage exactly as it is this particular Saturday in April.

A year later, you're back to square one. Everything is a mess again. Corporations are no different from garages.

Or glove compartments. Empty the glove compartment of your car and see what you find. Probably a lot of things you never knew were there. Maps, pens, sunglasses, gas receipts, portable telephone, chewing gum, change, Kleenex, vehicle registration certificate, insurance cards for the last three years, owner's manual. Everything except a pair of gloves. Corporations are no different from glove compartments.

Open the top drawer of your desk. Is it focused or unfocused? Enough said.

Like human nature itself, the destiny of corporations is to become unfocused. Peter Drucker paints a bleak picture of the typical corporation: "Analysis of the entire business and its basic economics always shows it to be in worse disrepair than anyone expected. The products everyone boasts of turn out to be yesterday's breadwinners or investments in managerial ego. Activities to which no one paid much attention turn out to be major costs centers and so expensive as to endanger the competitive position of the company. What everyone in the business believes to be quality turns out to have little meaning to the customer."

Does that sound like the company you are working for? Peter Drucker recommends focusing "scarce resources on the greatest opportunities." Or you might consider a strong dose of Ritalin for top management.

There are two reasons for this unfocusing. One has been widely discredited; the other is still alive, but showing signs of wear and tear.

The discredited reason is "diversification." Remember how wildly popular the management strategy of diversification once was? Literally every major corporation in America went out of its way to proclaim its belief in the philosophy of not putting all your eggs in one basket.

The stool was the favorite analogy. The three-legged stool representing the three major businesses a company was engaged in, or the four-legged stool representing four major businesses. (For obvious reasons the two-legged stool was not a favorite analogy of corporate planners.)

Financial services were a special favorite of the diversification crowd. Scores of companies went down the financial services chute, including Sears, American Express, Xerox, Prudential Insurance, and Westinghouse Electric.

The story at Westinghouse is particularly painful. Nearly crippled by its now defunct credit subsidiary (Westinghouse Financial Services), the company barely skirted bankruptcy court a few years ago. In the past five years Westinghouse has had four chairmen. They also had $2.4 billion in losses on $58.6 billion in sales. There are a lot of Westinghouses out there that could do better by turning the company's assets into Treasury bonds.

Then there's the unhappy experience at Xerox. In the early eighties, the Copier King decided to diversify into financial services. Under the name "The Xerox Financial Machine," the component companies included Crum and Forster property/liability insurance, Van Kampen Merritt mutual funds, Furman Selz investment banking, and Xerox Life insurance.

When The Financial Machine broke down in late 1992, the company took an after-tax charge of $778 million and announced its total withdrawal from the field. "The long-awaited decision was a humbling admission of failure from Xerox," said the *Wall Street Journal*, "which bought into the business at its peak only to watch the investment spoil the acclaimed comeback in its core copier operation."

Yet company after company continues to search for the magic acquisition that will drive sales and stock prices skyward. But in the end they usually find only disappointment and disillusionment.

- IBM bought Rolm in 1984. IBM sold Rolm in 1989.

- Coca-Cola bought Columbia Pictures in 1982. Coca-Cola sold Columbia Pictures in 1989.

- Metropolitan Life bought Century 21 Real Estate in 1985. Metropolitan Life sold Century 21 in 1995.

- Chrysler bought Gulfstream Aerospace in 1985. Chrysler sold Gulfstream in 1990.

- Eastman Kodak bought Sterling Drug in 1988. Eastman Kodak sold Sterling in 1994.

- Dow Chemical bought Marion Merrell Dow in 1989. Dow sold Marion Merrell Dow in 1995.

- Matsushita bought MCA in 1990. Matsushita sold MCA in 1995.

A study of these and other acquisitions/divestitures confirms the existence of a six-year itch. Six years is long enough for the acquiring company to be convinced it has bought a lemon. Six years is also long enough for the investing public to forget about the marvelous "synergies" promised when the acquisition was first unveiled.

If things go well on the public relations front, the "back to basics" divestiture announcement gets as much favorable publicity as the original acquisition announcement.

In retrospect, some of the diversification moves were almost comical. On November 7, 1985, Lee Iacocca unveiled the new Chrysler Corporation, now a holding company, with automobiles just one of its businesses. The company would become a "four box" corporation: Chrysler Motors, Chrysler Aerospace (Gulfstream), Chrysler Financial, and Chrysler Technologies.

Iacocca dubbed the latter "the empty box" because he hadn't yet purchased anything to fill it. But he would immediately start searching for a high-tech acquisition in the $1 billion range.

Later he would admit that his biggest mistake was to diversify. "We didn't need a holding company. That's what made us top-heavy. If we went astray—you know, people do go astray now and then in many areas—man, we got focused in a hurry."

Ford Motor Company went through the same drill. CEO Donald Petersen decided Ford should become a three-box company. One was cars, of course. The second was finance, and the third was high-tech. Petersen proceeded to beef up the finance box with the acquisition of a California savings and loan and two consumer-lending companies, one in Philadelphia and the other in Dallas. All told, Ford spent $6 billion on acquisitions between 1985 and 1989. With mediocre results, of course.

"Four-box thinking" is not an exclusive prerogative of the giant corporation. A small company often falls prey to the same kind of thoughts. When annual sales get in the neighborhood of $10 million a year (give or take a few million), a small company often hits the wall and becomes unfocused.

Ten million is about the time the founder decides the company is getting too big and delegates operating responsibility to three or four key people. Result: Each person takes his or her box and runs in a different direction.

To be fair, I should also mention megaconglomerate General Electric, which gets more than one-third of its pretax profits from GE Capital. The question is, does the $20 billion financial power-house benefit from its GE connection? Or is it successful in spite of its GE connection?

Just because two facts are related doesn't mean there's a cause-and-effect relationship. The longest field goal in National Football League history (sixty-three yards) was kicked by Tom Dempsey, a man with half a foot, on November 8, 1970, in a game between New Orleans and Detroit. If I wanted to kick field goals for an NFL team, would I get my kicking foot amputated? I think not.

Buying a lottery ticket is a losing strategy because most ticket buyers wind up losing money. But even a losing strategy can have its share of winners. GE Capital is a winner, even though the diversification strategy it represents might be a loser.

Furthermore, success in the past is no guarantee that you'll be successful in the future, especially if you're following a losing strategy. Will GE Capital continue to post those extraordinary gains? I think not.

Luck evens out. In the long run, winning companies are ones that are the most focused. Losing companies are ones that are the least focused. The guiding principle, the one that should drive your company's every decision, is the principle of focus.

If focus is so important, how come so few companies seem to be driven by it? How come focus gets so little attention in the management books? How come the principle of focus is generally ignored and even violated by most CEOs?

As dramatized by Edgar Allan Poe in "The Purloined Letter," sometimes the hardest thing to see is also the most obvious. And what is obvious to an outside observer about almost any company today is the constant, day-by-day, relentless march into an unfocused state. Call it entropy or whatever you like, unfocusing is a fact of corporate life. What to do about it is what this book is all about.

What makes the situation even worse is that most companies make a conscious effort to become unfocused. That sounds impossible, but it's not. We call this process "line extension," or in the immortal words of management consultants, "extending the equity of the brand."

Line extension is the second reason for the unfocusing of Corporate America. One that's still alive, but showing signs of wear.

Nobody has extended the equity of the brand quite so far as Donald Trump. At first, The Donald was successful. Then he branched out and put his name on anything the banks would lend him money for. Three casinos, two hotels, two condominiums, an airline, a shopping center, a football team, even a bicycle race.

Fortune magazine called Trump "an investor with a keen eye for cash flow and asset values, a smart marketer, a cunning wheeler-dealer." *Time* and *Newsweek* magazines put him on their covers. Today Trump is millions of dollars in debt. What made him successful in the short term is exactly what caused him to fail in the long term. Line extension.

What The Donald did in the United States, The Richard is in the process of doing in the United Kingdom. Richard Branson is the owner of Virgin Group, whose Virgin Atlantic Airways has created a lot of excitement in the North Atlantic airline market. Not satisfied with just owning an airline, Branson is now line-extending the Virgin name.

The Richard has licensed the Virgin name for personal computers and has set up joint ventures to market Virgin cola and Virgin vodka. (One of Virgin's Boeing 747s is being painted to look like a cola can.) On the drawing boards are Virgin water, in bubbly and non-bubbly form, and Seven Virgins, a fizzy lime beverage.

Then there's Virgin Lightships, which rents lightweight blimps to advertisers. Branson has also franchised the Virgin name to two European start-up airlines and is bidding to take over the running of all British train services from the state-owned rail network. There's also Virgin Financial Services, which includes an index fund and a payroll savings plan.

Meanwhile back at Virgin Atlantic, the airline has been losing money. To cover the losses The Richard has lent $50 million to the airline in the past two years. Is there any doubt the Virgin empire is going to come crashing down at some point in the future? It's hard enough to compete with British Airways and American Airlines without taking on Coca-Cola and Smirnoff on the side.

Branson is following in the slipstream of Sir Freddie Laker. Back in 1977, Laker Airways introduced the Skytrain to the North Atlantic market. A walk-on, walk-off discount flight service that charged for food and other frills, the Skytrain became known as the "cheap and cheerful" way to the UK. Two years later Laker began adding frills.

In the end, Sir Freddie was offering five types of fares, including one for an upscale "Regency" service aimed at the business market. "In addition to blurring the public's image of Laker Airways," said *Business Week,* "the new services added to the carrier's costs and destroyed the simplicity of the original concept."

Meanwhile in a typical "conquer the world" attitude, Sir Freddie ordered ten A300 Airbuses and filed a rash of European route applications, including one blockbuster to fly "among and between" thirty-five European cities. Just before his 1982 bankruptcy he also laid plans for a "Globetrain" that would circle the world and "assure competition on a substantial part of the world air-transport system."

While Sir Freddie Laker was going down in flames over the North Atlantic, Don Burr was starting a "no-frills" airline in North America. Called People Express, the new airline took off in the spring of 1981. Fares were low and the stewardesses charged for soft drinks and brownies. If you wanted your bags checked, the charge was $2 apiece.

Lured by the low fares, people would hop aboard the airline for weekend jaunts at the drop of a hat. Dubbed the "Trailways of the Airways," People Express was an immediate success. The stock went public in 1980 at $8.50 a share and less than three years later was near $50.

Then Don Burr made the predictable line-extension moves, including rapid expansion of routes and schedules. He bought 747s and started service to London. In 1985, he bought Frontier Airlines for $300 million (and sold it to United Airlines the following year).

Then he tried to shift from a no-frills low-cost carrier to a full-service airline. Flying in the face of almost certain bankruptcy, People Express was swallowed up by Texas Air in 1987.

What Burr, Laker, and Branson failed to realize is that the brand name is not a hunting license to go out and nail the big game (the more, the merrier), but a diamond that needs to be cut and polished. In other words, focused. Only when you focus a company or a brand over an extended period of time do you develop a powerful company whose future success is almost guaranteed.

Nowhere is this principle so clearly demonstrated than in the success of *Playboy* magazine and in the lack of success of all the *Playboy* spin-offs. The world's best-selling men's magazine, *Playboy* and the company's trademark bunny logotype are known around the world. With a circulation of 3.4 million, *Playboy* is bigger than *People,* Time-Warner's most profitable magazine. *Playboy* is also bigger than *Sports Illustrated, Newsweek,* or *Cosmopolitan.*

What an opportunity for Playboy clubs, Playboy books, Playboy videos and Playboy cable channels. Not to mention clothing, cologne, jewelry, eyewear, and condoms. Playboy Enterprises, now run by Hugh Hefner's daughter Christie, has tried all of these things and more, with little success. (The first Playboy Club opened in Chicago in 1960. The last Playboy Club was closed in 1986.)

Over the last six years, for example, the company racked up $1.1 billion in sales and managed to lose $6 million. But they never give up. Recently Playboy Enterprises hired Hollywood's Creative Artists Agency to help find investors to fuel an ambitious expansion into international television, casinos, and new media.

Playboy magazine is now forty-two years old. One wonders what could have been accomplished by keeping *Playboy* focused as a magazine. And then by introducing new magazines with different names. Which is exactly what Henry Luce did, starting with *Time* magazine. (See chapter 12, "Building a Multistep Focus.")

Instead of introducing new brands, companies fall in love with themselves and constantly look for ways to take advantage of their presumably all-powerful brand names. Reebok is the latest brand to make the club scene, opening a $55 million complex in 1995 called Reebok Sports Club/NY. Is there any doubt the Reebok clubs will go the way of the Playboy clubs? Not in my book.

Not to be outdone, Nike has announced that they will build a theme park in Irving, Texas, in and around the Dallas Cowboys' Texas Stadium. Will Nike's next move be to buy the team?

Comsat Corp. has bought a professional team. Created by the U.S. government in 1963 as a publicly traded company to link phone companies to the global network of Intelsat satellites, Comsat decided to diversify into sports and entertainment.

Since 1989, the communications company has bought the Denver Nuggets basketball team, a Hollywood film-production company, one-third of a Denver theme park, and a company that beams pay-television programs via satellite to nearly six hundred thousand hotel rooms. Recently Comsat picked up the Quebec Nordiques hockey team for $75 million.

With a partner, the company is building a $132 million Denver arena to house both the Nuggets and the hockey team, which has been moved from Quebec and renamed the Avalanche. Any wonder Comsat's stock price today is about where it was when it started the entertainment push in 1989?

Jostens, a $665 million company with 40 percent of the market for class rings, yearbooks, and other school graduation products, decided to get into the educational software business. It seemed to make sense. Software was booming, and the distribution channels were already there.

So in 1986 the company launched Jostens Learning Corp. and started to make big-time acquisitions. Education Systems Corp. for $65 million. Wicat Systems for $102 million. By 1992, Jostens had 60 percent of the computer learning market.

But what does a ring company know about computers? Apparently not much. Jostens was selling proprietary computer terminals as the market was turning to low-priced IBM-compatible personal computers and commercial software packages.

In 1994, Jostens took a $140 million pretax write-off, mostly for software development costs and cutting its salesforce. In 1995, Jostens went back to basics, selling its educational software division, its sportswear business, and its aviation-training division. Jostens, said the *Wall Street Journal,* "is shedding its remaining peripheral businesses and focusing on selling achievement and recognition products to schools and businesses."

Line extension doesn't need much encouragement. It's a process that takes place continuously in a corporation with no conscious effort. Companies seem to flow like a river into new directions or to fill holes in their existing line.

It's like a closet or a garage or a glove compartment or a desk drawer that becomes unfocused with no conscious effort. There are six different areas that seem to generate these line extension efforts.

1: Distribution. In the case of Jostens, it was the existence of well-established distribution channels that caused corporate executives to ask themselves, "What else can we be selling? What is the hot new product moving into our marketplace?" The more products a salesforce handles, the more likely it is to lose focus.

2: Manufacturing. "What else can our factories be making to increase our efficiencies and reduce our overhead burdens?" Dow Jones & Co. owns the *Wall Street Journal,* the world's most profitable newspaper. But the *Journal* publishes only five days a week, leaving two days free for other ventures.

So Dow Jones filled the presses with the *National Observer,* a weekly newspaper. After fifteen straight years of losses, Dow Jones finally folded the *Observer.*

3: Marketing. A company that successfully markets a consumer package-goods product assumes it can market any consumer package-goods product. Procter & Gamble, the mecca of marketing, took on Minute Maid and Tropicana with an orange juice brand called Citrus Hill.

Launched in 1981, the brand never had a profitable year. Killed in 1992, the Citrus Hill funeral cost Procter & Gamble $200 million. Marketing is marketing, but orange juice is orange juice.

4: Customer life cycles. "What happens when our customers outgrow our products?" That's the question many companies ask themselves. So the Gerber Products Company comes up with Gerber Graduates. McDonald's tries pizza. And Burger King tries main course dinners and table service. None of these introductions turn out to be profitable.

5: Geography. Sometimes geographic expansion can take place without loss of focus. Starbucks, for example, successfully moved out of its Seattle home market into the national arena. Other times, the geography is the focus. One of the most profitable newspapers in America is *Newsday* on Long Island. So *Newsday* decided to move to the city and introduced *New York Newsday*.

Over a ten-year period the paper won three Pulitzer Prizes and lost $100 million. You can't blame *Newsday*'s owner, the Times Mirror Company, for shutting the paper down. What you can blame them for is starting it up in the first place.

6: Pricing. "Some customers can't afford our prices. What do we do about that?" No problem, just introduce inexpensive versions of our brands. The biggest name in women's designer clothing is Donna Karan. But, let's face it, Donna Karan is expensive. So the company introduced DKNY, their less expensive clothing line. (Would Coca-Cola introduce CCAT, a less expensive cola? Actually, they might. Let's not give them any foolish ideas.)

In one year Donna Karan spawned five new companies: men's wear, DKNY men's and kids, intimate apparel, plus a beauty company that started life with Donna's own personal perfume.

Will Donna go the way of Liz? Back in the eighties, Liz Claiborne was the single most popular label in women's apparel, dominating the department store segment. The core sportswear label spun off myriad divisions designed to outfit a woman for virtually every phase of her life. Claiborne's Collection, Liz & Co., Lizsport, and Lizwear.

Today Liz Claiborne is in trouble. Recently the company hired a new vice president of merchandising "to refocus the clothing lines at the moribund apparel firm," according to *Crain's New York Business*.

Brand inflation is another reason for the raft of recent line extensions. Ask yourself, "What does our brand stand for?" Are you sure?

Gerber apparently thinks its brand stands for "babies." How else can you explain the company's losing line extensions into children's apparel, strollers, and high chairs? The company also spent millions trying to get into the day-care business.

Strange. Ask any mother what Gerber stands for and she will undoubtedly say "baby food." Food does not mean clothing or furniture.

Even successful companies with a reputation for successful line extensions are not all they seem to be. McDonald's is the leading fast-food company with a reputation as an innovator in menu additions. Since 1983, McDonald's has introduced Chicken McNuggets, ready-to-eat salads, McLean Deluxe, and a host of new products. In a decade, average revenue per U.S. restaurant unit has increased 35 percent.

Terrific. But over the same time period the consumer price index for food has increased 41 percent. If the average McDonald's had not added any new menu items in a decade, but just sold the same items but at inflation-adjusted prices, revenues presumably would have increased 41 percent, not 35 percent.

There are some assumptions here. Could the average McDonald's continue to sell the same volume of hamburgers, Big Macs, Cokes, and french fries? Maybe, maybe not. Certainly there was a strong trend toward out-of-home eating over the past decade, which should have helped McDonald's increase their volume.

If you can't maintain your volume when the tide is with you, how will you fare when the tide goes against you?

Mind you, McDonald's has enormous self-confidence and a sterling reputation in the financial community. "If we served beer and wine," CEO Michael Quinlan once said, "we might eventually have 100 percent of the food-service market."

Many companies mimic McDonald's. These are successful companies with reputations for substantial line and product extensions. But when you look under the covers, you find that most of their growth has been in the consumer price index. When you remove the effect of inflation, you also remove most of the growth.

The road to Unfocus can take many paths. Some companies go the McDonald's route by steadily increasing the number of products in their basic line. Others try to assemble a basket of many different products. It's the latter approach that causes most of the highly visible line-extension failures.

One day a company is tightly focused on a single, highly profitable product. The next day the company is spread thin over many products and is breaking even or actually losing money. Brand inflation strikes again.

Last year the world's largest manufacturer of brand-name condoms took $220 million in write-offs and reported an operating loss of $37 million. In this day and age of AIDS, how could the world's largest condom manufacturer lose money?

Easy. London International decided to diversify into retail photo processing, fine china, and beauty aids. Recently new management took over and out went diversification and in went focus. This year the world's largest condom manufacturer reported a net profit of $19 million on sales of $509 million.

Line extension is not a big-company phenomenon. Small companies are more prone to line-extend their brands than their big brothers. In 1988, Main Street Muffins was a $100,000-a-year retail business in Akron, Ohio, when a local restaurateur asked the owners to sell him frozen muffin batter rather than just fresh muffins. And a wholesale business was born.

Main Street bought new equipment, developed systems, and started selling to other restaurants. Things were looking so rosy, they opened a second store. But all was not what it seemed to be. Serving two different businesses was stretching their resources. Employee morale was falling. A year later both the retail stores and the batter business were bound for bankruptcy. It was decision time.

Confucius say: Man who chases two rabbits catches neither.

The owners, Steven Marks and Harvey Nelson, decided to chase one rabbit only. They sold the stores and focused on the frozen batter business, even though it represented only about a third of their total sales.

Within three months the wholesale business became profitable and has remained so ever since. And business has been rising at a rapid rate. Since 1990, Main Street's sales have increased an average of 100 percent a year. Currently the company does $10 million worth of muffin business a year.

"Instead of doing two things subpar," says Steven Marks, "we needed to do one thing exceptionally well. We reasoned that to be successful we had to be focused. We had to devote our energies to that part of the business that had the best chance for success."

Small companies like Main Street Muffins already have two strikes against them. Of the seven hundred thousand new businesses started this year, only thirty-five thousand (or one in twenty) will be around five years from now. And the primary reason for a small company's failure is trying to do too many different things at once.

If you do one thing, and do it well, you can build a reputation that almost guarantees success in the long term. (Unfortunately, you can also starve in the short term, which is why capital is the crucial component of any start-up.)

What's true in muffins is also true in computers. Years ago when IBM was focused on mainframe computers, they made a ton of money. Today IBM makes mainframes, midrange computers, workstations, desktop computers, home computers, and software (to mention some of their major product lines) and they are in trouble.

In 1991, for example, IBM's revenues were $65 billion. Yet they wound up losing $2.8 billion. In 1992, they lost $5.6 billion. In 1993, they lost $8.1 billion. (In 1994, IBM managed to make $3 billion, but the future looks anything but bright for Big Blue.)

Along the way, IBM dropped millions on copiers (sold to Kodak), Rolm telephone equipment (sold to Siemens), Satellite Business Systems (sold to MCI), the Prodigy network (limping along), SAA, TopView, OfficeVision, and OS/2. What's the justification for all these unfocusing moves?

In an attempt to maintain its industry leadership, IBM thinks it has to ride the "computer" horse. Wherever the computer industry goes, goes the thinking, IBM has to follow. In fact, there has been considerable criticism in the media that IBM didn't move fast enough. Networking, client-server, and desktop software are some of the areas that critics say IBM should have pursued more vigorously. (The critics even applauded the purchase of Lotus.)

When you try to ride an expanding industry, the way IBM has tried to ride the computer horse, you get pulled apart. It's like being on the rack.

Yet that's what most companies do. When they become incredibly successful, they invariably sow the seeds for their future problems. Take Microsoft, one of the most successful companies in the world. If ever a company is on top, it's Microsoft. (Even though it's one-thirtieth the size of General Motors, Microsoft's stock is worth more than GM's.)

Whom does that sound like? Sounds like IBM. Microsoft is setting itself up as the next IBM, with all the negative implications that term suggests.

There are ominous signs of softness in Microsoft's strategy. *The Economist* magazine reported in early 1992, "Mr. Gates is putting together a range of products, based on a common core of technology, that will compete across virtually the whole of the software industry: from big computers to small ones, and from operating systems in the information engine-room to graphics programs that draw every picture for executives. Nobody in the software industry has yet managed a venture of that complexity—though IBM has tried and failed."

When you try to be all things to all people, you inevitably wind up in trouble. "I'd rather be strong somewhere," said one successful manager, "than weak everywhere."

In a narrow sense, line extension is taking the brand name of a successful product (A.1. steak sauce) and putting it on a new product you plan to introduce (A.1. poultry sauce).

It sounds so logical. "We make A.1., a great sauce that gets the dominant share of the steak business. But people are switching from beef to chicken, so let's introduce a poultry product. And what better name to use than A.1. That way people will know the poultry sauce comes from the makers of that great steak sauce, A.1."

But business is a battle of perceptions, not products. In the mind, A.1. is not the brand name but the steak sauce itself. "Would you pass me the A.1.?" asks the diner. Nobody replies: "A.1. what?"

In spite of an $18 million introductory advertising budget, the A.1. poultry launch was a dismal failure.

There are as many ways to line extend as there are galaxies in the universe. And new ways get invented every day. In the long run and in the presence of serious competition, line extensions almost never work.

Back in 1978, when 7UP was simply the lemon-and-lime Uncola, it had a 5.7 percent share of the soft-drink market. Then Seven-Up added 7UP Gold, Cherry 7UP, and assorted diet versions. Today 7UP's share is down to 4.2 percent.

Wherever you look, you find line extensions, which is one reason stores are choked with brands. (There are 1,300 shampoos, 200 cereals, 250 soft drinks.)

Take Tab versus Diet Pepsi. The common assumption is that Coca-Cola introduced Diet Coke because Tab was losing the diet cola war to Diet Pepsi. Nothing could be further from the truth. The day Diet Coke was introduced Tab was leading Diet Pepsi in market share by about 32 percent. Today Diet Coke's lead over Diet Pepsi is still about that same percentage.

When two line-extended brands compete against each other, one line-extended brand has to win. So there's always plenty of line-extension successes like Diet Coke to brag about.

Invariably the leader in any category is the brand that is not line-extended. Take baby food, for example. Gerber has 72 percent of the market, way ahead of Beech-Nut and Heinz, the two line-extended brands.

In spite of evidence that line extensions don't work, companies continue to pump them out. Some examples:

- Listerine mouthwash. *Listerine toothpaste?*

- Mentadent toothpaste. *Mentadent mouthwash?*

- Life Savers candy. *Life Savers gum?*

- Bic lighters. *Bic panty hose?*

- Hostess Twinkies. *Hostess Twinkies Lights?*

- Tanqueray gin. *Tanqueray vodka?*

- Coors beer. *Coors water?*

- Continental Airlines. *Continental Lite?*

- Heinz ketchup. *Heinz baby food?*

- USA Today. *USA Today on TV?*

- Adidas running shoes. *Adidas cologne?*

- Levi's blue jeans. *Levi's shoes?*

According to *New Product News,* a leading trade publication, 20,076 new consumer goods appeared on the shelves of America's supermarkets and drugstores in 1994. This was an increase of 14 percent over the previous year. Approximately 90 percent of these new products were line extensions.

It may be just a coincidence, but only 10 percent of these new products are successful enough to be on the shelves two years after their introduction, according to Kevin Clancy, a leading marketing consultant.

Supermarkets today make a substantial part of their profits not by selling products to consumers but by selling services to manufacturers. Under a ubiquitous category called "trade promotion," manufacturers are paying for displays, promotions, advertising, discounts, and a variety of creative schemes designed by supermarket and drug chains to extract money from their vendors.

The latest is the slotting fee, which presumably pays for putting a new product on retailer shelves. Even a modest national launch of a new product can call for $2 million in slotting fees. And if the product fails, retailers sometimes demand a "kill fee" to take the product off the shelves.

Line extensions are unfocusing both the manufacturers that produce them and the retailers that sell them. One supermarket chain counted 240 analgesics on its shelves. Customers don't need that many pain relievers. All they create is a headache for the people who have to stock and maintain the shelves.

Most new products are line extensions. Most new products fail. These are the two immutable facts that management should keep in mind the next time someone recommends the umpteenth line extension of the product.

Why does management believe in line extension in spite of the overwhelming evidence to the contrary? One reason is that while line extension is a loser in the long term, it can be a winner in the short term.

But you can't measure success in the short term only. Every Miller line extension was pronounced a success. First there was Miller Lite, followed by Miller Genuine Draft and Miller Genuine Draft Light. And then, of course, Miller Reserve, Miller Reserve Light, and Miller Reserve Amber Ale. Not to mention Miller Clear, Miller High Life Light, and Miller Genuine Red.

Miller Lite also has had its share of extensions. Lite Ultra and Miller Lite Ice.

Did Miller increase its share of the beer business? Short-term, yes, but long-term, no. Furthermore, in the wake of its line-extension successes, Miller has fallen farther behind Anheuser-Busch.

Not that Anheuser-Busch hasn't been busy on the line-extension front. After the launch of Miller Lite in 1974, Anheuser-Busch waited eight years to launch Bud Light. By 1994, Bud Light had become the largest-selling light beer in America, but mostly at the expense of their regular beer.

In the six years between 1988 and 1994, for example, Bud Light gained five million barrels and Budweiser lost seven million barrels. And the decline of Budweiser is likely to continue.

Momentum is the most powerful force in business today. The big mo is the hardest force to capture and the easiest force to lose. One sure way to kill a brand's momentum is by line extensions. Coors was brewing a curious malt-beverage product called Zima. By 1994, the brand had 2 percent of the beer market.

Then Coors introduced Zima Gold. Since Zima, with a gin-and-tonic taste, appeals to women, the idea was to broaden the appeal to men with Zima Gold, which has a bourbon-and-soda taste. Lots of luck.

Today Zima Gold is dead and the original Zima has less than 1 percent of the market.

Managers frequently fall for the fallacy that customers are demanding more flavors, more variety, more choices. Hence, more line extensions. Oddly enough, you find more line extensions in categories that are declining in sales than in categories that are increasing in sales.

Beer, coffee, and cigarettes, three categories that have been steadily declining in sales, have had the most line extensions. (There are a dozen or so varieties of Marlboro cigarettes.)

Per-capita beer consumption, for example, has declined eleven out of the last thirteen years. When customers are walking away from your category, why would you need more brands to satisfy those customers? Logic suggests you would need fewer brands.

But that's customer logic. Manufacturer logic is different. Since our volume is declining, the manufacturer concludes, we need more brands to maintain or increase our sales. When a category is increasing in sales, there's opportunities for new brands, but manufacturer logic suggests they're not needed.

As a result, the marketplace is filled with line extensions in areas where they are not needed and is starved for new brands in areas where they are needed. Go figure.

One of the loonier line extensions was put in the nation's drug-stores a few years ago by Sterling Winthrop, when it was the pharmaceutical products subsidiary of Eastman Kodak. Sterling's big brand is Bayer aspirin, but aspirin was losing out to acetaminophen (Tylenol) and ibuprofen (Advil).

So Sterling launched a $116 million advertising and marketing program to introduce a selection of five "aspirin-free" products. The Bayer Select line included headache pain relief, regular pain relief, nighttime pain relief, sinus pain relief, and menstrual formulations. All products contained either acetaminophen or ibuprofen as the core ingredient.

Results were painful. The first year Bayer Select sold $26 million worth of pain relievers in a $2.5 billion market, or a little over 1 percent of the market. Even worse, the sales of regular Bayer aspirin have been falling about 10 percent a year. Why should you buy Bayer aspirin if the manufacturer is telling you that their "select" products are "aspirin-free"?

Management can also be blinded by an intense loyalty to the company or brand. Why else would PepsiCo have introduced Pepsi XL, Pepsi Max, and Crystal Pepsi in spite of the failures of Pepsi Light and Pepsi AM?

Another reason you find so many line extensions on the market is the belief that they are less expensive to launch than new brands. Not true, according to one chief executive who ought to know. "It costs as much to introduce a line extension," says John MacDonough, CEO of Miller Brewing, "as it does to introduce a new brand."

The hottest new beer on the market is not a line extension at all. It's Red Dog from Miller Brewing. In its first five months, Red Dog amassed a 1.4 percent share of major supermarket beer sales in the United States, exceeding the combined volume of all the microbrewers.

Furthermore, look at the "ice" beer category. Every major beer brand has an ice line extension: Miller Lite Ice, Bud Ice, Molson Ice, Labatt Ice, Coors Artic Ice, Schlitz Ice, and Pabst Ice Draft. So what is the leading ice beer? Icehouse, the only major non-line-extended brand in the category.

But the issue at any company is not line extensions versus new brands. The issue is whether a company should emphasize growth above all other factors.

The more products, the more markets, the more alliances a company makes, the less money it makes. "Full speed ahead in all directions" seems to be the call from the corporate bridge. When will companies learn the lesson that line extension ultimately leads to disaster?

If you want to be successful today, you have to narrow the focus in order to stand for something in the prospect's mind.

What does IBM stand for? They used to stand for "mainframe computers." Today they stand for everything, which is another way of saying they stand for nothing.

Why is Sears in trouble? Because they tried to be all things to all people. Sears was big in hard goods, so they went into soft goods and then into fashion. They even hired Cheryl Tiegs. (Do fashion models really buy their miniskirts at Sears?)

In the conventional view, a business strategy usually consists of developing an "all-encompassing vision." In other words, what concept or idea is big enough to hold all of a company's products and services on the market today and planned for the future?

In the conventional view, strategy is a tent. You stake out your tent big enough so it can hold everything you might possibly want to get into.

IBM has erected an enormous computer tent. Nothing in the computer field, today or in the future, will fall outside the IBM tent. This is a recipe for disaster. As new companies, new products, new ideas invade the computer arena, IBM is going to get blown away.

You can't defend a rapidly growing market like computers even if you are a financial powerhouse like IBM. From a strategic point of view, you have to be much more selective, picking and choosing the area in which to pitch your tent.

Technological change accelerates the arrival of the specialist. As time goes on, and new technologies arrive on the scene, business becomes more specialized. In place of a shoe-manufacturing plant, we now have factories that specialize. In men's shoes, women's shoes, children's shoes, work shoes, casual shoes, boots.

As time goes on and lifestyles change, opportunities are created for new specialists who know how to take advantage of change. It wasn't Florsheim or U.S. Shoe that benefited from the arrival of the athletic shoe. It was the athletic-shoe specialists Nike and Reebok.

Power lies with the specialist, not the generalist. As new technologies change the nature of the marketplace, existing companies try to encompass the new technologies within the framework of their organizations. As a result they become unfocused and are easy targets for the specialists.

Technological change in the computer industry heralded the arrival of the specialists who focused on one type of computer and in the process carved out significant pieces of business that Big Blue considered to be its private domain.

Digital Equipment in minicomputers. Sun Microsystems in UNIX workstations. Silicon Graphics in 3-D computing. Compaq in office personal computers. Packard Bell in home personal computers. Dell and Gateway 2000 in mail-order personal computers.

"It's one of the great mysteries of the computer industry," said the *Wall Street Journal* in 1995. "Why has the world's biggest computer maker—the company that practically created the personal computer market—floundered in PC software?"

Is it really a great mystery? *None* of the other personal computer manufacturers are a big factor in PC software. Not Compaq. Not Dell. Not Gateway. Not Packard Bell. Not Digital Equipment. Not Hewlett-Packard. Why should IBM be big in PC software?

Who is big in personal computer software? The specialists, of course. Microsoft, Novell, Adobe, Intuit, Borland, Broderbund, and dozens of other software companies, none of which make personal computers.

(Every computer company, of course, has a software business to the extent that they can "tie" software sales to hardware. This bundling practice creates a barrier that competitors find hard to penetrate. Even IBM has an $11 billion software business, two-thirds of which is mainframe related.)

Strategically, General Motors is in the same boat as IBM. GM is into anything and everything on wheels. Sedans, sports cars, cheap cars, expensive cars, trucks, minivans, even electric cars. So what is GM's business strategy? If it runs on the road, or off the road, we'll chase it.

If there were nothing but general surgeons and you were the only brain surgeon, you would have an incredible business and you could charge outrageous prices. Companies that find themselves in similar situations think the opposite.

Imagine a medical practice saying to itself: "We are known as terrific brain surgeons, so let's get into the heart, liver, lung, and limb business." In other words, they turn themselves into general surgeons. It never happens in medicine. It does happen in management.

What's the primary purpose of a brand? The number one objective of a brand, according to a recent survey of senior executives, is "to provide an umbrella for products and services." Whether you call it an umbrella or a tent, putting everything under one roof is a dangerous practice. It's the management theory that leads directly to the line-extension trap.

For many companies line extension is the easy way out. It's perceived as the inexpensive, logical way to grow. Only when it's too late does a company turn around and notice that they have become unfocused, perhaps precariously so.

THE DRIVING FORCE
OF GLOBALIZATION

The biggest story in the business world today is the rise of global trade. To take advantage of dramatically lower trade barriers brought about by treaties like GATT, NAFTA, APEC, and Mercosur, every country in the world is trying to increase its export business.

How will globalization affect your business?

It will tend to unfocus your business . . . even though you make no changes in your line of products or services.

Why this is so is best explained by an analogy. Let's say you're living in a small town in Wyoming with a population of fifty people. What kinds of retail stores are you likely to find?

Exactly. One "general" store that sells everything: food, clothing, gasoline.

Now move to New York City with a population of eight million. What kinds of retail stores are you likely to find?

Exactly. Many highly specialized retail establishments. Not just shoe stores, for example, but men's shoe stores, women's shoe stores, children's shoe stores, athletic shoe stores.

The larger the market, the more specialization that takes place. The smaller the market, the less specialization that takes place and the more generalized the companies. As the world moves to a global economy, companies are going to have to become more specialized.

Some industries are going global faster than others. The cola industry, the computer industry, and the commercial airplane industry are virtually global now. Others will take decades or longer to achieve the same degree of globalization. Retail might never get there, although the television shopping channels and the catalog houses are hastening the process.

The boom in global trade has been astonishing. Take a trip to any major city in the world and read the billboards from the airport into town. "Sharp, Canon, Samsung, Xerox, Philips, Marlboro, Shell, IBM, Coke." What country are you in?

If you just read the billboards, you wouldn't know what continent you were on, let alone which country or city you were in.

You often can't tell by the clothing worn by the natives either. Especially the younger natives. Jeans, T-shirts (with appropriate advertising slogans), and sneakers are the uniforms of the teenage crowd in Europe, Asia, Latin America, and the United States.

Foreign trade is healthy for a country's economy. The Far East is the most spectacular example of what can be accomplished by a global focus. Japan, Taiwan, Hong Kong, Singapore, and Korea have all gotten relatively rich through the medium of trade. Trade is driving virtually every business of any significant size into world markets. A company either competes against imports only at home, or competes around the world in markets of increasing sophistication.

While many companies have benefited, the globalization of business is also rapidly unfocusing many companies that have yet to understand the long-term implications of a world based on free trade. Again, it's back to the basic principle of specialization: The larger the market, the more specialized a company must become if it is going to prosper. When we have truly free trade on a worldwide basis, every company in the world will have to specialize in order to survive.

Except that many companies don't see it that way. They see the rise of a global economy as an opportunity to broaden their lines, not narrow them.

Take the example of a German food company late in 1992. At the beginning of 1993, with the abolishment of border controls and other barriers to free trade, Germany, with a population of 81 million, was going to become an integral part of a "single market" European Union with a population of 347 million people.

In other words, the German company found that its "home" market more than quadrupled overnight. How did most companies respond to that kind of overnight population explosion? The temptation to broaden the line must have been overwhelming.

"Let's see, we'll need a sweet-tasting version for the English, a tart-tasting version for the Italians, an herbal version for the Dutch," etc. While this might be logical thinking, it's also diametrically opposed to the principle that the larger the market, the more specialized a company must become. As your market expands, your product line must contract.

As a result, many corporations all over the world are in trouble. But globalization affects companies in some areas more than it does companies in other areas. Compare Europe with America. Of the two, which area is the scene of more corporate disasters?

Europe, of course, but the reasons are not readily apparent. Most observers tend to blame Europe's high cost of employee benefits, the rigidity of labor laws, the high taxes needed to support the welfare states, and especially the inability to hire and fire at will. While these factors undoubtedly contribute to the economic malaise that has swept the Continent, there's another factor that's often overlooked.

Compared with U.S. companies, most European concerns have a much broader product line. Siemens makes many of the same electrical products that General Electric makes. Plus Siemens also makes a wide range of computers, telecommunication switches, and electronic equipment, products that General Electric doesn't make.

As a matter of fact, intense competition in mainframe computers drove General Electric out of the computer business in the United States. Much tamer competition in Germany helps keep Siemens *in* the computer business.

Take Philips Electronics of the Netherlands. Here is a $39 billion company trying to compete in the chip business (against Intel), in the video game business (against Sega and Nintendo), in the lighting business (against General Electric), in the VCR and camcorder business (against Sony and a host of others).

Along the way, Philips has dipped its toes into the computer business, the cable television business, and the video rental business. Not to mention the $175 million investment in Whittle Communications, which was almost a total loss.

In 1990, Philips lost $2.3 billion and nearly went under. Needless to say, the stock has gone nowhere the past decade. The current boom in semiconductors is keeping the company healthy in the short term, but Philips desperately needs a focus for the long term.

Take Daimler-Benz, the largest industrial company in the most economically successful country in Europe, the Federal Republic of Germany. Along with those natural advantages, Daimler-Benz owns the world's best automotive brand name, Mercedes-Benz. You would think that Daimler would be rolling in deutsche marks, but they're not. In 1995, the company lost substantially more than $1 billion.

The problem is not cars. The Mercedes-Benz division has been consistently profitable. The problem is diversification. During the eighties, Daimler-Benz got into everything from jets to helicopters to trains to satellites. (The latest is a minivan project in China estimated to cost $1 billion.) If you had bought Daimler stock a decade ago and sold it today, you would have had a substantial loss.

As business goes global, Daimler-Benz should have been driving in the opposite direction. It should have been narrowing its focus to luxury cars only and using its car profits to build assembly plants around the world instead of using them to prop up its money-losing subsidiaries.

Or take Fiat, Italy's largest company. The $40 billion Fiat car group makes a full line of automobiles much like $155 billion General Motors. But the Agnelli family, which controls Fiat, also has interests in everything from motor scooters to farm equipment to trucks. Also chemicals, insurance, food, publishing, sports, railroads, and defense. (Listed companies in the Agnelli aggregation represent more than 25 percent of the value of the Milan Stock Exchange.)

The Fiat/Agnelli combination has a much wider product line than General Motors, with much smaller sales. As globalization drives companies into becoming specialists, this combination is going to be under intense pressure to break up.

In 1993, Fiat alone lost $1.1 billion. In 1994, thanks to a 25 percent devaluation of the lira (which helped Fiat abroad while making imported cars more expensive at home), Fiat posted $612 million in profits. More and more, however, it looks like Fiat is organized for the past with its feudal network of so-called *salotto buono*, or business insiders, linked to state banks and political parties. Fiat's future is far from bright.

There's more to come. Recently, a new $28 billion conglomerate was announced that would combine the chemical interests of Fiat with the Ferruzzi Finanziaria group and its chemical subsidiary,

Montedison. The conglomerate would be under the control of Mediobanca, the powerful Milan investment bank, and the Agnelli family. Ferruzzi itself is a sick company that nearly collapsed two years ago under $20 billion of debt. It was saved only because the banks swapped debt for equity.

The Ferruzzi deal "makes no sense," said one financial expert. It created a huge conglomerate "at a moment when the formula is growing obsolete almost everywhere in the world." (Thanks in part to scathing reports in the media, the ill-conceived merger was recently called off.)

Olivetti is going down the same path. Europe's second largest computer manufacturer (after Siemens Nixdorf), Olivetti has not had a profitable year since 1990. In the past four years the company lost $1.5 billion. Managing director Corrado Passera agrees that Olivetti "used to do too many things." At home, it was a typewriter-to-mainframe company, while overseas it was trying to run a worldwide personal computer business.

Instead of narrowing its focus, Olivetti looked around for other businesses it could enter. It found three: services, telecommunications, and multimedia. As business becomes more global, Olivetti should have looked for ways to reduce, not expand, its product offerings.

In addition, Olivetti suffers from the same organizational problems that Fiat does. The company is controlled by Carlo De Benedetti, a younger version of Gianni Agnelli. De Benedetti's holding company, Compagnie Industriali Riunite, has interests in electronics, retailing, and other fields. It's hard to compete with IBM, Apple, and Compaq when you have a portfolio of other products to worry about.

Currently, Olivetti has 4 percent of the European personal computer market versus 14 percent for Compaq Computer.

Highly profitable Compaq is more than twice the size of its Italian rival, but unlike Olivetti, Compaq has not diversified into telecommunications, multimedia, or services. Not necessarily by choice, however.

It's the larger size of the U.S. market and therefore the driving force of specialization that has made American companies like Compaq more focused. As the globalization of business continues, the pressure will increase on European companies to narrow their focuses or they will increasingly be at a relative disadvantage. You can expect to see a lot of turmoil taking place in the European business community.

Of course, the European Union is technically a larger market than the United States. But it's not a single market in the true sense of the word. It will take time for the EU market to become "homogenized" to the same degree that the U.S. market is. Maybe decades.

The same is true of the globalization of business. It will take many decades for the world to approach a truly single global market, even if all governments cooperate in the establishment of such a market. Even then there will probably be many countries that stay on the sidelines in order to protect their home businesses. ("No nation," said Benjamin Franklin, "was ever ruined by trade.")

The same principles apply on the other side of the globe. Japan has been in an economic slump for several years. One reason is that Japanese companies, to a large extent, have product lines that are much too broad.

This is so not only because the Japanese market is smaller than that of the United States, a factor that accounts for part of the broadening of the lines, but also because the control-minded Japanese government has encouraged the trend. It's easier to keep track of a few companies making a broad range of products than it would be here in the wild and woolly United States, where many narrowly focused companies compete for a slice of the market.

Of the top ten corporations in the United States, only one (General Electric) is a classic conglomerate. Of the top ten corporations in Japan, eight are conglomerates. Only two are not (Toyota Motor and Nippon Telegraph & Telephone, a recently privatized government monopoly).

Six of the top ten corporations in Japan are *sogo shosha*, or trading companies. In total they account for revenues of almost a trillion dollars, or one-fourth of Japan's gross domestic product. Yet they operate on paper-thin margins. Net income is less than one-tenth of 1 percent of sales. Prediction: The sun will soon be setting on some of these Japanese-style conglomerates.

The Japanese Big Six are as unfocused as one could possibly imagine. They are commission agents, dealers, financiers, venture capitalists, and investors in the stock of their *keiretsu* members. In addition the *sogo shosha* have been pouring money into oil and gas production facilities, power plants, satellite communication ventures, and cable television systems.

Many of their *keiretsu* members are already falling behind the curve. Mitsubishi Electric, for example, is a $29 billion company that makes everything from semiconductors to consumer electronics, from space equipment to transport systems. Sales and profits have been declining since the early nineties.

As brand names become more important, companies like Mitsubishi Electric are going to suffer even more. Annual revenues of some of the companies that share the name include Mitsubishi Motors ($34 billion), Mitsubishi Bank ($30 billion), Mitsubishi Heavy Industries ($29 billion), Mitsubishi Chemical ($13 billion) and Mitsubishi Materials ($10 billion). A name that tries to stand for everything winds up standing for nothing.

The Japanese practice of fielding a wide variety of products under the same name has drawn favorable comments from many business writers who don't always look under the financial covers to find the real story. One particular favorite has been Yamaha. "How a motorcycle manufacturer manages to successfully sell pianos" is the general nature of their stories.

In the first place, Yamaha Motors is a separate company, only one-third owned by the piano company, Yamaha Corporation. In the second place, Yamaha Corporation has been far from financially successful. A typical Japanese-style conglomerate, Yamaha Corp. makes archery equipment, golf clubs, audio equipment, kitchens, skis, electric bicycles, and, of course, musical instruments.

As a matter of fact, Yamaha is the world's largest maker of musical instruments. In the past decade Yamaha sold about $46 billion worth of products at current rates of exchange. Yet net income has been less than 1 percent of sales. Profitless prosperity seems to be the Japanese style of business, consistent with their philosophy of massive line extensions and a marketing emphasis on low price.

Japan is a land of a thousand Yamahas. Companies that make everything under a common brand name and sell on price. Hitachi ($76 billion), Toshiba ($48 billion), Sony ($40 billion), NEC ($38 billion), Canon ($19 billion), Sanyo ($16 billion), Sharp ($14 billion), and Ricoh ($10 billion). Collectively these eight Japanese conglomerates did $261 billion in sales in a recent year and managed to almost break even.

A big contributing factor was a $2.9 billion loss at Sony, but none of the eight conglomerates were particularly profitable. The best performance was at Sharp, with net income of $295 million, or a little more than 2 percent of sales. (With a similar sales volume, Caterpillar had net profits of almost 7 percent of sales.)

In the long run, Japanese conglomerates are going to be no match for narrowly focused companies with strong brand names and even stronger bottom lines. The stock market reflects the poor prospects of Japanese companies. Since 1990, the Japanese market has fallen by 50 percent while the U.S. market was rising by 75 percent.

The situation is even worse in countries like Korea with stronger government control of the economy. Four giant *chaebols* dominate the Korean economy: Samsung ($63 billion), Hyundai ($63 billion), LG ($48 billion), and Daewoo ($40 billion).

"From chips to ships" said a recent Hyundai advertisement. Here is a company that literally makes everything except the kitchen sink. According to Hyundai, the company is in the following industries: "automobiles, electronics, shipbuilding, engineering and construction, machinery and equipment, petrochemicals, trading, and transportation."

Or look at the Samsung line: consumer electronics, shipbuilding, computer chips and screens, aerospace, petrochemicals, engineering and construction, life insurance. Recently Samsung paid $378 million for a 40 percent stake in AST Research, a money-losing U.S. manufacturer of personal computers.

Even more astonishing is Samsung's 1994 decision to start producing automobiles in a joint venture with Nissan. In autocratic Korea, of course, that decision required government permission, obtained only after a hard-fought campaign by Chairman Lee Kun-Hee, son of the founder.

What if General Electric decided to build automobiles? The stock market would have a fit, and rightly so. The role of the market is not just to supply capital and liquidity to corporations and investors but also to control managements' flights of egomania.

The LG Group is in double trouble. Not only has it given up its name (Lucky Goldstar) for a set of meaningless initials, but the group is also expanding in all directions at once.

In Southeast Asia and India, LG is getting into oil refineries, petrochemicals, communications, and real estate development along with its core electric and electronics businesses, which include television sets, audio/video products, home appliances, computers and office automation equipment, semiconductors, and liquid crystal displays.

Recently the company spent $351 million to buy 58 percent of television set manufacturer Zenith Electronics. Zenith is no bargain. The company hasn't posted a full-year profit from continuing operations since 1984.

While its protected home market (where LG is number one in television sets, refrigerators, and washing machines) will keep the company relatively healthy, its broad product line is a serious disadvantage in the worldwide market.

In search of synergy, the company has invested $10 million in 3DO to work on the next generation of game hardware, and it's working with Oracle to develop video-on-demand set-top boxes. It's also producing and marketing household appliances with General Electric and developing new operating software with IBM.

Daewoo is following in the footsteps of the other three *chaebols*. Debt-laden Daewoo recently spent $1.1 billion for a 60 percent stake in a state-owned Polish automobile factory. That's in addition to the $340 million Daewoo invested in another Polish car manufacturer.

The company also put up $156 million to establish a joint venture to build its Cielo family car in Romania. Daewoo already builds the Cielo in New Delhi and plans to invest $5 billion in India's auto industry in the next five years. Daewoo also earmarked $2 billion for a joint-venture auto-parts plant in China. Two years ago, the company broke ground on a $500 million car plant in Uzbekistan.

Mind you, Daewoo isn't just an automobile company. Daewoo is a trading/consumer electronics/construction/shipbuilding/computer/telephone/financial services/automobile company.

Nor is Daewoo a profitable automobile company. In spite of a protected domestic market, Daewoo has lost more than $450 million in the past four years. Meanwhile the company is preparing a 1997 entry into the highly competitive U.S. automotive market. Good luck.

The *chaebol* system in Korea and the *keiretsu* system in Japan help dampen competition in home markets but don't do anything to make the home teams globally competitive, aside from furnishing the funds domestically to lose abroad. (Using domestic profits to subsidize export sales is "dumping," and is illegal under international trade rules.)

If anything, by encouraging a broadening of the product line, the *chaebol* and *keiretsu* systems destroy a company's power outside of its home country.

China seems to be following the same pattern. Zheng Dunxun, president of Sinochem, China's largest company, thinks the $15 billion giant is too small. "We must diversify in all areas and very rapidly to compete." So he's turning Sinochem into a Japanese-style multinational trading, industrial, and financial giant, known in the Chinese media as an "aircraft carrier."

Other Chinese chief executives are rushing to park their aircraft on the deck of a carrier. "Big is beautiful" seems to be the buzzword in management circles.

Big is beautiful, but only if a company is narrowly focused. As a developing country, China offers many opportunities for intra-industry mergers, much like the one that created General Motors in 1908.

The Chinese automotive industry is highly fragmented. Few people can name even one of China's 130 makers of cars and trucks. As it happens, the United States had approximately the same number of car manufacturers the year GM was formed.

Big is beautiful, but not when it's a collection of unrelated businesses. As a matter of fact, General Motors was a financial mess until Alfred Sloan found a way to focus the company in the twenties (chapter 12).

Further complicating the long-term problems of countries like Japan, Korea, and China is the globalization of money. In the future, companies cannot count on low-cost money anymore. It's too easy for investors to shift their capital to companies in other countries where the returns on their investments are higher.

In the past, Japanese companies have benefited from favorable interest rates. Currently the Bank of Japan's discount rate is 0.5 percent. The prime rate is around 1.5 percent. But these low rates are unlikely to continue.

Like products and services, money in the future will flow into those countries that offer the highest returns. Unless the *keiretsus* and *chaebols* find a way to increase their profits, they are going to be starved for capital. Without profits, there is no way for a conglomerate to meet its future capital requirements.

Many companies in the U.S. market are creating their own *keiretsus* with alliances or "soft mergers," which have become extremely popular. According to management-consulting firm Booz, Allen & Hamilton, the number of formal alliances jumped from 750 during the seventies to 20,000 in the five-year period from 1987 to 1992.

Quick, name one alliance that has been a spectacular success. The truth is, most alliances have been disappointments to their principals. They drain money, resources, and management time into unproductive areas. Alliances unfocus a corporation.

Take Apple's alliance with IBM. This "computer *keiretsu*" has produced two joint ventures in the software area, Taligent and Kaleida, which have yet to produce a profitable product. (Nor are they likely to do so in the future.) Out of this alliance has emerged the PowerPC chip, a product produced by IBM and the third partner in the deal, Motorola, Inc.

The PowerPC chip has been a mixed blessing. It has helped Motorola sell a few more chips, but it has done nothing positive for Apple Computer. For IBM the new chip is a definite negative because Big Blue must now support two chip standards, the Intel and the PowerPC.

The numbers reinforce this conclusion. The day the pact was announced on October 2, 1991, at an elaborate San Francisco event beamed around the world via satellite, Apple and IBM were number one and number two with 35 percent of the U.S. personal computer market. Four years later the two protagonists were number two and number four with 21 percent of the market.

The hype that accompanied the announcement was awesome. "IBM-Apple could be fearsome," boasted *Business Week*. "Their final agreement is a sweeping array of joint efforts in hardware, software, and networking that could profoundly alter the $93 billion personal computer industry's balance of power." It never happened.

Furthermore, the two executives who negotiated the deal (John Sculley of Apple and James Cannavino of IBM) are both gone.

One wonders whether the same hype accompanied the creation of the dinosaur some hundreds of millions of years ago. "The ten-ton Tyrannosaurus rex will rule the world." Which is exactly the hype that accompanied the planned merger of Walt Disney and Capital Cities/ABC. (The ABCDisneysaurus rex.)

Also the Time Warner and Turner Broadcasting System merger. (The Timeturnersaurus rex.)

Where have all the dinosaur reptiles gone? Will the same question be asked about the dinosaur corporations? I think so. Corporate size is not a measure of corporate power. Size is a weakness if the company is not focused.

IBM was a $35 billion powerhouse when Compaq was just a sketch on a paper place mat. Yet today, thirteen years later, Compaq leads IBM in personal computers by a wide margin. Compaq is focused. IBM is not.

The dinosaur is a good image to keep in mind for companies in smaller countries trying to break into the global market. These companies often complain of the difficulties of exporting to the larger, developed countries. They fear the challenge of competing with larger, more established companies.

But the real problem is not the size of the country but the focus of the company. In a small country, the typical company is far more diversified than the typical company in a large country. The small country is paying the price in export markets for its companies' lack of specialization or focus in its home markets.

To effectively compete in export markets a company has to narrow its product line and concentrate on establishing both a reputation and a market presence. Be it tomatoes or baseball bats, radios or leather coats, the most globally successful companies based in small countries are those with a razor-sharp focus and a dedication to selling in the global marketplace.

With global specialization and focus comes change in the composition of economies and industries. Companies cannot compete effectively in every sector of the market and neither can countries. Change is the order of the day.

When you see industries such as the U.S. television set industry shift offshore, it does not mean that America is any worse off. In fact, it means that the country is better off. Specialization requires sacrifice. In America, capital and workers are better employed in such industries as aircraft, motion pictures, and computers, where the focus of American firms allows them to dominate world markets.

The globalization of business is driving both companies and countries into greater specialization, a trend that is good for everybody. A country that devotes 100 percent of its resources, human as well as material, to a handful of industries is a country that has become a specialist.

And a country that is probably exceptionally wealthy, too.

THE DRIVING FORCE
OF DIVISION

Like amoebas dividing in a petri dish, business can be viewed as an ever-dividing sea of categories.

A category starts off as a single entity usually dominated by one company. IBM dominated the computer category, for example, with the mainframe.

But over time, the category divides into two or more categories. Mainframes, minicomputers, supercomputers, fault-tolerant computers, personal computers, workstations, laptops, notebooks, palmtops, file servers. And more to come.

Beer used to be beer. Then the category divided. Today we have domestic beer and imported beer. Regular beer and light beer. Draft beer and dry beer. Expensive beer and inexpensive beer. Red beer and ice beer. Even nonalcoholic beer. And more to come.

Ford once dominated the automobile category with the Model T, a car that represented basic transportation. Then the category divided. Today we have luxury cars, moderately priced cars, and inexpensive cars. Full-size, intermediates, and compacts. Imported cars, domestic cars. Sports cars, sport-utility vehicles, RVs, and minivans. And more to come.

Bayer once dominated the pain reliever category with aspirin. Then the category divided. Today we have acetaminophen, ibuprofen, and naproxen sodium. And more to come.

Each segment is a separate, distinct entity. Each segment has its own reason for existence. And each segment has its own leader, which is rarely the same as the leader of the original category. Bayer leads in aspirin. Tylenol leads in acetaminophen. Advil leads in ibuprofen. And Aleve leads in naproxen sodium.

Division is a fact of life, a driving force of business. Division is happening in every product category from computers to communications to consumer electronics to cable television.

Why then do so many corporate executives believe just the opposite? Why do they believe that categories are coming together and not dividing? And why are these beliefs causing them to rapidly unfocus their companies?

What concept has such a powerful lock on their imaginations it's causing them to see things that are not happening?

It's the concept of *convergence*, the latest and greatest in a long line of management fads.

Every recent decade has had its own management fad that history proves to have been misguided at best. In the sixties, it was *conglomerization*, the notion that a professional manager could manage anything. Textron, AM International, ITT, LTV, Litton, and a long list of other conglomerates had their moment in the sun and then faded away.

"The conglomerate theory," according to the *Wall Street Journal,* "held that companies operating in many different businesses would be less vulnerable to downturns in individual sectors and could benefit from centralized management. But the fad was discredited when conglomerate stocks collapsed, along with the rest of the market, in the 1970s. Indeed, much of the takeover activity of the 1980s involved breaking up multi-industry companies and selling off the pieces."

According to UCLA professor David Lewin, the share of the economy controlled by the big conglomerates has declined dramatically from roughly 45 percent in the sixties to about 15 percent today.

In the seventies, it was *diversification*, the notion that every company needed a countercyclic business to balance out its business cycle. Xerox, Westinghouse, and a host of other companies got into the financial services business to balance out their basic hard-goods products. The losses are still being tallied up.

The latest example is Seagram, with a beverage business and an entertainment business. Sometimes you can get lucky. But as a corporate strategy, diversification has almost nothing going for it.

After studying the performance of thirty-three big American firms between 1950 and 1986, Michael Porter concluded that diversification had done more to destroy shareholder value than to create it. Most of the companies had divested many more acquisitions than they had kept.

Diversification, of course, was based on the idea of combining two *different* entities so they would "balance" each other out. When one was down, the other might be up. And vice versa. That's why an electrical company like General Electric bought a mining company like Utah International. (Since sold.) The next decade's fad was based on the opposite idea. Buy a company that's *similar* to yours.

In the eighties, it was *synergy*, the notion that a company could exploit the similarities between such products as magazines and motion pictures (Time Warner), cola and wine (Coca-Cola's acquisition and divestiture of Taylor Wine Co.), or consumer electronic and motion pictures (Sony's acquisition of Columbia). The results are still coming in, but the first returns have been dismal.

Synergy and its kissing cousin, the corporate alliance, are still popular buzzwords in the boardrooms of Corporate America. AT&T bought NCR but failed to find any synergy between communications and computers. (Recently AT&T has given up on synergy and split up into three parts, an example of the driving force of division.)

The fad of the nineties is *convergence*, the notion that digital technologies are coming together. So naturally companies have to merge or set up alliances in order to take advantage of this powerful trend. The media hype behind the convergence fad is enormous. Every major management publication has jumped on the convergence bandwagon.

Fortune: "Convergence will be the buzzword for the rest of the decade. This isn't just about cable and telephone hopping into bed together. It's about the cultures and corporations of major industries—telecommunications (including the long-distance companies), cable, computer, entertainment, consumer electronics, publishing, and even retailing—combining into one mega-industry that will provide information, entertainment, goods, and services to your home and office."

Wall Street Journal: "Shock is a common feeling these days among leaders of five of the world's biggest industries: computing, communications, consumer electronics, entertainment, and publishing. Under a common technological lash—the increasing ability to cheaply convey huge chunks of video, sound, graphics, and text in digital form—they are transforming and converging."

New York Times: "It's no mystery why telephone and cable are pursuing each other. The technological differences that separate telephone, television, and computer transmissions are rapidly disappearing, so one company can now provide all three."

Who will be hurt by the digital revolution?

Michael Crichton, author of *Jurassic Park* and other best-sellers: "To my mind, it is likely that what we now understand as the mass media will be gone within ten years. Vanished without a trace." And Mr. Crichton has some specific candidates in mind. "The next great American institution to find itself obsolete and outdated will be the *New York Times* and the commercial networks."

Reminds one of a 1913 prediction by Thomas Edison. "Books will soon be obsolete in the schools," to be displaced by the far more efficient medium of "motion pictures," which instruct "through the eye." (Books have never been more popular, with annual growth rates of 2 percent and more.)

One highly touted combination that has yet to come together is computers and communications. This concept was first publicly articulated in 1977 by Japan's NEC Corporation. A pet project of former CEO Koji Kobayashi, computers and communications, or C&C as it is widely called at NEC, has become well-nigh a religion inside the corporation.

C&C didn't seem to help NEC. The world's fifth largest maker of telecommunications equipment, the world's fourth largest maker of computers, and the world's second largest maker of semiconductors, NEC makes everything but money. In the last decade, NEC shares have lagged behind the Japanese stock market by 28 percent.

AT&T pursued a C&C strategy for more than a decade before throwing in the towel. Back in 1983, chairman Charles Brown said: "The driving force of this revolution, of course, is the convergence of communications and computer technology, which is literally redefining the telecommunications industry."

The 1982 consent decree spinning off local telephone service to seven newly formed Baby Bells included one "benefit" for AT&T. The Justice Department allowed the company to go into the computer business.

Big deal. So far that benefit has cost AT&T billions of dollars. The first iteration of the C&C strategy was the formation of AT&T Information Systems and the less-than-successful marketing of a line of personal computers and workstations. In eight years, the unit rang up $2 billion in losses.

The second iteration of the C&C strategy began in 1991 with the $7.4 billion purchase of NCR Corporation. With NCR, AT&T would "link people, organizations, and their information in a seamless, global computer network," vowed chairman Robert Allen.

NCR (since renamed "Global Information Solutions") has been a financial disaster for AT&T, bleeding losses ever since its acquisition. In five years Global Information Solutions has had four CEOs.

Another sign of trouble was the full product line, from desktop to midrange to mainframe. Global Information Solutions also tried to market a line of "massively parallel" computers, thanks to the $520 million purchase of Teradata Corp.

Personals? Midrange? Conventional mainframes? Massively parallel mainframes? Where's the focus? No wonder AT&T decided to spin off the entire mess. "AT&T abandoned yesterday its once-grand vision of combining communications and computers into a single corporate empire," reported the *New York Times*. "In the end, that vision proved to be a costly illusion."

Some people call convergence "the broadband-cyberspace-interactive-multimedia-full-service-network-500-channel-digital-information-superhighway revolution." Whatever you call it, the reality is quite different. The driving force in business today is not convergence, it's division.

Convergence is against the laws of nature. In physics, the law of entropy says that the degree of disorder in a closed system always increases. By contrast, a pattern of convergence would make things more orderly.

In biology, the law of evolution holds that new species are created by the division of a single species. Convergence, on the other hand, would have you believe that species are constantly combining, yielding such curiosities as the catdog.

Actually, it's the opposite. Instead of combinations like the cat-dog, new breeds of dogs are coming into existence. Currently the American Kennel Club recognizes 141 breeds of dogs, with a new breed added to the list about once a year.

Take the computer again. According to the convergenists, the computer is going to combine with the telephone, cable, and television industries, producing what is likely to be called "telecableputervision." Note that these revolutionary developments are always going to happen sometime in the future.

What about the past? Good question. After all, the computer industry is now pushing forty-five years old, starting with Remington Rand's launch of Univac in the early fifties. In more than four decades has the computer converged with any other product?

Not that I can recall. On the other hand, the computer has certainly done a lot of dividing.

"Those who cannot remember the past," wrote George Santayana, "are condemned to repeat it." The first computer, if you remember, was known as a computer. It was never called a mainframe until Digital Equipment Corp. launched the minicomputer. With that development the computer industry had divided into mainframe computers and minis.

Over the years the computer industry divided again and again. Today we have personal computers, portables, laptops, notebooks, palmtops, pen computers, workstations, supercomputers, super minicomputers, fault-tolerant computers, fault-tolerant minicomputers, parallel processing computers.

If we are to believe the convergenists, all of this division is going to suddenly come to a halt and computers are going to *converge*? With what? Is someone forgetting the past? It would certainly seem so.

Is the computer going to merge with television? Bill Gates thinks so. "The device we're talking about here has all the benefits of a TV. It is fairly inexpensive; you can stick it in your living room and use a little remote control to control it. But inside are chips that are even more powerful than today's PCs. And if you add a keyboard or a printer you can do PC-like things. So it's a device that needs a new name. We call it the TV/PC."

The TV/PC? Great idea, but doomed to failure. Technologies don't converge, they divide. But companies seem willing to spend millions of dollars exploring these technological dead ends. A few years ago Hewlett-Packard and Time Warner announced plans to jointly develop technologies that would allow a television set to print out sales coupons, advertisements, magazine articles, and color stills of TV shows. Expect nothing of the sort to occur.

Pretty soon they might be introducing a combination TV/VCR. Why not? It's a natural. As a matter of fact there are combination television and videocassette recorders on the market, but very few are bought. The problem is people don't usually buy a new TV or a new VCR until their old one breaks down. Unfortunately for the manufacturers of these combination products, your television set and your videocassette recorder seldom give up the ghost at the same time.

And how about the microwave oven? Did it combine with the electric or gas oven? No, because of the same problem. Why do I have to throw out a perfectly good oven to buy a combination microwave/gas or microwave/electric oven?

Take another example. If any two products should merge, it's the washer and the dryer. Sure, you can buy a combination washer/dryer, but almost nobody does. There are too many advantages with separate units, starting with the revolutionary feature of being able to wash the second load while you are drying the first.

Another favorite convergence concept is "one-stop shopping." Many companies have dropped a bundle trying to make this one work. Saatchi & Saatchi, one of the world's largest advertising agencies, became enamored of the idea. So they bought a basket of design and consulting firms in an effort to handle all of their corporate clients' needs.

Soon after, with losses mounting, Saatchi was forced to sell its nonadvertising businesses. (The stock fell from $80 a share eight years ago to around $2 today.)

Gates has another convergence idea that he calls the Wallet PC. This one combines keys, charge cards, personal identification, cash, writing implements, passport, and pictures of the kids! Not to mention a global positioning system so you can always tell where you are and how to get where you want to go.

Silly? Of course, but the media makes enough of a fuss about the concept that many ordinarily unflappable people get all worked up about the electronic wallet. The truth is that the driving force in business is not convergence. It's division.

When convergence products are introduced, they usually attract only a small market. Witness Apple's Newton, a combination pen computer, electronic calendar, fax machine, and wireless communicator. Few new products received so much media attention as the Newton. And, unfortunately for Apple, few Newtons are being bought.

One of the most persistent predictions is that cable television and local phone service will converge. After all, both industries wire up houses in similar ways. Why not combine the two operations, reduce overhead, and make the system interactive? Both the Baby Bells and the cable companies have explored mergers and set up joint ventures to explore the possibility.

Bell Atlantic's $32 billion planned takeover of Tele-Communications Inc. was the most visible example of this kind of convergence thinking. The deal collapsed but convergence lives on. Cable companies are talking about offering phone service. Phone companies are talking about offering "movies on demand."

"Every cable company today has a business plan," says a Bell Atlantic vice chairman, "that calls for it to get 10 percent of the market from the local telephone company." Time Warner's chairman predicts that by the year 2000 his company's telephone revenues will surpass $1 billion, about one-third of the company's current cable income.

What's technically feasible isn't always acceptable in the marketplace. Aside from low price, what's the number one customer requirement for telephone service?

Reliability, of course. If your house is burning down, you want to be able to reach the fire department in a hurry. Ditto the police department or the 911 emergency line.

Ask someone the last time their telephone service was out. "Seldom, if ever" is the typical reply. Ask someone the last time their cable service was out. "Last Tuesday" is the typical reply.

Why would anyone switch from a reliable Bell company to an unreliable cable company for telephone service? Highly unlikely. You can live without *ER*. You might die without EMS.

While cable companies are broadening their services to include telephone and two-way communications, the cable industry itself is dividing. More than a million customers are now getting HBO, CNN, NFL games, Showtime, MTV, and other cable channels via digital satellite systems, or DSS.

DSS was pioneered not by the cable industry but by Hughes Electronics, a subsidiary of General Motors. (Primestar Partners, a consortium of six cable operators and General Electric, is struggling to catch up.) DirecTV, the Hughes service, is currently outselling Primestar by two to one.

It's typical. The cable companies are so busy trying to get into somebody else's business they don't have the time to see the division taking place in their own business. Leaders are almost never overthrown from the outside. Leaders are almost always toppled from within as the category divides beneath them.

Also on the horizon is wireless cable, which provides a high-quality signal where conditions are favorable. Cable used to be cable. Now we have three kinds: regular cable, wireless cable, and DSS. And more to come.

Why has convergence gained such acceptance in the absence of tangible evidence that it is happening? Again, it's the enormous emphasis that chief executives place on growth. They want to believe in convergence because it promises to double their size. "If my business is converging with somebody else's business, then I can put the two together and be twice as big."

Traditionally, convergence can be thought of as a horizontal combination, the coming together of two equal partners. Lately another kind of convergence has captured the imagination of business leaders everywhere. It could be called vertical integration or vertical convergence.

Vertical convergence is best illustrated by the Walt Disney deal to buy Capital Cities/ABC for $19 billion in stock and cash. It's a merger of content and distribution. "One plus one equals four," said Michael Eisner, Disney CEO.

His thinking is as faulty as his math. Competition is the driving force in improving the breed, not sweetheart distribution deals. From ABC's point of view, the network should be searching for the best content. They should not be forced to take the Disney output.

From Disney's point of view, they should sell their content to the highest bidder. They should not be forced to take the ABC distribution deal. One plus one equals maybe one and a half.

Ask Matsushita. They thought they needed content to fill their Panasonic hardware, so they bought MCA, a major motion-picture studio. While MCA did well under Matsushita's hands-off management, they found precious few synergies with hardware. So they sold the movie business to Seagram.

Ask Sony. They also thought they needed content to fill their hardware, so they bought Columbia Pictures. Five years and a string of box-office flops later, Sony was forced to take a whopping $2.7 billion write-down.

Sony surrender? Never. The new president of Sony Corporation, Nobuyuki Idei, is going one step further. He plans to move into the distribution of movies, television shows, music, computer software, and other forms of programming to fill in the missing link between Sony's two existing main businesses: creating the programming and building the electronic boxes to play, or consume, the programs.

"My dream," said Mr. Idei, "is to fill the gap between content creation and content consumption."

Whether you call it filling the gap or line extension or vertical convergence, it's just another route toward unfocusing a corporation. Companies that broaden their line, for whatever reason, are vulnerable to narrowly focused competition that takes advantage of division, not convergence.

Since no one can predict the future, how can one be so sure that convergence won't take place?

A study of history is the best place to start. If the computer was the defining product of the second half of the twentieth century, then the automobile was the defining product of the first half. If convergence is a natural effect of technological progress, then what similarities can we find between cars and computers?

In other words, if the computer is going to converge with another product, then perhaps the automobile has already done so.

Most historians credit the invention of the automobile to Karl Benz in 1885. In more than one hundred years, has the automobile converged with any other vehicle?

No, of course not, although many people have tried. In 1945, Ted Hall developed the Hall Flying Car, which was introduced to a wildly enthusiastic public with grandiose predictions.

Roads would become obsolete, traffic jams a thing of the past. You could go anywhere, anytime, with complete freedom of movement. Every major airplane manufacturer in America hoped to cash in on Hall's invention. The lucky buyer was Convair.

In July 1946, Convair introduced Hall's flight of fancy as the Convair Model 118 ConvAirCar. Company management confidently predicted minimum sales of 160,000 units a year. The price was

$1,500, plus an extra charge for the wings, which would also be available for rental at any airport.

In spite of the hype, only two ConvAirCars were ever built. Both now rest in a warehouse in El Cajon, California.

Three years later, Moulton Taylor introduced the Aerocar, a sporty runabout with detachable wings and tail. The Aerocar received a great deal of fanfare at the time. The Ford Motor Company even considered mass-producing it. But the Aerocar met with the same predictable fate as the Flying Car.

A bad idea never dies. Recently Paul Moller, president of Moller International, introduced the M400 Volantor, a "sky car" that Moller has spent twenty-five years and $25 million developing. A former professor of aeronautical engineering at the University of California at Davis, Mr. Moller has taken seventy-two orders for the craft, with a $5,000 deposit each, at a projected price of $800,000 each. (Not exactly a mass-market vehicle.)

Designed to hover motionless in midair and to take off and land vertically from a standing start without a runway, the Volantor is more of a cross between a helicopter and an automobile. Will the product take off? Very unlikely.

If it wouldn't work in the air, maybe it would work on the water.

In 1961, the Quandt Group of West Germany introduced the Amphicar, which was sold around the world until 1965. This was not a flight of fancy; there was a serious marketing effort put behind the product. But the Amphicar foundered for the same reason that almost all combination products go under. It combined the worst of both worlds. Owners said it drove like a boat and floated like a car.

They keep trying. Recently a group of California entrepreneurs demonstrated the Aquastrada Delta, a $25,000 surf-and-turfmobile with a fiberglass hull, a 245-horsepower Ford truck engine, and wheels that retract into watertight compartments. Will it sink or swim? History has a habit of repeating itself.

Then there's the fax/phone that Canon introduced with a big advertising and publicity campaign. These combination ideas sound terrific in the boardroom, but they usually have a fatal flaw that keeps them from gaining wide acceptance. Do you own a fax/phone? Most people don't. Why? It's a mediocre fax combined with a mediocre phone.

If the fax won't work with the phone, maybe it will work with the copier and computer printer. Currently the media is getting all worked up about the combination copier, facsimile, and computer printer (with a scanner sometimes added as an extra feature). The hype is enormous, but sales remain modest.

So what do you think? Do categories divide or do they converge?

Many otherwise intelligent people have a personal philosophy that they call "the law of the middle." If half the people say "black" and half the people say "white," then the correct answer must be "gray."

Therefore, we're likely to get some convergence, which is going to take longer than many people believe. That's the gray answer to the convergence question and the one that's most likely to be wrong.

"Yet while convergence has diverged from the high road of early expectations," reported the *Wall Street Journal* recently, "it remains the way of the future. It's only that the journey, executives in multimedia businesses say, will take longer, cost more money, and be far more complicated than first imagined."

It's the Vietnam syndrome. Once we have decided to take action, we cannot be wrong. Therefore, we have to redouble our efforts, convinced of the rightness of our cause and our confidence in the ultimate outcome.

Do categories divide or do they converge?

Does the Earth revolve around the Sun, as Copernicus thought? Or does the Sun revolve around the Earth, as Ptolemy thought? The gray answer is that half the time the Sun revolves around the Earth and half the time the Earth revolves around the Sun.

Is capitalism the better economic system for a country? Or is communism? The Middle Way has been an economic disaster for countries that have tried it.

Do categories divide or do they converge?

Gray is usually the worst of both possible worlds. Focusing a corporation requires courage. You have to look the *Wall Street Journal* in the eye and say, "You're wrong."

There is no middle way.

ENCOURAGING SIGNS FROM THE CORPORATE FRONT

The *Fortune* 500 list of the largest industrial corporations is a fairly accurate barometer of the health of American business.

- 42 out of the *Fortune* 500 companies lost money in 1988.

- 54 companies lost money in 1989.

- 67 companies lost money in 1990.

- 102 companies lost money in 1991.

- 149 companies lost money in 1992.

At the rate the barometer was falling, every *Fortune* 500 company in the year 1997 would have been losing money.

In 1993, things started to change. Only 114 of the 500 companies lost money. (That's still 23 percent losers, however.)

And in 1994, forty companies lost money, although the list is not comparable with previous years because service companies were added for the first time.

One reason for the improvement might be a change in corporate philosophy. With diversification dead in the water and synergy looking more and more like a lame strategy, there seems to be a movement in the opposite direction. Yes, the business world is getting focused.

Underneath the hype of convergence, alliances, and mergers, another story is unfolding. Thoughtful business leaders are quietly beginning to bring their companies into focus. Some recent stories that illustrate this trend:

Wall Street Journal, May 4, 1994. "Eastman Kodak Co., in a surprisingly sweeping reorganization, said it will put up for sale its big Sterling Winthrop drug unit and two other businesses to focus on its core film operations."

Wall Street Journal, May 27, 1994. "While much of corporate America is racing to produce electronic data products and services, Mead Corp. is chasing more mundane markets such as paper and notebooks. Last week, Mead decided to put its Lexis/Nexis electronic data services division on the block and beef up its old-line paper, packaging, and pulp businesses. Rather than searching for the next hot technology to pursue, Mead believes there's lots of money to be made in paper products if done right."

New York Times, June 21, 1994. "Citicorp, continuing to shed nonstrategic assets in an effort to build capital and focus on its core financial businesses, said yesterday that it had sold I/B/E/S Inc."

Wall Street Journal, September 29, 1994. "Just when its office-paper business is finally on the upturn, James River Corp. has decided to shed that operation and possibly its profitable packaging business. Instead, the Richmond, Va., company plans to concentrate on its core consumer-paper business, which includes Dixie paperware and Brawny paper towels. Not a bad idea, analysts say."

International Herald Tribune, November 5–6, 1994. "Bowater PLC said Friday it was selling its tissue and timber business in Australia as part of its drive to focus on its core printing and packaging sectors."

Wall Street Journal, November 11, 1994. "Sears, Roebuck & Co., completing a return to its retailing roots, plans to spin off its $9 billion controlling stake in its huge Allstate Corp. insurance unit. The Allstate spin-off will return Sears to its retailing roots dating to 1886, when it opened its mail-order business. Since September 1992, the company has shed its Dean Witter, Discover Corp. holdings and its Coldwell Banker real-estate unit."

Advertising Age, November 14, 1994. "R.L. Polk & Co. is getting out of the full-service direct marketing business as part of a plan to bolster its core operations, gathering and interpreting data."

Wall Street Journal, March 2, 1995. "St. Joe Paper Co. saw its stock jump 14% as investors cheered the expected sale of more than

$800 million in assets and the company's new focus on transportation and real estate."

New York Times, April 27, 1995. "Pitney Bowes Inc., in the midst of a restructuring program to cut costs and focus on core businesses, said it agreed to sell its Dictaphone Corp. unit for $450 million to a New York investment group."

International Herald Tribune, June 22, 1995. "After wild buying sprees in the 1970s and 1980s, Guinness PLC has decided that Guinness is good for it. It has divested itself of virtually everything but beer and liquor, because 'I have a strongly held point of view that you can only be good at a limited number of things,' the chairman, Anthony A. Greener, said in a recent interview."

New York Times, August 23, 1995. "Domtar Inc. is planning to shed its gypsum and decorative-panel divisions as part of a new strategy focusing on lumber, papers, and packaging."

Wall Street Journal, August 30, 1995. "Fisons PLC neared completion of a six-month drive to divest itself of noncore operations by agreeing to sell most of its Laboratory Supplies division to Fisher Scientific International Inc. of the U.S. for $311.9 million."

Finally, business is getting around to doing what Peter Drucker recommended years ago: "Concentration is the key to economic results. Economic results require that managers concentrate their efforts on the smallest number of activities that will produce the largest amount of revenue. . . . No other principle is violated as constantly today as the basic principle of concentration. . . . Our motto seems to be: let's do a little bit of everything."

"We've had some real problems," said a Colgate-Palmolive executive recently. "We may have tried to do too much in the past year with new products, manufacturing changes, and organizational changes. There may have been too much activity with not enough focus on the base businesses. We have to refocus now."

Does that sound like a company you might know? My experience tells me this complaint could be heard at almost any company in the United States.

Too many corporations today are a mile wide and an inch deep. Maybe this formula could work in an era when there were fewer companies and less competition. But not today. Today a company needs a narrow focus to compete in a marketplace that is rapidly going global.

TRW is a good example. Once a conglomerate with eighty different businesses, TRW has shed nearly half its units. Says TRW executive vice president William Lawrence: "The key words for the nineties are focus and flexibility."

Union Carbide is another. Before the Bhopal disaster a decade ago, Union Carbide had 110,000 employees and sold $10 billion worth of Eveready batteries, Glad bags, and countless industrial chemicals. It was an unwieldy, barely profitable mishmash. After Bhopal and a failed takeover attempt by raider Samuel Hayman, things got worse.

"We had too many diverse businesses competing for capital and management attention," says Robert Kennedy, Carbide's CEO since 1986. So Kennedy sold noncore assets such as the battery and consumer products units, reduced debt to less than $1 billion, and shed 90 percent of the workforce. Sales are now approaching $5 billion and profits nearly $500 million. Less is more. Half a focused loaf is better than the whole loaf with slices that are spread too far apart.

Merck bought Medco, a drug benefit-management company, because it promises to help the company reduce the cost of its drug distribution systems. But Merck has been dropping its noncore businesses like Calgon Vestal Laboratories (sold to Bristol-Myers Squibb for $261 million) and Calgon Water Management (sold to English China Clays for $308 million). It also sold Kelco, its chemical company, to Monsanto for $1.1 billion.

Merck's only nondrug unit left in its portfolio is Hubbard Farms, a turkey breeding company. Want to bet that turkey will soon hit the chopping block?

Fingerhut, a $1.8 billion Minnesota company, has sold its computer service bureau and its deep-discount cataloger and is about to sell its food catalog in order to concentrate on its direct-marketing business.

Quaker State sold its insurance company to GE Capital for $85 million and then turned around and bought a specialty oil company for $90 million. According to Herbert Baum, the company's CEO, the moves fit into Quaker State's strategy to refocus on lubricants and lubricant services.

After a review by McKinsey & Co., Shoney's said it was selling four of its seven food divisions. CEO Taylor Henry said that the company's resources were "spread too thin." As a result, he said,

"We need to reduce the complexity of our business and focus on the Shoney's flagship."

Looking to become a pure restaurant company and also to reduce its debt, Flagstar sold most of Canteen Corp., its contract-feeding business, to Compass for $450 million. "It really was a strategic decision to focus on the restaurant business as opposed to being a more broad-based food-service company," said vice president Coleman Sullivan.

Philip Morris sold its Kraft Foodservice unit to Clayton, Dubilier & Rice for $700 million. "Food service is a business of relatively low margins and nonbranded items, whereas Kraft sells branded items through supermarkets," said Barry Ziegler, a securities analyst. "The sale is a good move since the food service is so different from the Kraft core business."

In 1991, Boole & Babbage, one of the oldest companies in the software field, lost $11 million on sales of $101 million. Over the years Boole had accumulated a hodgepodge of businesses, including a time-sharing company. Newly appointed president Paul Newton decided it was time to focus.

"We decided we were only going to sell two kinds of products to one kind of customer," says Newton. "Anything else had to be sold off or written off." In their latest fiscal year Boole reported sales of $132 million and an $8 million profit. The stock has quadrupled.

There are encouraging signs from the banking industry. Today's bankers speak eloquently of their own bank's "focus" and sense of direction. The days of everything for everybody seem to be disappearing from the typical banker's agenda. Which is surprising because most bankers have been fighting the Glass-Steagall Act (which restricted activities of commercial banks) ever since Congress passed the law in 1933. On their own, most commercial banks today are voluntarily restricting their target markets.

There are encouraging signs in the political arena. No recent president of the United States has been as focused on a single issue as Bill Clinton . . . before he was elected. "It's the economy, stupid," was James Carville's famous rallying cry.

But after the election it was a different story. No issue was too small for Mr. Clinton to be involved with. When asked what three things Bill Clinton had to do to get back the public's confidence, one practical politician said: "Focus, focus, focus."

There are encouraging signs from Europe, a continent noted for the notion that companies should be as diversified as they possibly can. Volvo, Sweden's largest company, has been paring down to its original role as a manufacturer of cars and trucks by getting rid of a 26 percent interest in Hertz and a 44 percent interest in Cardo, a Swedish investment company.

Companies like Volvo are not helped by a raft of magazine articles suggesting that it cannot survive without increasing its 1 percent share of the worldwide market. For years, automotive editors have encouraged Volvo to explore mergers, including one with Renault, which would have been disastrous.

By itself a 1 percent share of market doesn't make a company vulnerable. It all depends on how focused the company is. Volvo is focused on "safety," an enormously powerful and profitable position for any automobile company. Share of market isn't the driver here; share of mind is. For a company its size, Volvo has an outsized share of mind.

Tata Iron & Steel, India's largest company, is a good example of the problems facing third-world companies. Although it has $5 billion in annual revenues, Tata is not one company. It's a collection of forty-six companies that make everything from tea to trucks, from cosmetics to computer software.

But Tata's dream is to become a major player in passenger cars. Is this possible? Sure, as long as you can get a little help from your government to keep the competition out. But this is exactly what a developing country like India doesn't need. More tariffs and government regulations.

Ratan Tata, the new chairman at Tata, seems to understand the nature of the problem. "Our critical task is to refocus," he says. "We must restructure and divest noncore businesses." He wants to make his group a leader in a few key industries: trucks, autos, computer services, steel, and construction engineering as well as a domestic pioneer in multimedia and telecommunications. Sounds like a company biting off more than it can chew.

The same problems can be found in virtually all of the developing countries. The small size of these countries (economically speaking) and their high tariff barriers have combined to produce companies that are far too unfocused to compete in global markets. Only by making wrenching changes will many of these companies survive.

There are encouraging signs from the many corporate mergers that have occurred recently. Actually, there are two kinds of mergers: the good and the bad.

The bad mergers are the ones that emphasize market coverage or "fit." They are the ones that combine two dissimilar operations in order to increase the range of a company's operations.

Let's say you combine a company that specializes in the high end of the market with a company that specializes in the low end. Or perhaps a cable company with a phone company. Or in the entertainment industry, you might combine a content company with a hardware or a distribution company. None of these mergers, in the long run, are going to be very successful.

The good mergers are the ones that emphasize market dominance. In theory, the ideal merger, sure to be frowned on by the Justice Department, would combine two competitors, each with 50 percent of the market, into one company with 100 percent of the market.

In practice, companies can achieve a degree of market dominance by merging with competitors that match their own product or service offerings. Some recent mergers that illustrate this trend include:

- Lockheed merged with Martin Marietta to form Lockheed Martin, the world's largest defense company.

- Cineplex Odeon merged with Cinemark USA to create the world's biggest movie theater chain.

- First Data acquired First Financial Management in a $6.6 billion deal to create America's largest independent processor of credit card transactions.

- Interstate Bakeries bought Continental Baking to become America's largest baker.

- Rite Aid is buying Revco for $1.8 billion to cement its position as the nation's largest drugstore chain.

- Crown Cork & Seal acquired CarnaudMetalbox for nearly $4 billion to become the world's largest packaging company.

- International Paper bought Federal Paper Board for $2.7 billion to become the U.S. leader in bleached board used for packaging.

- Glaxo bought Wellcome for more than $14 billion to become the world's largest prescription-drug company.

- United HealthCare bought MetraHealth for $1.65 billion in cash and stock to become the largest U.S. health care management company.

- Abbey Healthcare merged with Homedco to create the largest U.S. home health care provider.

- Medpartners acquired Mullikin Medical Enterprises for $360 million in stock to create the nation's largest physician-management company.

But the most spectacular series of mergers is the one started by Rick Scott with the purchase of two large hospitals in El Paso, Texas. Eight years later, his company was the largest private health care provider in the country with 326 hospitals and more than 100 outpatient surgery centers.

Called Columbia/HCA, the company has annual revenues in excess of $15 billion and is three times the size of its closest for-profit competitor. This is focus and this is dominance.

Mergers are either good or bad depending on whether or not they increase a company's focus. Every merger with a similar company increases the focus of the resultant combination. Every merger with a dissimilar company decreases the focus.

There used to be a perception that a company was better off if it was in two lousy businesses rather than one good one, but that perception is changing.

Andrew Grove, CEO of $10 billion Intel, sums up the thinking of many chief executives today: "I'd rather have all my eggs in one basket and spend my time worrying about whether that's the right basket, than try to put one egg in every basket."

How to put all your eggs in one basket is what this book is all about.

ENCOURAGING SIGNS
FROM THE RETAIL FRONT

If you want to be an expert prognosticator of trends, go to the movies, listen to popular music, and keep your eyes on retailing. Especially retailing.

No other segment of the market is as sensitive to trends as retailers. As retailing goes, so goes the nation. So how is retailing going?

In a word, specialization. The era of the generalist seems to be over.

Let's go back a few decades when the generalists, the department stores, ruled the retailing roost. Macy's in New York; Marshall Field's in Chicago; Garfinckel's in Washington, D.C.; Rich's in Atlanta; I. Magnin in San Francisco.

As a matter of fact, every major city in America had a glittering array of department stores. In New York City, you could find Abraham & Straus, Alexander's, B. Altman, Arnold Constable, Bergdorf Goodman, Best & Co., Bloomingdale's, Bonwit Teller, EJ Korvette, Galeries Lafayette, Gimbel's, Henri Bendel, JC Penney, Lord & Taylor, Macy's, Ohrbach's, Saks-Fifth Avenue, and Stern's, to name a few.

Today, Abraham & Straus, Alexander's, B. Altman, Arnold Constable, Best & Co., Bonwit Teller, EJ Korvette, Galeries Lafayette, Gimbel's, and Ohrbach's are gone. Macy's and Bloomingdale's have been in and out of bankruptcy. And Saks-Fifth Avenue has required a substantial capital infusion.

What caused the decline of the department store?

Critics are often quick to criticize the stores themselves. They neglected

customer service. They didn't keep up with fashions. Their prices got
out of line. They were mismanaged. And so on. To a certain extent all
of these factors may have been true. But have department store customers given up buying?

Of course not. Today more and more people are shopping at specialty stores. It wasn't the department store that caused the decline
of the department store. It was the specialty store. Focus strikes
again.

The department store versus the specialty store. It's a fundamental principle of business that the more focused competitor usually
wins. You can apply that same principle to your business. Compared
with your major competitor, which company is the more focused?
The advantage always lies with the more focused operation.

Nor did Wal-Mart cause the decline of the New York City department store. (There are no Wal-Mart stores in New York City.)
Although Wal-Mart has wiped out many inefficient stores in smaller
cities and towns, they are just starting to move into the larger cities,
where they will face the same specialist competition that has deci-
mated the department stores.

Nationwide, the department store has been suffering for a decade
or longer. Many have clogged the courts seeking financial relief. In
1989, L. J. Hooker, owner of the Bonwit Teller and B. Altman
department stores, filed for bankruptcy. (B. Altman & Company,
whose 124-year-old flagship establishment was on Fifth Avenue,
was one of the first stores to cater to Manhattan's carriage trade.)

Rights to the Altman name went for $1.75 million, prompting
Alan Milstein, a retail newsletter editor, to comment, "In my opinion Altman's died fifteen years ago. Why would anyone want to res-
urrect it? It's stuck in the 1960s."

In 1990, Campeau Corporation collapsed, bringing such department store jewels as Bloomingdale's, Abraham & Straus, Stern's,
Jordan Marsh, Burdines, Rich's, and Lazarus into bankruptcy court.
In April that same year, Ames Department Stores Inc., with 680
stores east of the Mississippi, filed for Chapter 11 bankruptcy. That
summer, Garfinckel's, the pride of Washington, D.C., found its way
into bankruptcy court.

In 1991, Hills Department Stores Inc., with more than two hundred stores mostly in the Midwest, filed for Chapter 11 bankruptcy.
Also that same year Carter Hawley Hale Stores Inc., the largest

department store operator on the West Coast, filed for Chapter 11 bankruptcy.

Later the same year P.A. Bergner & Co., one of the Midwest's largest department store operators, including sixty-eight Carson Pirie Scott units, sought bankruptcy-court protection.

In 1992, tony retailer Saks-Fifth Avenue was forced to seek an additional $300 million in funding from its owner, Bahrain-based Investcorp. According to news stories, Saks had lost $398 million in the preceding two years.

In 1994, Woodward & Lathrop Holdings Inc. filed for Chapter 11 bankruptcy. Joining the filing was John Wanamaker Inc., a Philadelphia retailer and Woodward subsidiary. Woodward & Lothrop, with sixteen stores in the Washington-Baltimore area, and Wanamaker, with fifteen stores in the Philadelphia area, are venerable retailers with strong reputations.

A good reputation is not enough when the tide is against you. We have entered the era of the specialist. A store that sells everything is living in the past.

Sears also has a good reputation. In a way, Sears is also living in the past because it has gone against the trend toward specialization. For exactly one hundred years, Sears steadily expanded the scope of its operations. In 1886, Sears mailed out its first catalog. It wasn't until 1925 that Sears opened its first retail store. Six years later it established Allstate Insurance, at first to sell auto insurance and then property, casualty, life, and even mortgage insurance.

In 1959 Sears formed Homart Development Co. to develop shopping centers. In 1981 Sears bought Dean Witter Reynolds, a stock brokerage firm, and Coldwell Banker, a real estate firm. In the eighties Sears opened Financial Network Centers in many of its retail stores, the infamous "socks and stocks" strategy. Also in the eighties the company opened Sears Business Systems Centers to sell computers and software.

In 1986 came the nationwide launch of the Discover credit card. This was the high-water mark; from now on everything would be downhill. On Wall Street analysts were calling on Sears, Roebuck to break up into separate companies that would be worth more individually than as parts of the retailing giant.

In 1988 Sears sold Coldwell Banker's commercial real estate business. In 1992 Sears spun off Dean Witter, including the Discover credit card. In 1993 Sears shut down its Business Systems Centers and its general catalog business. It also sold its mortgage operations to PNC Bank Corp. and Coldwell Banker Residential business to The Fremont Group.

Size is not the determining factor in creating a profitable business. Focus is. The general catalog operation was a $3 billion business. That's right, three billion dollars, but it managed to lose $450 million in the three years before the ax fell.

In 1994 Sears announced plans to spin off the rest of Allstate and to seek a buyer for Homart. What's left at Sears? A retailing company with eight hundred department stores, a credit company, and twelve hundred specialty stores, including Western Auto Supply Company and Homelife furniture stores.

Even the real estate venture, Sears Tower in Chicago, turned out to be a disaster. Sitting with an $850 million mortgage on real estate worth only about $400 million, Sears literally walked away from the property.

What has replaced the department store?

A host of specialty stores, each with a narrow focus. The Limited focuses on upscale clothing for working women. The Gap focuses on basic clothing for the younger crowd. Victoria's Secret focuses on expensive women's undergarments. Circuit City and Best Buy focus on consumer electronics and major appliances. The Home Depot on household products. Office Depot on office supplies.

Then there are the catalog houses, each with a narrow focus. L.L. Bean, Sharper Image, J. Crew, and others.

Most fair-minded observers of the retail scene have concluded that the golden age of the department store has passed. Those that remain will be under constant pressure to cut costs to stay alive. Prognosis: more department store bankruptcies to come.

This is not to say that some department stores won't succeed. Many will. In a declining industry the few survivors that remain can be fabulously profitable.

There's always a market, even though small, for almost any product or service. And the advantage of serving a declining industry is the fact that you can develop a semimonopoly. A declining industry attracts almost no fresh, new competitors.

The horse, for example, has been almost totally replaced by the automobile. But the cost of saddles, bridles, and reins has gone up, not down. Reason: little competition for a small market. In the New York area you can buy four car shoes (tires) for the installed price of four horseshoes ($250). And the car shoes will last a lot longer than the four to five weeks the horseshoes are good for.

One department store weathering the storm is Nordstrom. The ninety-four-year-old Seattle-based retailer has burned its way into the mind of the department store customer by emphasizing "service." But isn't service the essence of the department store concept? Why couldn't all department stores do what Nordstrom has done?

Because there are only so many people who want to shop at a place that sells everything. A big-name consultant once suggested that American department stores had a customer base of perhaps 30 percent of the market. "Yet their failure to pay attention to the 70 percent who were not customers largely explains why they are today in a severe crisis."

Maybe it's just the opposite. Maybe by trying to appeal to the 70 percent of the market that doesn't shop at department stores with sales and special promotions, they lost sight of their core customer, the market that Nordstrom is targeting.

The numbers prove the point. Nordstrom figures that 90 percent of its retail business comes from 10 percent of its hard-core, repeat customers.

Many department stores have gotten the message and are beginning to focus on not just their customers but their high-volume customers. (The Nordstrom 10 percent, for example.) Known in retailing circles as "clienteling," the strategy involves plying these hardcore customers with personal attention and special services, an approach traditionally used by boutiques.

For some shoppers, Bloomingdale's sends reminders to husbands to buy birthday or anniversary presents. Other shoppers get free alterations and gift-wrapping service. Helping in this effort are new computer programs that allow stores to tap their vast databases to identify their most profitable customers.

Bloomingdale's, for example, has 1.8 million credit card users. Yet the store estimates that 20 percent of credit customers account for 75 percent of sales.

While department stores have been declining in importance, specialty stores have been booming. One chain in particular has served as a pattern for all the rest: Toys "R" Us. Today the company has 618 stores in the United States and sells 22 percent of all the toys in the country.

In addition, Toys "R" Us is moving its concept overseas with 293 units outside the United States. Already the company is the largest toy retailer in Germany.

Ironically, Toys "R" Us started as a children's furniture store to which founder Charles Lazarus added toys. The original name: Children's Supermart.

Now here comes the interesting dilemma. How does a children's supermart grow? The obvious answer is to add children's clothing, bicycles, diapers, baby food, etc. In other words, broaden the base of the merchandise.

But that's not what Charles Lazarus did. He threw out the furniture and opened another, larger store with discount toys only. In other words, he narrowed the focus to toys. How unusual and how effective. No wonder *Forbes* magazine calls Mr. Lazarus "without question one of his generation's most brilliant retailers."

Toys "R" Us pioneered a pattern since adopted by every retailer trying to create a category killer.

There are five key steps in the Toys "R" formula: (1) Narrow the focus. (2) Stock in depth. (3) Buy cheap. (4) Sell cheap. (5) Dominate the category.

Let's discuss each of these five steps in more detail.

NARROW THE FOCUS

This is the most difficult step of all, because it is counterintuitive. Most managers and entrepreneurs look for ways to expand their product offerings. If you want faster growth, you should offer fewer product lines? How can this be? It seems obvious that if you want faster growth, you should offer more products and services.

What's obvious and logical is also not true. In business, more is less and less is more. If you want faster growth, you must first narrow the range of products and services you offer. Or if you are planning a start-up company, you must offer a narrower range of products than existing stores.

Take housewares, just one of the many products for the home traditionally bought in department stores. By focusing on housewares only, Gordon Segal and his wife Carole built a robust business. Because they couldn't afford store fixtures, the Segals opened their first store selling European-designed tableware displayed on packing crates and barrels. Hence the name, Crate & Barrel.

Today, the chain has fifty-five stores with revenues of about $275 million and, according to Mr. Segal, is "at the upper end" of retail operating margins.

What Crate & Barrel did in housewares, Lechters is doing in kitchenware, but at the lower end and with smaller stores. With more than six hundred stores (80 percent of them located in malls), Lechters does $400 million in annual volume. Recently Lechters abandoned its sharp focus on the kitchen and started to stock a hodgepodge of stuff for other rooms in the house.

Earnings per share promptly declined 28 percent and the stock dropped 40 percent. New management is now refocusing the Lechters chain on, what else, kitchenware.

Take athletic shoes. Traditional shoe stores sell all kinds of shoes, but the most successful shoe store chain in America is Foot Locker, which sells just athletic shoes. The fifteen-hundred-store chain sells more than $1.6 billion a year in athletic shoes and plans to open another thousand stores by the end of the decade.

Take coffee. Years ago every town in America had one or more coffee shops that served everything from hamburgers to apple pie à la mode. So what did Starbucks do? They opened a coffee shop that specialized in, of all things, coffee. Amazing.

Today Starbucks has turned into megabucks for its principal owner, Howard Schultz. In a recent year Starbucks took in $285 million from its 425 company-owned stores. Currently it has 680 stores and plans to have "2,000 by 2000," when Starbucks will be a billion-dollar company.

Taking another bite out of the traditional coffee shop market is Cinnabon. The chain sells huge nine-ounce cinnamon rolls fresh from the oven, rich and sticky and dripping with frosting. So what if a bun costs $1.89 and has 810 calories. The chain now has 276 shops (about half franchised) and does about $100 million in sales with a 500-store goal by the year 2000.

Take manicures. Every community has a handful of "beauty salons," many of which are convinced that the road to success lies in adding products like wigs, clothing, handbags, jewelry, health and beauty aids, and services like facials, body massages, body waxing, and other personal services.

At the same time, the industry is seeing a growing trend based on narrowing the focus. This is the "nails only" salon. While the traditional beauty salon manager was figuring out how to increase sales by broadening his or her business, the business itself was dividing into two categories, hair and nails. (In the New York area, the nail salons are dominated by Korean immigrants.)

Take cigarettes. Virtually every retail establishment sells them, from drug and grocery stores to restaurants and convenience stores. Yet one of the fastest growing retail categories in America is the cigarettes-only superstore carrying more than three hundred brands. Today there are about two hundred such stores, and they have doubled their share of the market in the past year.

Take sunglasses. Like cigarettes, you can find sunglasses everywhere, displayed on those ubiquitous kiosks. No matter. Sunglass Hut International has opened more than fourteen hundred locations, from shopping malls to airport terminals, to sell Oakley, Armani, Revo, and other top-of-the-line products.

With an average price of $80 a pair and an average margin of 60 percent, Sunglass Hut has been extremely profitable. The stock has tripled in the past two years. (Currently 33 percent of all sunglasses are sold through sunglass specialty stores.)

Some critics point to companies like Amway, with five thousand products and $3.5 billion in sales, as an example of a successful company "without a focus." While it's true that Amway sells everything but the kitchen sink, the company does have a focus. It's their unique multilevel direct-marketing system.

You don't have to focus everything to be successful. But you do have to focus something.

STOCK IN DEPTH

The second step in the Toys "R" Us formula is to stock in depth. A department store at Christmas time might stock three thousand or so toys. Toys "R" Us on a week-in and week-out basis stocks about eighteen thousand toys. Variety is one reason that one out of every five toys is purchased at a Toys "R" Us store.

Variety (and low cost) are also the reasons that one out of every five video rentals takes place in a Blockbuster Video store. While a mom-and-pop video store might carry a thousand titles, a Blockbuster superstore carries more than five thousand titles. In addition, Blockbuster stores carry more than a thousand video games in all popular formats.

Bed Bath & Beyond focuses on bed linens, blankets, towels, bathroom accessories, and basic housewares in open, warehouse-style stores that carry up to thirty thousand different items at 20 to 40 percent off department store prices. Revenues have been growing at 30 percent a year, and net income is a healthy 7 percent of sales.

Stocking in depth is an important concept and is a direct result of taking the first step, narrowing the focus. If your focus is wide, you can't stock in depth. Even the largest department store can't handle eighteen thousand toys.

Stocking in depth is the reason latecomers like Toys "R" Us and Blockbuster Video have come to dominate their categories. Normally the company that pioneers the category goes on to become the leader. (Hertz was the first company to rent cars; Hertz went on to become the rent-a-car leader. H&R Block was the first income tax service; H&R Block became the leader. Charles Schwab was the first discount brokerage firm; Charles Schwab became the leader.)

The video rental pioneers never learned this lesson. The first rental stores were either small mom-and-pop operations, or they were video rental departments tacked onto drug, grocery, or convenience stores.

One way to get rich is to walk through any retail operation and look at the new items that have been added to the store. Ask yourself, what would happen if you took that item, stocked it in depth, and then built a nationwide chain to dominate the category?

You used to buy donuts at a bakery or a grocery store until Dunkin' Donuts came along and built a nationwide brand to dominate the category. You used to buy watches at a jewelry store, but today most watches are bought at specialty watch stores like Tourneau in New York City. You used to buy television sets at department stores, but today most TV sets are bought at electronic stores like Circuit City.

In most cases the specialty stores stock in depth. How many kinds of donuts does a bakery sell? Three or four at the most. A big Dunkin' Donuts outlet will sell more than fifty varieties. Your friendly neighborhood "coffee shop" will sell two kinds of coffee: regular and decaffeinated. Starbucks sells thirty kinds of coffee.

That same coffee shop will sell ice cream in the three flavors:

vanilla, chocolate, and strawberry. A Baskin-Robbins outlet will sell ice cream in five different varieties (regular, light, sugar-free, yogurt, and fat-free yogurt) and in thirty-one different ice cream flavors (31-derful flavors).

New opportunities are created every day. The FCC's 1968 Carterfone decision, which for the first time allowed phone customers to use any company's equipment on Bell system lines, created a market for privately owned telephones. Up popped a retail phone market, dominated not by existing department or electronic stores but by telephone stores. The rise of the personal computer created an opportunity for retail computer chains.

Sears and others made the classic mistake of just adding computers to their stock of things to sell. After that didn't work, the big retailer opened Sears Business Systems Centers, which proved to be a business disaster.

In Sears's case, it was typical big-company thinking to call their new stores "business" instead of "computer" centers. "Why limit ourselves to computers when we can sell copiers and other office equipment, too?"

Why indeed? It's because the future belongs to the retail chain with the narrow focus, not the broad one.

Radio Shack made the same mistake. They first added computers to their stock of things to sell. Then as competitors like ComputerLand, Businessland, and other specialized computer retailers started to take off, the company put up signs at many of their outlets that read "Radio Shack Plus Computer Center."

None of the early computer retailers understood the Toys "R" Us concept of stocking in depth. As a result, they lost out to the latecomers like CompUSA and Microcenter. Today Tandy is striking back with plans to open a host of Computer City stores, but it may be too late. CompUSA, with fewer than a hundred stores, already has sales approaching $3 billion.

Tandy had all the natural advantages, including an early lead in the personal computer market with the Radio Shack TRS–80. But they threw away their lead in an effort to protect the Radio Shack name. They should have left Radio Shack as an electronic knick-knack store and put their computers, their money, and a new name into a nationwide chain of computer-focused retail superstores.

In other words, Tandy should have exploited the emerging personal computer market with a nationwide chain of stores that stocked all computers, including the TRS-80, in depth. And this is the crucial point. They should have also invented a new name to capture the public's fascination with the emerging new computer category.

"Will CompUSA be the next Toys "R" Us?" said a headline in a recent issue of the *New York Times*. My answer is yes. Mark Mandel of Salomon Brothers agrees: "We believe that CompUSA has the potential to dominate the retailing of personal computers much like what Circuit City, Toys "R" Us, Staples, and Office Depot have accomplished in electronics, toys and office supplies, respectively."

What CompUSA is trying to do in computers, PetsMart, Petstuff, and Petco are trying to do in pet supplies. Pets are an enormous business in the United States. Twice as big, for example, as the home computer business. Nearly half of all U.S. households have a dog or a cat, and they spend about $400 a year on average on their pets. The total pet bill: $17 billion.

There are about twelve thousand pet stores in the United States, 85 percent independently owned. Until recently, however, there were very few pet superstores. That's changing fast. Two years ago there were 250 pet superstores. Today there are more than 600.

These pet emporiums are big, ten thousand square feet or more, compared to less than three thousand square feet for the traditional pet shop. And they have been taking business away from supermarkets at a rapid rate. Ten years ago supermarkets sold 95 percent of all pet food. Today that number is down to 65 percent and falling.

PetsMart wants to be to pet lovers what Home Depot is to homeowners. Recently it got a jump on its competition by buying out Petstuff as well as two smaller competitors, Pet Food Giant and Sporting Dog Specialties.

A typical PetsMart store is a huge twenty-thousand-square-foot space with ten thousand items in stock. Forty-pound bags of pet food are stacked twenty-five feet high. Dogs, cats, and owners prowl the aisles filled with everything they could desire, including dental floss bones, pet cologne, dried pigs' ears, and the ubiquitous squeaky toys.

Most pet superstores offer the two high-end pet foods (Hill's Science Diet and Iams) at substantial discounts. But they don't just sell one kind of dog food. They stock in depth. In addition to regular dog food, a pet superstore will stock diet dog food, all-natural dog food, gourmet dog food (venison or lamb), puppy food, geriatric dog food, and vegetarian dog food.

PetsMart's annual sales currently exceed $1 billion, but the company still has lots of opportunities to grow in a $17 billion market.

What the pet superstores are trying to do in pet supplies, Baby Superstore Inc. is trying to do in baby supplies. Stuffed to the rafters with everything from cribs to crayons, Baby Superstore operates forty-eight warehouse stores that carry more than twenty-five thousand items, many priced 10 to 30 percent less than at traditional specialty and department stores. (Motto: Prices are born here and raised elsewhere.)

What can small, independent stores do to compete with category killers like Toys "R" Us? One way is to outstock them. The Tattered Cover, a highly successful bookstore in Denver, keeps half a million volumes in stock of 155,000 different titles. Zabar's, Balducci's, and Dean & DeLuca in New York City use a similar strategy in gourmet food. So does FAO Schwarz in gourmet toys.

When you narrow your focus and stock several times as many items as your nearest competitors, you become an "institution" like Zabar's, FAO Schwarz, and the Tattered Cover, virtually immune from competition by the big, national chains.

BUY CHEAP

While most retailers make money selling products, Toys "R" Us and other dominant retailers make money buying products. When you do one-fifth of all the toy business in the country, you have enormous leverage on the prices you pay for your merchandise. You even have a vote on the kinds of products you get to sell.

When Hasbro developed Project Nemo, a home video game system designed to compete with Nintendo, it took a prototype to Toys "R" Us. Too expensive and not exciting enough, was the retailer's reaction. Even though Hasbro had poured $20 million into Nemo, it canceled the project and took a $10 million write-off.

One cloud on the Toys "R" Us horizon is Wal-Mart. While Toys "R" Us has seen its market share erode from roughly 25 percent of the domestic toy business in 1989 to about 22 percent today, the reverse is true of the Bentonville behemoth.

In the same time period Wal-Mart has almost doubled its share of the domestic toy market to about 16 percent. A 16 percent slice combined with Wal-Mart's legendary ability to buy cheap should be striking terror into Toys "R" Us management ranks.

When you buy cheap, you can operate your stores on markups similar to those of your smaller competitors, sell for less, and still make a lot of money.

Overall, Toys "R" Us markups average about 45 percent, although they vary depending on the product. On high-profile toys like video games, Barbie dolls, and Mighty Morphin Power Rangers, markups are a lot less.

And, of course, there is a lot of "razor and blades" pricing. The video game machines are the razors that are sold with minimum markups and the games are the blades that carry higher markups.

You can also use your size to squeeze discounts from everything you buy, including advertising media and credit card commissions. Tandy, for example, was able to cut its American Express commission by a fourth of a percent, saving more than $500,000 a year.

Another point. If you're big enough, you don't have to compete on price. You can get your suppliers to tailor their products to your specifications. Crate & Barrel, for example, seldom takes products off their suppliers' racks. Outside of a few areas like cookware, the company's offerings are designed and manufactured exclusively for Crate & Barrel. Other retailers that dominate their categories use similar strategies.

SELL CHEAP

The other half of the price equation is selling cheap. By both buying and selling cheap, you put tremendous pressure on the competition.

An independent pet store, for example, might sell a case of a premium pet food brand like Hill's Science Diet for $32. A super pet store might sell that same case for $19.95.

In the final analysis the ultimate objective of having a focus is to dominate your category. When you dominate a category, you will ultimately be rewarded with your full share of profits.

Just selling cheap is not enough, as Toys "R" Us competitors have found out. Both Child World and Kiddie City have been chopping prices for years without making much progress against Toys "R" Us. One reason is they're not able to do both: buy cheap and sell cheap.

What protects a leader is its dominant position. "In the final analysis," says Charles Lazarus, "we say market share, market share, market share."

But is Toys "R" Us following its own strategy? I think not. Take another look at the markup percentage. Toys "R" Us averages about 45 percent versus an overall 26 percent for Wal-Mart. (It could be a few percentage points higher for toys.) As a result, Wal-Mart has been undercutting the toy titan on price.

Not only does Wal-Mart take a smaller markup, it also has a lower cost structure. Selling, general, and administrative expenses at Wal-Mart are about 15 percent of sales versus 19 percent of sales for Toys "R" Us.

One reason SGA costs have been drifting higher at Toys "R" Us is the chain's loss of focus. The net effect of launching Kids "R" Us and Books "R" Us has been an increase in the percentage spent on selling, general, and administrative costs. Robbing Peter to pay Paul undermines a company's financial power.

Recently, the company announced it will open five new stores to compete with Baby Superstore to be called, of course, Babies "R" Us. A typical line-extension mistake.

Another factor is the net profit margin at the two chains. Wal-Mart's net income is 3.5 percent of sales versus 6.1 percent at Toys "R" Us. While it's nice to be putting 6 percent into your shareholders' pockets every year, it's even better to maintain your toy leadership. What Toys "R" Us should do is to cut prices to increase their overall share of the toy business.

In the long run the only thing that really matters in business is leadership. With leadership anything is possible. Without it you're under constant pressure from your competition.

DOMINATE THE CATEGORY

Who will win the pet supermarket battle? It may not be the best player with the best strategy and the best people. It may be the first chain to dominate the category, which looks to be PetsMart.

When you study the history of big retail successes, the chain that dominates the category is the one that usually walks away with most of the marbles.

One way to dominate a retail category is by rapid expansion. When Wayne Huizenga bought into Blockbuster Video in February 1987, the chain had eight stores and eleven franchised units. In rapid succession, Huizenga bought out Southern Video Partnership and Movies to Go, increasing the number of Blockbuster outlets to 130 by year's end.

In 1988 the company bought Video Library chain. By the end of the year, Blockbuster had 415 stores. The following year Blockbuster passed the 1,000 mark by gobbling up Major Video (a 175-store chain) and Superstore MLA (its biggest franchise owner).

In 1990 Blockbuster bought chains in Arizona, California, Florida, Kansas, Nebraska, Texas, and Virginia, bringing the store total past fifteen hundred. Blockbuster Video was now the largest U.S. video-rental chain. "The faster we grew, the more stores we had open, the more money we made," says Huizenga.

He even took the concept overseas, opening 1,250 video stores outside the United States, including 775 stores in the UK that were operating under the Ritz name before Blockbuster bought them.

Today Blockbuster Video has fifty million members and rents 4.6 billion videos every year. What made Blockbuster such an overwhelming success was the fact that they dominate the video rental category in the mind of the customer.

Name another video chain. Pretty hard to do, isn't it?

Huizenga had done the same thing with Waste Management, Inc. After two years of college, he returned home in 1960 to join a family friend's garbage-hauling business. Within three years he bought out his friend, and in 1971 joined forces with two partners to form Waste Management.

They took the company public and embarked on an aggressive acquisition program, buying ninety garbage companies in the first year. In 1975 the company won a contract in Saudi Arabia. Other foreign contracts followed, and the company now operates in twenty foreign countries.

Today, Waste Management (now called WMX Technologies) is the Blockbuster of garbage, the world's largest waste collection and disposal company, with annual revenues in the neighborhood of $10 billion.

Unfortunately, when a retail chain reaches the end of the line and dominates its category, the chain's management often starts looking for new fields to conquer. They tend to forget what made them famous. Instead of continuing to focus on their core business, they go off on a tangent. It happened to Toys "R" Us. It happened to Blockbuster Video.

In rapid succession Blockbuster acquired a movie producer (Republic), 78 percent of a television producer (Spelling), and 49.9 percent of a children's indoor playground (Fun Centers). Huizenga also launched a joint venture with BET to produce black-family-oriented films as well as a joint venture with Virgin Retail Group to open eighteen megastores in Europe, Australia, and the United States.

Then there is the joint venture (with Sony and PACE) to develop musical concert theaters, a majority interest in an entertainment software company (VIE), and a 2,500-acre theme park/sports complex in Florida.

Plans for Blockbuster Park (what else?) call for a domed baseball stadium, an arena for hockey, a golf course, an amusement park, theaters, clubs, restaurants, movie and television studios, a sports museum, a lake for water sports, and a community park. Also included is Block Party, an indoor entertainment complex for adults age eighteen to forty-five.

To fill the stadiums, Huizenga invested $95 million in a professional baseball team (Marlins) and paid $128 million for a professional football team (Miami Dolphins). He also put up $50 million for a professional hockey team (Panthers).

Before the chickens could come home to roost, Blockbuster Entertainment Corporation merged with Viacom Inc. and dumped the potential problems on the back of Viacom chairman Sumner Redstone, who promptly pulled the plug on the Blockbuster Park project.

While announcing his intentions to retire, Wayne Huizenga invoked his vision of a global entertainment company that will "make a movie, put it in our theaters, rent it in our video stores, sell it on our pay-per-view channels, show it on our cable networks, and play it on our television stations. And we'll publish the book, release the soundtrack, make the video game, and sell them all in our stores."

Sure, Wayne.

With all its successes, Blockbuster's share of the video-rental market is only about 15 percent. Logic would suggest that the other 85 percent of the market is a much easier target for Huizenga than the movies, music, and entertainment fields, which have powerful and dominant competitors.

Back in 1989, one financial analyst predicted that Toys "R" Us would eventually have a 40 percent share of the toy market. Actually that ought to be the goal of any company that wants to dominate its marketplace.

Toys "R" Us is far short of that goal. Yet it is plunging into kids' clothing and books, losing focus and losing market share in toys. A good rule of thumb for the dominant chain is to shoot for 50 percent of the market. That's the lion's share, which is usually achievable by any company with a powerful focus.

Federal Express has a 45 percent share of the domestic overnight package market. Coca-Cola has a 45 percent share of the domestic cola market. For market shares higher than 50 percent, you usually need multiple brands (chapter 12).

From a strategic point of view, it's much better to have 50 percent of one market rather than 10 percent each of five markets. Yet traditional thinking often leads a company's management down the diversification trail. The grass is always greener on the other side of the fence. Managers often think they have reached the limit in their existing market, so they are eager to try for something new.

They see a big market out there and their minds shift into Chinese logic. "It should be easy to get 5 percent of that market and since the market is so huge, 5 percent is a very big number."

If it were that easy, there would be a lot of companies out there with a small piece of many different pies. But they're not.

Look at the *Fortune* 500. If getting into everything is the key to success, conglomerates should be leading the list. Of the top ten companies, three are automobile companies, three are oil companies, one is a computer company, one is a chemical company, one (Philip Morris) is into two businesses (tobacco and food).

That leaves only one company (General Electric) that fits the classic conglomerate mold.

Even mighty General Electric has been cutting back and refocusing itself. In the past dozen years, GE has sold or shut down literally hundreds of businesses. "Only businesses that are number one or number two in their markets could win in the increasingly competitive global area," says CEO Jack Welch. "Those that could not were fixed, closed, or sold."

In 1983, for example, GE had 340,000 employees. Ten years later the company employed only 220,000. Refocusing didn't seem to hurt the company. In the process, General Electric moved up five notches on the *Fortune* list, from tenth place to fifth place.

Furthermore, General Electric is a relatively old company, founded in 1878. Creating a conglomerate when competition was sparse is not the same as trying to build a conglomerate today when the competition is intense. Furthermore, GE has had 117 years to burn its name into the mind. GE is an unfocused company with a powerful brand name, an advantage that tends to compensate for its faults.

Chinese logic never works. Run the numbers. The United States is a $7 trillion economy. Any company that succeeded in getting 5 percent of every market would be a $350 billion company. There are no $350 billion companies.

Retail is the mirror of America. It's the most sensitive industry and the quickest industry to reflect changing customer wants. In virtually every category, retailers are narrowing their focus in order to capture a larger share of the market.

But that's not all. In order to dominate their category, retailers are expanding in order to become nationwide or even global chains. As a result, the small, independent retail establishment is rapidly becoming an endangered species. In category after category, the small independents have been replaced by a national chain of franchised or wholly owned outlets.

These national chains are beginning to dominate virtually every retail category, including fast food, convenience stores, hotels and motels, drugstores, shoe stores, office supplies, pet supplies, books, computers, consumer electronics, housewares, hardware, music, video rental, car rental, clothing, furniture.

Even professional service organizations are now in the process of becoming national chains. It's happened in the accounting, advertising, stock brokerage, real estate, and optical professions. The legal profession is headed in this direction, and so is the medical profession. As soon as state and federal laws permit, national chains will dominate the banking business.

Some retailers are in denial. They refuse to see what is happening all around them. They circle the wagons and hope for the best. Yet in the long run, the local store that sells everything is no match for the national chain with a powerful focus that can buy cheap, sell cheap, and dominate the category.

The local retailer has only two choices. Join a national chain or start one of their own.

What retailers are doing, so should you.

A TALE OF TWO COLAS

No two companies illustrate the power of a focus better than PepsiCo, Inc., and The Coca-Cola Company.

PepsiCo is a company driven by growth at all costs. "We're not at all backing off our commitment to 15 percent long-term growth," said PepsiCo's CEO Wayne Calloway recently. Over the years Calloway and his predecessors have worked hard at fulfilling this commitment to growth by buying a collection of companies.

In addition to Frito-Lay, the world's largest snack food company, PepsiCo owns three of the seven largest fast-food chains in the United States: Pizza Hut, the world's largest pizza chain. Taco Bell, the world's largest Mexican food chain. And KFC, formerly Kentucky Fried Chicken, the world's largest chicken chain.

The sun never sets on a PepsiCo restaurant. In addition to the three big chains, PepsiCo also owns Hot'n Now, Chevys, California Pizza Kitchen, D'Angelo Sandwich Shop, and East Side Mario's. Together, PepsiCo's 24,000 restaurant units make up the world's largest restaurant system. (By comparison, McDonald's has only 14,000 restaurant units worldwide.)

To drink in all these restaurants, PepsiCo has a full line of beverage brands including Pepsi-Cola, Diet Pepsi, Pepsi Max, Pepsi XL, Slice, Mountain Dew, Lipton teas, All Sport, and 7UP (outside the United States). Just for kicks, the company also imports Stolichnaya vodka from Russia.

It should come as no surprise that PepsiCo is a much larger company than The Coca-Cola Company, which has pretty much stuck to its beverage heritage. In a recent year PepsiCo had sales of $28.5 billion versus $16.2 billion for Coca-Cola.

What might come as a surprise is the relative "value" or worth of the two companies. Using one measure of value, the stock market, PepsiCo, the larger company, is worth $44 billion, and Coca-Cola, the smaller company, is worth $93 billion, or more than twice as much. Per dollar of sales, Coca-Cola is worth almost four times as much as PepsiCo. That's the power of a focus.

Not that Coca-Cola hasn't fooled around a bit over the years. In 1982 they bought Columbia Pictures (sold to Sony in 1989). They also bought and sold Taylor Wine Company. Today, The Coca-Cola Company is a beverage company. Period.

Well, you might be thinking, that's not fair. PepsiCo is bogged down by its relatively low-profit fast-food chains.

Let's try another comparison. McDonald's Corporation versus PepsiCo. McDonald's has some fourteen thousand restaurant units, which do $7.4 billion in sales compared to PepsiCo's more than twenty-four thousand units, which do $9.4 billion in sales. If given a choice, why wouldn't an investor want to own the PepsiCo fast-food chains rather than McDonald's?

One reason is profits. On its $7.4 billion in sales, McDonald's keeps a hefty $1.1 billion in net income, or 15 percent. On its $9.4 billion in sales, PepsiCo manages to keep only some $400 million in net income, or 4 percent.

The stock market tells the same story. McDonald's is a much smaller company than PepsiCo's restaurant chains, yet the market values McDonald's Corporation at $31 billion. How much the KFC, Taco Bell, Pizza Hut combination is worth is a matter of conjecture.

One way to estimate their market value is to take their net income as a percentage of PepsiCo's total net income and then calculate what that would represent as a percentage of PepsiCo's total market value. On this basis, the PepsiCo restaurant chains would be worth $10 billion.

Note again the power of a focus. McDonald's, with $7.4 billion in sales, is worth $31 billion. PepsiCo's restaurant chains, with $9.4 billion in sales, are worth $10 billion. The smaller, more focused company is worth three times as much as the larger, less focused operation.

Maybe even more. Market valuations are just numbers that represent the price at which investors are willing to buy or sell an individual company's stock. If they truly understood the power of a focus, they might be willing to pay even more for the more focused company's stock.

In PepsiCo's case, its fast-food units are doubly unfocused. First of all, they are a collection of competing brands versus the singularity of the McDonald's operation. Second, the fast-food brands are buried in a beverage company, a disadvantage McDonald's doesn't have.

It's not fast food that is slowing PepsiCo down. It's the fact that the company, for all its successes, is fundamentally unfocused. Why does an unfocused company like PepsiCo have so much trouble competing against a more focused Coca-Cola?

First, and foremost, there's the management problem. If any concept has been discredited recently, it's the notion that a professional manager can manage anything. Management is a discipline that requires people skills (which can be applied to any industry) and conceptual skills (which can be applied to any industry).

So far so good. But management also requires knowledge (which can be learned on the job) and experience. It's the latter that's the Achilles' heel of the professional manager. There's just no way of cramming twenty years of experience into six months of on-the-job training.

That's the inherent problem at PepsiCo. What the company needs is a beverage expert to run the beverage business, a snack-food expert to run Frito-Lay, and a fast-food expert to run the restaurant chains. But who selects the people to run each of these operations? The chief executive, who may be an expert in one of the three businesses but not the other two.

When Coca-Cola owned Columbia Pictures, it hired and fired a series of top executives as studio results steadily turned sour. Coke finally gave up and sold the studio.

PepsiCo tries to solve its management problems by shuffling promising managers from division to division. But the mathematics are against this arrangement. On average, a promising manager at PepsiCo will have one-third the experience of his or her counterpart at Coca-Cola.

Unless you have a deep knowledge and experience in a given

business, it's difficult to select the right person to run that business. "It takes one to know one," goes the old saying.

It's been my experience that most divisional leaders in large corporations (field commanders in military jargon) don't have the right experience or the right personality for their jobs. They're too eager to please their chief executives and they're too focused on short-term results.

Then there's the morale problem. Traditionally, diversified companies shift people between divisions in order to prevent insular thinking. They want to develop well-rounded corporate executives rather than narrow-minded divisional managers. Many managers who are eager to move up in their organizations play along with the game and try to avoid being tagged as a "specialist."

But being a specialist is exactly where the power in business lies. That's why the organization that is focused also develops managers who share the company's focus.

At PepsiCo, the objective of the game is to become the chief corporate executive. At Coca-Cola, the objective of the game is to become the chief beverage executive.

Perhaps the most difficult management problem in an unfocused company is the promotion process. Having observed hundreds of companies "up close" for many years, I'd have to say that the wrong people are promoted to management positions at least half the time. Maybe more.

Look at Burger King. Here is a company that has had ten chief executives since 1980. One reason they don't last very long is that Burger King is a fast-food operation buried in a traditional food company (Pillsbury), which is now part of a United Kingdom conglomerate (Grand Metropolitan PLC) whose major business is alcoholic beverages. It's easy for top management at Grand Met to get out of touch with what's happening in hamburgers.

When it comes to selecting people for promotion, chief executives make two classic errors. They promote either "by the numbers" or "by the personality." Neither approach works very well.

Guess what happens in a company that promotes by the numbers? Everyone goes after short-term results and sacrifices the long-term gains. It's the philosophy espoused by Harold Geneen and a host of professional managers who brought us the conglomerate concept. ("Managers must manage," said Geneen. Translation: Make your numbers or you're out of here.)

It's no secret that conglomerates lost their luster by becoming unfocused. They tried to become all things for everyone. If you want to make your short-term numbers, the best strategy is to launch new products and services. In other words, to unfocus the company.

Damn the long term and full speed ahead. "Why are you line-extending your brand when you know that line extension is going to hurt you in the long run?" I asked one manager. His answer: "If I don't make my numbers this year, I'm not going to be around for the long run."

Instead of the numbers, some companies promote "by the personality." They select people according to their ability to inspire and motivate others. There's nothing wrong with a great personality, especially when it's coupled with the knowledge and experience that great leaders usually possess.

It's been my experience that great leaders, in spite of a multitude of distractions, know how to keep things focused. They know how to inspire and motivate their followers to keep pushing "the main chance." They don't let side issues overwhelm them.

But a great personality alone is not usually the mark of a good leader. Most of the successful leaders in fields other than business, from politics to warfare, usually have a dark side to them. (Winston Churchill and George Patton are two examples.)

Great leaders tend to be introspective rather than "extrospective." They observe their environment but don't always relate well to it. They seem to be driven by their own inner demons, which perhaps accounts for a great leader's ability to focus on a single issue in spite of a thousand distractions.

There is a third way to select leaders. Instead of measuring numbers or personality, you can ask the troops who would make the best leader of their particular operation. I'm not suggesting a popularity contest because that won't work either.

What does work is selecting individuals who have already exhibited elements of leadership in their environment. Natural leaders tend to be those individuals who are quick to "seize" leadership in a vacuum. (Nobody ever appointed a dictator.)

Another major disadvantage of the unfocused company is the additional layer of management needed to knit the company together. On top of PepsiCo's presidents of beverages, snacks, and restaurants sits an array of functional vice presidents. These people don't just sit there and review the numbers; they actively participate in the operation of the divisions.

In addition, the corporate staff's frequent requests for information consume a considerable amount of management's time. Much like the federal government's "paper tax" imposed on the nation's corporations, a diversified company imposes an internal "paper tax" on its operating divisions. This is in addition to the frequent meetings to review operating results, present budgets, etc.

Perhaps the most important problem faced by an unfocused company like PepsiCo is that it competes with its customers. Instead of finding synergy in multiple product lines, most companies find the opposite: One of their product lines tends to undermine the other. In PepsiCo's case, their restaurant chains compete with their beverage prospects.

Why should Domino's Pizza or Little Caesars buy their soft drinks from PepsiCo when PepsiCo's Pizza Hut chain is their biggest competitor?

Coca-Cola has exploited this connection in a series of memorable advertising campaigns. "Has PepsiCo opened a restaurant near you yet?" said one Coca-Cola ad. "Wait four hours." The advertisement went on to say, "Every four hours PepsiCo adds another unit to their restaurant empire. Another unit that competes with your business and feeds your customers."

Not only are the restaurants a competitive problem, they are also a financial drain. PepsiCo pours $1 billion annually into capital expenditures for building and acquiring restaurants, an amount far in excess of its restaurant operating profits. The company is on the horns of a dilemma here. Without substantial annual capital investments, the restaurant chains wouldn't have much of a long-term future.

But this is money that PepsiCo needs to fight Coke on a global basis. Take the Soviet bloc, for example. Thanks to its political connections, PepsiCo got a big head start in the Soviet Union. It all began with a meeting between Donald Kendall, the company's chairman, and Nikita Khrushchev during a 1959 visit to Moscow by Vice President Nixon.

But things are changing. Coke opened for business in Romania in late 1991 and now is outselling Pepsi by more than two to one. Pepsi has also given way to Coke throughout most of Eastern Europe and the rest of the former communist world. Pepsi is number one only in Hungary, the Ukraine, and in Russia itself.

In China, a hundred thousand retail outlets currently offer Coca-Cola. After Hitachi, Coca-Cola is the most widely recognized brand name in the country. Coke has 19 percent of the Chinese soft drink market, three times the share of Pepsi.

One reason for Coke's rapid progress in the global arena is its investment levels. So far, Coca-Cola has poured $1.5 billion into Eastern Europe, $150 million into Romania alone. Coke's 1995 budget for international investment is roughly $700 million, compared with $300 million or so for PepsiCo.

It makes sense. Coca-Cola already gets 80 percent of its net income from operations outside the United States, versus 15 percent for PepsiCo. (Coca-Cola is the number one consumer product currently sold in Europe.) And the potential is even greater. Globally, consumers drink only one-tenth the soft drinks they do in the United States.

The disadvantages of an unfocused company like PepsiCo are obvious. The real question is, what should PepsiCo do about them?

The conventional answer is to try harder. If only Pepsi-Cola could duplicate its U.S. beverage success outside of the United States. If only the restaurant chains could become as profitable as McDonald's. If only PepsiCo could hit pay dirt with one of its new products like Pepsi Max or Pepsi XL. If only . . .

Trying harder seldom works. Nor should PepsiCo continue to fight a three-front war. The better approach is to concentrate the company's resources on one of its three major product lines. My choice would be cola.

Let's look at the cola market. Where is Pepsi-Cola's only hope of making a major move against Coca-Cola? Conventional wisdom says overseas, where Coca-Cola has an enormous lead over Pepsi.

My analysis of the problem suggests just the opposite. Cola consumption in the United States is a staggering 32.5 gallons per person per year. A supermarket in the United States will move a lot of cola in a given week, thereby justifying the stocking of the three brands (Coke, Pepsi, and Royal Crown) plus at least one private-label brand. Overseas the situation is different.

In Indonesia, a country where per-capita cola consumption is one-fifth that of the United States, a Jakarta supermarket might stock only one brand, invariably Coca-Cola.

In many countries of the world, just getting on the shelf is enormously difficult for Pepsi-Cola. And you can't win the battle unless you're in the ball game.

Here at home the beverage business is really two businesses. One is traditional outlets like supermarkets, convenience stores, delicatessens, and vending outlets. The other is the fountain and restaurant trade. Over the years, Pepsi-Cola has actually outsold Coke in supermarket chains.

Where Pepsi isn't in the game is the fountain and restaurant trade. (Why buy your beverages from a competitor?) The fountain business, where Coca-Cola outsells Pepsi-Cola some two to one, accounts for 26 percent of the overall market.

The tragedy of Pepsi-Cola is that their supermarket leadership has never been converted into overall cola leadership. Nor is it ever likely to occur unless something can be done about Pepsi-Cola's fountain business.

Solution: Spin off Pizza Hut, Taco Bell, KFC, and the other PepsiCo restaurants into a separate company. (See chapter 11, "Divide and Conquer.")

This one move neatly solves two problems. It focuses PepsiCo on beverages, and it removes a barrier from selling beverages to the fountain trade. (Frito-Lay should also be sold or spun off to generate the resources necessary to fight the cola war.)

Owning the fast-food chains not only blocks PepsiCo from ever dominating the U.S. market, but it also blocks them from exporting their U.S. leadership overseas where the real cola growth is likely to come from.

By focusing on beverages, PepsiCo has a chance to do both. The first and more difficult move would be to try to wrest the cola leadership from Coca-Cola in the United States. The second and easier move to make would be to take the message "America's number one cola" overseas.

(Pepsi-Cola is already advertised in parts of South America as *"El auténtico sabor americano,"* or the authentic American taste. It would be more authentically American if Pepsi were the largest selling cola in the United States.)

Leadership alone is the most powerful message in marketing. Check the bars and restaurants in your neighborhood. Chances are a typical bar or restaurant might carry Budweiser, Bud Light, Miller

Genuine Draft, Heineken, Amstel Light, Michelob, Corona Extra, Samuel Adams, etc.

In other words, the number one domestic beer (Budweiser), the number one domestic light beer (Bud Light), the number one draft beer (Miller Genuine Draft), the number one imported beer (Heineken), the number one imported light beer (Amstel Light), the number one premium domestic beer (Michelob), the number one Mexican beer (Corona Extra), the number one microbrew (Samuel Adams), etc.

When you see a bar or restaurant heavily promoting lesser brands, you can be sure the brewery is buying its way into the account.

Would it be easy for a restaurant-less PepsiCo to wrest the cola leadership in the United States away from Coca-Cola? No, it would be extremely difficult. But, at least, this is a strategy that clarifies the situation. It allows PepsiCo to concentrate all its resources on one enemy (Coca-Cola) in one country (the United States) with one objective (market leadership).

Actually, Pepsi-Cola already has a powerful strategy to cope with the power of Coke. It's the "Pepsi Generation," a marketing concept first introduced in the early sixties. "You don't want to drink what your parents drink, you're the Pepsi Generation."

The best way to reach the younger generation is with music. Pepsi's biggest successes occurred in the eighties when they hired Michael Jackson, Lionel Richie, and other icons of the younger crowd.

This takes money, and PepsiCo is not spending nearly enough marketing their core product. Currently Coca-Cola spends almost twice as much on beverage advertising in the United States as Pepsi does.

Spinning off Frito-Lay and the restaurant chains would free up resources for PepsiCo to put into sponsoring the top-rated music groups. Hopefully, they could outspend Coca-Cola and capture the cola leadership in the U.S. market. In other words, they could sacrifice short-term profits for a long-term leadership position.

Cola is perceived as an American product. Once leadership is established in the U.S. market, PepsiCo could take this leadership position around the world. First, America. Next, the world.

That's what a focus is all about.

THE QUALITY AXIOM

To increase sales, you need to improve your product or service. Everybody knows *the better product or service will win in the marketplace*. This is the quality axiom, the basic axiom of business today.

An axiom, of course, is a truth so self-evident it doesn't need to be proved. Everybody knows an axiom is true. Everybody knows the better product will win.

What's self-evident, what's obvious, what everybody knows, is also what's invisible. Nobody ever questions an axiom, nobody ever discusses an axiom, nobody ever talks about what everybody knows.

Only controversies get discussed. Axioms get ignored. As a result, over time an axiom becomes invisible.

Then, all of a sudden, someone comes along and turns the old axiom upside down. The truth wasn't really the truth after all.

In geography, the old axiom was: "The world is flat." It looks flat, so everyone thought the world was flat. No longer. Ever since Nicolaus Copernicus the flat world has become round.

In geometry, the old axiom was: "Parallel lines meet only at infinity." But nobody traveled to infinity to check the lines, so nobody questioned what seemed to be an obvious truth. That is, nobody did until Albert Einstein formulated the general theory of relativity.

Now it seems that space is curved and that parallel lines do meet . . . somewhere this side of infinity. And all of Euclidean geometry becomes just another concept that collapsed when the axiom fell.

In business, the current axiom is: "The better product will win."

Since everybody knows the better product (or service) will win, companies around the world search for ways to make their products better.

The search leads to quality.

Quality has become an icon for an entire generation of managers. No single management concept has generated as much acceptance as "total quality management," or TQM as it is more popularly called.

At last count 87 percent of American companies practice some form of TQM. In a recent survey nearly 80 percent of U.S. managers thought that quality would be a fundamental source of competitive advantage in the year 2000.

When 455 senior managers in the electronics industry were asked what their top competitive success factor was, "quality" was the number one answer. (Quality has been at the top of the survey for six years in a row.)

Quality is busting out all over. The most prestigious award a company can win today is the Malcolm Baldrige National Quality Award, handed out annually by the National Institute of Standards and Technology. Thirty-one states also have set up quality award programs based on the Baldrige pattern.

The prestigious American Management Association runs no fewer than eight programs on the subject of quality management. There's even a mutual fund that invests only in companies that practice TQM.

Books, articles, and speeches on quality are flooding the bookstores, business magazines, and podiums of America. At Powell's City of Books in Portland, Oregon, there are five shelves of "quality" books, more than a hundred different titles.

Jack Covert, the phenomenally successful president of Schwartz Business Books in Milwaukee, reports that "quality" books are his biggest sellers, accounting for 31 percent of all books sold to his sixty thousand customers.

In the past five years, 1,777 major magazine and newspaper articles on quality have been published, including 931 on TQM.

What is quality? Good question. And who decides what quality is? Another good question. Maybe the customer?

Let's say the customer walks into an appliance store to look at television sets. He or she looks at three television sets side by side.

Does the customer open up the back of each set and compare the quality of the circuitry? Of course not. Does the customer read the brochure on each set and compare the sets, feature by feature? Of course not.

Does the customer look at the three sets and compare the quality of the three pictures? Of course, but you know what? Nine times out of ten, you can't tell the difference.

Everybody talks about quality, but nine times out of ten the customer can't tell the difference. Most products that cost the same also look and feel about the same.

Is a Mercedes better "quality" than a BMW? Is a Honda better "quality" than a Toyota? Is a Coca-Cola better "quality" than a Pepsi-Cola? Is a Nike better "quality" than a Reebok?

Sure, there are preferences, especially when it comes to style, taste, appearance, and other product attributes you can see, feel, or taste. But quality?

Quality in the abstract is easy to define. Quality in the specific is a lot more difficult to pin down.

Go back to the appliance store. Most customers concerned about quality do the same thing. They ask the salesperson what set to buy. Which is the highest quality brand? And what set does the salesperson recommend?

It all depends. If one of the manufacturers is having a special promotion with a free trip to Italy for the salesperson who sells the most television sets, you know which television set is the quality set. Quality is the free trip to Italy.

Don't worry. While customers listen to what salespeople have to say about products and brands, they don't usually take their advice at face value. They look for corroborating evidence. Maybe it's a special feature available only on the recommended brand, maybe it's an attractive price, maybe it's the only brand on sale this week.

One bit of corroborating evidence is particularly effective. "It's the largest selling brand."

There's a double whammy at work here. The manufacturer believes the better product will win; the customer believes the better product will win. Therefore the best-selling product must be the better quality product.

But there's precious little evidence to show that this is true. Take automobiles, for example. Every year one of the leading consumer-rating services does extensive testing of car models, both on and off the track.

They comb through reliability reports and frequency-of-repair data from owners. They road-test the cars, considering such factors as handling, engine performance, seating comfort, braking ability, and fuel consumption. Then they rank the models, within each category, in order of overall quality.

Take the small-car category. In a recent buying guide, the consumer-rating service listed sixteen small, passenger car models. The number one model in quality was the Volkswagen Jetta. Number two was the Acura Integra, and number three was the Volkswagen Golf.

How did these three top-ranked models do in sales in the same year? Well, the number one Volkswagen Jetta was number twelve in sales, the number two Acura Integra was number nine in sales, and the number three Volkswagen Golf was number sixteen in sales. Not much correlation there.

On the other hand, the number one car model in sales, the Ford Escort, was number eleven in quality. The number two selling car, Saturn, was number six in quality. The number three selling car, Honda Civic, was number seven in quality.

If you take the cars in order of quality (1, 2, 3, etc.) and then list them in order of sales, here are the rankings: 12, 9, 16, 5, 7, 2, 3, 4, 15, 6, 1, 11, 8, 10, 13 and 15. Not much correlation there, either.

If you're an automotive expert, you might recognize many problems with my oversimplified analysis. Most people buy brands, not models. Some brands have many more dealers than other brands. Some cars are more expensive than others. But if the better car usually wins the sales battle, there should be some general relationship between "quality" rankings and "sales" rankings. But I don't find much.

This is not an isolated instance. In reviewing quality ratings with sales over a host of different products, I find very little correlation between the two.

Part of the reason is the increasing complexity of the products themselves. The people that test high-tech products like automobiles, television sets, and computers have an impossible job. What's important and what's not? How much of the differences are due to variations in the individual samples selected for the tests?

Furthermore, many of the attributes are highly subjective. Just what is a "good-riding" car? And how much influence do brand names have on a tester's subjective ratings?

Yet quality has its own cheering section. Wherever you turn, from the top of the corporation to the bottom, there's an emphasis on quality. "Quality is Job 1" say the Ford advertisements. Then there's Motorola, which *Fortune* magazine calls the "titan of TQM" and the winner of the first Malcolm Baldrige award.

Chief executives of the elite Business Roundtable ranked Motorola the country's top practitioner of total quality management. Books and business-school case studies have chronicled the company's fanatic pursuit of six sigma quality (3.4 mistakes per million).

Yet all this emphasis on quality hasn't helped Motorola in the computer business. In 1985, the company launched a line of personal computers that went nowhere. In 1990, Motorola introduced a line of workstations that never got airborne. In 1992, they tried the mainframe business with similar results. In 1994, Motorola announced its intention to build a broad line of desktop computer systems called PowerStack.

Currently Motorola is pushing the Envoy, a personal wireless communicator in the Newton category. Prognosis: not good.

One of the prime promoters of quality is the Strategic Planning Institute of Cambridge, Massachusetts, which maintains the PIMS (Profit Impact of Market Strategy) database. Four hundred and fifty companies contribute confidential information on some three thousand strategic business units to PIMS without identifying them by name.

One comparison will give you a flavor of the PIMS findings. Companies with a high perceived product or service quality have an average return on investment of 29 percent. Companies with a low perceived product or service quality have an average return on investment of 13 percent.

Twenty-nine versus 13 percent. Quality pays . . . or does it? Notice the innocuous word "perceived." Is there any way to determine whether or not the high-quality companies actually had high-quality products or just a perception for high-quality products?

Suppose you could find a few companies with high-quality products and a low quality perception and also a few with low-quality products and a high quality perception. Now compare the two groups.

Is there any doubt that the latter will win? Is there any doubt that perception is more important than quality?

Perception is reality. The real driving force in the business world is not quality but perception of quality.

Another example. During the sixties, Schlitz and Anheuser-Busch fought for leadership in the beer business, with Schlitz eventually falling behind the big brewer from St. Louis.

Then in the early seventies Schlitz substituted corn syrup and hop pellets for traditional ingredients and shortened the brewing cycle by 50 percent. As a result the company achieved higher returns on sales and assets than Anheuser-Busch. "Does it pay to build quality into a product," asked *Forbes* magazine, "if most consumers don't notice?"

And they didn't. Schlitz continued to pick up market share from 12 percent in 1970 to 16 percent in 1976 (when the company was only three percentage points behind the leader, Anheuser-Busch). Then the Schlitz hit the fan.

The brand tumbled to 8 percent market share in 1980. Acquired by Stroh in 1982, the brand continued its free fall to less than 1 percent of the market today. And, of course, Anheuser-Busch went on to become the leading brewery in America, with 45 percent of the market.

What happened to Schlitz? Most business analysts have said that the company downgraded the taste of the product and beer drinkers rebelled. But sales of Schlitz actually *increased* after the product change.

A far likelier reason for the decline of Schlitz was that the publicity about the product change caused beer drinkers to switch to Budweiser and Miller. The perception is the reality.

How do we know it was the publicity and not the beer?

Because it took a while for the word to get around, that's why. It always takes time for bad publicity to takes its toll, especially in the case of Schlitz. Since the publicity was in business media only, it took years for the bad publicity to reach the general beer drinker. If it were the beer, one sip would have alerted the beer drinker to look for another brand.

What happened to Schlitz also happened to New Coke. But the difference in New Coke's case is that the product was "improved" with the addition of more corn syrup to give it a sweeter taste. As a matter of fact, Coca-Cola spent $4 million on two hundred thousand taste tests that proved that New Coke tastes better than Pepsi (and Pepsi tastes better than the original formula, now called Coca-Cola Classic).

Taste is tricky. The perception of good taste is as important as good taste itself. When consumers found that Coca-Cola had changed its formula, they said to themselves, "It's not going to taste as good." So they tasted New Coke and said, "It doesn't taste as good." Coca-Cola was forced to bring back the original formula. The perception is the reality.

Not to be left out, Royal Crown Cola did a million taste tests that proved that RC Cola tastes better than Coke Classic (57 percent to 43 percent) and better than Pepsi (53 percent to 47 percent).

Do you believe those numbers? I do, but it doesn't really matter. People drink the label, not the contents, which is another way of saying that the perception is the reality.

"What's in a name?" wrote Shakespeare. "That which we call a rose by any other name would smell as sweet." Maybe not. Certainly taste is just as much in the mind as in the mouth. Maybe smell is just as much in the mind as in the nose.

In spite of the dominant role played by perception in the success or failure of a corporation, quality remains the most popular belief in business today. One reason is the tendency to think an argument through to its ultimate absurdity.

"If you bought a new car and the wheels fell off when you drove the car out of the dealer's showroom, you'd never buy that brand again. Therefore quality must be the most important factor in the success of a business."

Have you ever bought a new car? Have the wheels ever fallen off as you drove the car out of the dealer's showroom? It could happen, but it almost never does.

The truth is that competitive products tend to be similar. The differences in quality, if they exist at all, are difficult to measure. The differences in perception, however, are substantial and easy to measure.

The objective of your business should be to improve the quality perceptions of the products or services you sell. Sometimes that includes making changes in the manufacturing process itself. (Are the wheels falling off the cars that you make? If so, you have to make some changes in the manufacturing process.)

Furthermore, it stands to reason that companies will want to emphasize quality internally. You're asking for trouble when employees think that management doesn't care about quality.

But don't bet the company on a better-quality product; it's not the key to success. It's like the old golf adage: Drive for show, putt for dough.

Drive for a quality product in the plant. Putt for a quality perception in the mind.

Don't misunderstand. There's nothing wrong with quality. There's no reason why a company should not try to build the highest quality into every product it sells. But building a quality product and building a quality perception are two different things.

As luck would have it, when you focus a company, you improve its quality perception. When you unfocus a company, you do the opposite. You undermine its quality perception.

Having a focus can improve a company's quality perception in the mind in four separate ways.

THE SPECIALIST EFFECT

If you go to a medical doctor (an internist or a general practitioner) and you have a real problem, chances are you'll wind up in the office of a specialist. A cardiologist for a heart problem. A dermatologist for a skin problem. An ophthalmologist for an eye problem.

Everybody knows a specialist knows more about his or her specialty than a general practitioner does. Whether it's true or not doesn't really matter. The perception is the reality, and everyone knows that specialists know more about heart problems, skin problems, eye problems, etc.

The same thing is true in business. Specialization drives quality. Buyers know this, but sellers often forget. Otherwise, why would companies fall all over themselves trying to become generalists when the power lies in specialization?

When IBM was a mainframe specialist, it had a powerful perception of quality in the mind of the mainframe buyer. "Inevitable" was the word most often associated with IBM. Today, IBM has become a computer generalist. As a result, IBM has lost its perception of inevitability.

When you are the leader like IBM was in the mainframe world, you develop the perception that you are an all-powerful company.

That you cannot do anything wrong. It becomes inevitable that you will maintain that leadership. As a result, prospects had a powerful incentive to continue to buy from IBM.

When you expand your business and get into other areas where you are not the leader, you destroy that perception of inevitability. Customers who perceived IBM as an all-powerful company were distraught to find that IBM couldn't repeat its mainframe successes in other areas.

And, of course, they couldn't. They were first in mainframes, which was the key factor in their success, but they weren't first in most of the other computer products they jumped into.

Like many companies, IBM was the victim of change. Markets change. Products change. New technologies make existing technologies obsolete. What's a company to do?

First of all, you have to recognize that change is a natural phenomenon. Change happens to people, change happens to companies. To stay competitive, a company may have to change its focus. (See chapter 10, "Coping with Change.")

THE LEADERSHIP EFFECT

Whether it's true or not, the consumer believes the better-quality product will win. Therefore the simplest, easiest, and most direct way to achieve a quality perception in the mind is to become the leader and then communicate your leadership. (You communicate your leadership, not just your quality.)

It's not inconsistent for Ford to tell its employees that Quality is Job 1 and to tell its prospects that Ford is the best-selling car in America. "Fords must be better because more people buy Ford cars than any other brand."

Leadership alone is the most powerful driver a business can own. Leadership communicates quality. What's the best photographic film? Kodak, the leading brand. What's the best imported beer? Heineken, the leading brand. What's the best ketchup? Heinz, the leading brand.

Not only does leadership drive quality, leadership drives leadership. The leading brands tends to keep their leadership, year after year.

A marketing firm compared the leading brands of 1923 in twenty-five product categories with the leading brands of today. Would you believe that in more than seventy years only five brands lost their leadership? Twenty of the twenty-five brands are still market leaders today.

Does quality makes you a leader, or does leadership build a quality perception? History seems to favor the latter explanation.

The fat cats of the corporate world are the market leaders in categories that have seen few fundamental changes. Coca-Cola in cola. Gillette in razors. Goodyear in tires, although they could have lost their leadership to Michelin if they had not jumped quickly into radial-ply tires.

Be careful. If you ask customers why they buy the leading brand, they almost never say, "Because it's the leader."

Customers always claim to buy the leading brand "because it's better." Customers as well as companies believe the quality axiom that the better product will win. Therefore, if you have the leading brand, you must have the better product.

Leadership is one of the best ways to create a quality perception in the mind.

THE PRICE EFFECT

What's the best automobile in the world? Rolls-Royce. What's the most expensive automobile in the world? Rolls-Royce.

If you want a high quality perception, you need a high price. Why is a Mercedes-Benz better than a Cadillac? One reason is that a Mercedes-Benz can cost twice as much as a Cadillac. (The base price of a Cadillac Seville STS is $45,935. The base price of a Mercedes-Benz S600 is $130,300.)

Of course, the higher the price, the smaller the market. In 1995, Cadillac sold 181,000 cars in the United States, Mercedes sold 77,000 cars, and Rolls-Royce (plus Bentley) sold just 300 cars.

You can't have it both ways. You can't have "high quality at a low price." Customers say: "Hey, wait a minute, that can't be. It has to be one or the other." It's what psychologists call cognitive dissonance, the conflict that goes on in the mind when a person tries to hold two opposing viewpoints at the same time. Normally, one concept has to be tossed out to resolve the dissonance.

Chilean wines, for example, have a good reputation for quality in the worldwide market. But the leading Chilean brand, Concha y Toro, can be bought for $2.99 a bottle in supermarkets and liquor stores in the United States. To establish a quality perception, Concha y Toro needs a higher price (and a better name, too).

A high price is not a negative. It's a benefit to the customer. If a Rolex watch were cheap, there would be no stature or prestige in wearing one.

THE NAME EFFECT

Other ways to improve the perception of quality is by changing the "look" of the product, the packaging, and the name. Perhaps the most important aspect of quality is the name itself. It's especially important to use a specialist name rather than a generalist name.

Would you rather buy a Sears, Roebuck battery or a DieHard battery? DieHard, sold by Sears, is the best-selling automobile battery in the country. Is it the best? Who knows? But it has the best name.

Polo by Ralph Lauren is a great name, and it has become a powerhouse brand in upscale clothing. Wonderbra, Starbucks, Easy-Off, Super Glue, Oil of Olay, Häagen-Dazs, and Duracell are also powerful and memorable names.

While your strategy might be the primary reason for your success, a good name tends to protect your company from competitive encroachments into your territory.

A bad name, on the other hand, is a millstone around your neck. Can you imagine trying to get a new airline off the ground with the name Kiwi International Air Lines?

No, the airline doesn't fly anywhere near New Zealand; it flies up and down the East Coast of the United States.

Kiwi, which calls itself "America's Best Airline," has been flirting with bankruptcy and desperately needs a cash infusion to survive. Fundamentally you cannot be perceived as America's best airline unless you have a reasonably good name.

Other airlines with bad names include Allegheny, Mohawk, and Piedmont. Why would you name an airline after a mountain range? Is it a death wish? (All three are no longer flying.)

Some names get out of date, like Ayds diet candy, whose sales fell in half when the AIDS epidemic hit. A popular soft drink in France, for example, is called Pschitt!, a name that would likely torpedo the brand in the United States.

The most distinguishing characteristic of a good (or bad) name is its sound. In the English language, there are many sounds that connote negative ideas or concepts. In particular, you have to be careful of words that end in a vowel. *A*, *E*, and *O* are all right, but *I* and *U* are potentially dangerous, especially *U*.

Take automobile brands. Cars that end in *A* have a quality perception: Acura, Honda, and Toyota. Cars that end in *E* also have a quality perception: Dodge, Eagle, Oldsmobile, and Porsche. (The weakest name is Oldsmobile. Who wants to buy a new car named "Olds"?)

Cars that end in *O* are also all right: Alfa Romeo and Volvo.

I endings can be dangerous: Audi, Hyundai, Infiniti, Mitsubishi, and Suzuki have not done well in the American market.

But the worst ending of all is a *U*: Daihatsu, Isuzu, and Subaru. To an American ear the letter *U* is the worst-sounding vowel in the alphabet.

Both Daihatsu and Isuzu failed to penetrate the passenger-car business in the United States and have been withdrawn from the market, although Isuzu continues to sell light trucks under the Trooper name.

If the Lexus were named the Lexsu, the car would not have been nearly as successful.

Names like Isuzu have three strikes against them. Isuzu not only has a double *U*, but also an initial *I*. In spite of a massive and widely praised advertising campaign, Isuzu sales in the United States have been dismal.

The high-water mark for the brand was 1987, when the company managed to sell only 39,587 passenger cars. This was the same year that the Big Three (Toyota, Honda, and Nissan, not a *U* in the crowd) sold 1,597,153 passenger cars in the U.S. market.

Some names don't travel well, like Yugo from Yugoslavia or Kia from Korea. What undermines names like Yugo and Kia is the fact that they suggest the country of manufacture. Unlike Japan and Germany, Yugoslavia and Korea do not have good reputations as car countries.

Some names are bad because they are similar to much larger companies in the same field. BFGoodrich, for example, which reminded tire buyers of the leading company in the field, Goodyear.

Goodyear is still around, the leading U.S. brand of tires, but BFGoodrich no longer makes tires, having sold the tire brand to focus on engineering and chemicals.

What do you do about a bad corporate name? Change it. Corporate name changes are more common than you might think. In a recent year 11 percent of 8,286 public and privately held companies changed their names, according to a survey conducted by Anspach Grossman Portugal, a New York–based corporate-identity consulting firm.

Most of the changes, of course, were the result of mergers, acquisitions, divestitures, spin-offs, and so on, but 170 corporations, or 2 percent of the sample, changed their names for marketing reasons.

FINDING YOUR WORD

The first paragraph of an obituary column in the March 12, 1995, issue of the *New York Times* read: "Victor Dorman, who helped change the way Americans buy cheese by putting 'the Paper Between the Slices' as chairman of the Dorman Cheese Company, died on March 4 at his home in Delray Beach, Fla. He was 80."

A naval officer, businessman, and philanthropist, Mr. Dorman lived eight decades. Yet his obituary sums up a lifetime of achievements as the man who put "the paper between the slices."

Perhaps a thousand people a year are written up in the obituary pages of the *Times*. Most of these obituaries are eminently forgettable. Yet once in a while someone manages to put the paper between the slices.

If you want to be famous in life as well as death, you should follow the same strategy: Own a word in the mind. That's true of an individual; it's also true of a company.

Why this is so is best explained by examining the human mind. When you study the mind, you find two opposing dynamics at work: complexity and simplicity.

The human mind is undoubtedly the most complex organism in the universe, certainly more complex than the largest and most expensive supercomputer. A mind has perhaps one hundred billion neurons plus more than forty different chemicals that function as neurotransmitters, giving the one-quart container that sits on top of your neck thousands of times more processing capacity than a Cray C90.

It needs it. To survive in today's complex world, the average mind has a reading vocabulary of about twenty thousand words and an active speaking vocabulary of about eight thousand words.

But look what the average mind has to cope with in the marketplace. A typical supermarket will have some thirty thousand products to choose from. (A hypermarket will have fifty to sixty thousand products.) A typical chain drugstore will have fifteen thousand products for sale. A department store might have forty thousand products on display. A large Toys "R" Us store will have eighteen thousand toys to sell. A Blockbuster outlet will have five thousand different videos to rent. A large Borders bookstore will have 130,000 book titles in stock. And so on. The list is endless.

The average mind is deluged by an avalanche of words in the media. According to the latest data, the average mind consumes nine hours of television, radio, newspapers, magazines, books, and videos a day. That translates into 40,000 words a day, 280,000 words a week, more than 14 million words a year.

Minds have become addicted to mass media. The average person's day is essentially divided into three parts: work, sleep, and the media. Neither work nor sleep is as time-consuming as the media part.

Media is often combined with other activities. We listen to the radio when we get dressed. We watch television when we eat breakfast. We read a newspaper when we commute. We listen to the radio, a tape, or a CD when we drive a car. And we often take a book to bed.

We are drowning in an overcommunicated society.

Yet individual words are important. Most products are bought verbally, not visually. Sure, at the supermarket you might visually compare one head of lettuce with another and then buy the one that looks the freshest and the best. But most of what you buy is bought verbally.

You pick up a can of Campbell's chicken noodle soup or a bottle of Heinz ketchup and read the words. Then decide whether to buy the product or not. If you make a list to take to the supermarket, you don't draw pictures. You write words.

Even lettuce (Foxy), oranges (Sunkist), bananas (Chiquita), and other products are coming to market with names attached. The mind pays attention because the words add meaning to the products.

How does a human mind cope with the avalanche of words that descend on it daily? The only way it possibly can. It selects what it wants to remember based on simple psychological principles.

The answer to the problem of the overcommunicated society is the oversimplified message.

Ask someone why they buy Kodak film and you never get a specific answer like: "It's because Kodak uses T-grain technology to deliver flatter silver halide crystals in the emulsions."

Most people buy Kodak film because they think it's the best. But how do they know it's the best? "Because everybody knows it's the best" is the answer you usually get.

A professional photographer might shoot several rolls of a specific Kodak film and also several rolls of a similar Fuji film and then compare the results. The amateur would never do this, because life is too short. How would one cope with the hundreds of other buying decisions a person makes in a month?

If Fuji were the largest selling photographic film in America, most people would be buying Fuji film. And if you asked people why they bought Fuji film, they would say, "Because it's the best."

How do we know this to be true? Because Fuji is the largest selling photographic film in Japan and the Japanese prefer Fuji film "because it's the best."

Many, many other companies and products illustrate this same phenomenon. They are widely preferred and purchased because they are perceived to be the best.

Yet many customers cannot name any single, tangible attribute to justify their purchases except for general comments like: It's the best. I like the taste. I like the texture. I like the look. Everybody knows it to be the best. It's the best quality. It's better than the other brands. Et cetera.

Gillette, Goodyear, General Electric, Kellogg, Hershey, Wrigley, Coca-Cola, and Xerox are some of the companies that sell products perceived to be "the best." These companies own the quality position where it really counts, in the mind.

Are they the best? Does it really matter? And who's to say which product is the best? Furthermore, if you asked their competitors, I'm sure you would get a different answer.

But in a deeper sense, leaders like Gillette, Goodyear, General Electric, and the others own a word in the mind. And these words are the source of their power in the marketplace.

If I asked a thousand amateur photographers to name the first company that comes to mind when I say "photographic film," would it be any surprise that the overwhelming answer would be Kodak?

If I asked a thousand business owners to name the first company that comes to mind when I say "copier," would it be any surprise that the number one answer would be Xerox?

Or that "gum" produces Wrigley? And that "chocolate bar" produces Hershey? I don't think so.

While no one is quite sure exactly how the mind works, it seems obvious by these and other experiments that the leading brand in any category *owns the category*.

By that I mean that when you think "ketchup," your mind jumps to the name "Heinz." You might then say, Heinz owns the word "ketchup" in the mind.

The mere fact that your company is the leader in your category might have no meaning to the customer. It's not your leadership that matters. What matters is owning the word in the prospect's mind that defines the category. This is the residual effect of leadership, and it's your most powerful way to dominate a category.

There's further proof of this phenomenon. It's the mind's tendency to telescope two names together, the company or brand name and the category name.

Instead of saying "Please give me a Kleenex tissue," people will say "Please give me a kleenex," even when the tissue box in front of them says "Scott." Kleenex owns the word "tissue" in the mind.

Instead of "Xerox copy," people will say "xerox" as in the expression "Make a xerox of this letter."

(I expect to get letters from both Kimberly-Clark and Xerox for using their brand names in lowercase letters, but it's not my fault. It's the penalty of leadership. The mind links the brand name with the category name and then uses the brand name generically. In the mind, it's kleenex, not Kleenex.)

An even more powerful verbal expression of a leadership position in the mind happens when someone uses a brand or company name as a verb, as in: "Please xerox this proposal and fedex it to Los Angeles." Nobody says: "Please canon this proposal and united parcel it to the Coast."

(Xerox is the leader in copiers, and Federal Express is the leader in overnight delivery service, which is why these nouns can be used as verbs.)

Not every company or brand name can be used generically. On April 15 nobody says "Let's H&R Block it," although income tax and H&R Block are strongly linked in the mind. In the same way, discount broker and Charles Schwab are linked in the mind, although nobody says "Let's Charles Schwab it."

Even though both H&R Block and Charles Schwab are the clear-cut leaders in their fields, their names are too "far out" to be used generically.

Who owns pizza, fried chicken, and hamburgers in the mind? Pizza Hut, Kentucky Fried Chicken (now KFC), and McDonald's. You could prove this by conducting word-association tests, but it's not really necessary.

Just ask yourself what brand names come to mind when you hear these product categories:

"Aspirin?"

"Cola?"

"Canned soup?"

"Instant photography?"

Chances are your answers to these four categories were Bayer, Coke, Campbell's, and Polaroid. Right?

How about "microbrewed beer"? This is a relatively new category, introduced by the Boston Beer Company in 1987. If you answered "Samuel Adams," you probably have downed a few bottles of this fabulously successful brew. Samuel Adams, the first microbrew and the leader in the category, outsells the next eight microbrews combined.

How about "rent-a-cars"? This is a relatively old category, introduced in Chicago in the year 1918 by Walter Jacobs, age twenty-two, with twelve Model T Fords. In 1923, John Hertz became president, and the following year the company changed its name to, you guessed it, Hertz System, Inc.

Leaders own their categories . . . literally. By that I mean that a leader owns the word that defines the category in the mind of the prospect.

Owning a word in the mind is a leader's fundamental strength, more valuable than its offices, its factories, its warehouses, its distribution systems. You can always replace a physical facility that burns down, but you can't easily replace somebody else's word in the prospect's mind.

If you're not the leader, you tend to see the problem as trying to produce a better product than the leader. I've worked with many number two, three, and four companies and invariably they see their products or services as either better than the leader's product or service or at least comparable to it, but at a lower price.

Yet they seldom make much progress against the leader, and they rarely, if ever, overtake the leader.

It's not enough to produce a better product or a cheaper one than the leader offers. It's helpful, but it's not enough. What you must do is develop a corporate strategy that allows you to cope with that powerful position in the mind.

That's what focusing is all about. If someone else "owns the category," your only viable strategy is to narrow your own focus and own a piece of the category.

Pizza Hut was first in the pizza category and owns the category. The number two and number three pizza chains are not companies that compete "across the board." They are companies that focus on one piece of the pizza pie. The number two pizza company is Little Caesars, which focuses on "takeout." The number three company is Domino's Pizza, which focuses on "home delivery."

When you have a focus, you can greatly increase the effectiveness of your strategy by taking the focus one step further: owning a word or concept in the mind. At its high-water mark, Domino's Pizza had 45 percent of the pizza delivery market by virtue of its famous pledge: "Home delivery in thirty minutes, guaranteed."

Safety considerations, including a number of fatal accidents involving Domino's drivers, convinced the company to drop the guarantee. Sales dropped, too. What Domino's Pizza needs to do is replace the guarantee with another word or concept they can own in the mind by virtue of their home delivery focus.

One of the fastest growing fast-food chains in America is Little Caesars. Little Caesars focuses on take-out pizza, the least expensive way to sell a pizza pie. No tables, no waiters or waitresses, no delivery trucks, no drivers.

Little Caesars focuses on its take-out segment with a concept called "two pizzas for the price of one." Or in the vernacular of Little Caesars advertising: "Pizza. Pizza."

The rise of Little Caesars has coincided with two powerful trends that have greatly increased the company's business. It's partly luck, partly foresight, partly brilliance that put Little Caesars' strategy so in tune with the times.

The first trend is the dramatic increase in restaurant take-out food. Take the dinner category, for example, where pizza accounts for a substantial portion of the market.

A decade ago, takeout accounted for 36 percent fewer dinner meals than the sit-down category. While dinners eaten inside restaurants have remained roughly constant, take-out meals have skyrocketed. Today takeout represents 12 percent more dinners than those eaten inside restaurants.

The second trend is the dramatic increase in take-out pizza. A decade ago, take-out hamburgers represented 30 percent of the take-out market, with pizza in second place at 26 percent. Today, pizza is the top meal in the take-out category by a substantial margin.

(Unfortunately, Little Caesars has recently entered the home delivery business, a serious mistake. Success often tempts a company to extend its line, which in turn unfocuses the company.)

Little Caesars demonstrates the importance of selecting your "word" carefully. If possible, pick a word with a future, not a word with only a past.

Again, look at the fast-food business. Who owns the word "chicken" in the mind? Kentucky Fried Chicken. But there's a problem. With the trend toward healthier eating, the "fried" in Kentucky Fried Chicken was a major liability. Hence the new name: KFC.

One company's liability is another company's opportunity. In 1985 two entrepreneurs in Newton, Massachusetts, opened Boston Chicken. Instead of fried chicken, the new chain focused on a healthier alternative, "rotisserie" chicken.

But it wasn't until 1991, when three ex-Blockbuster executives (Scott Beck, Saad Nadhir, and Jeffry Shearer) took over, that the company really started to cook. In 1993 Boston Chicken went public with the hottest initial public offering of the year. Its first day on the market, the stock more than doubled in price.

Growth has been spectacular. At last count, Boston Chicken had six hundred outlets, with plans to open more than three thousand restaurants in the next decade. There's still room to grow. KFC has more than five thousand units, for example.

Rotisserie chicken is riding a strong health trend. In virtually every category healthier alternatives are taking a substantial share of the market. It's not uncommon to watch someone add skim milk and Equal to decaffeinated coffee, bite into a Snackwell's cookie, and then light up a Marlboro Light cigarette.

Healthy Choice is the number one upscale frozen dinner brand. Thirty-five percent of all colas consumed are diet colas. Thirty percent of all beer guzzled is light beer. Supermarkets are filled with fat-free cookies, salt-free pretzels, low-cholesterol eggs. Healthy is the name of the food game today.

Then what does Boston Chicken do? The chain drops the chicken part of their name and adds roast turkey, ham, and meat loaf to the menu. In addition to its traditional "home-style" meals with mashed potatoes and corn bread, the chain also offers deli-style sandwiches. New name: Boston Market.

Prediction: Nothing good will come of this move. What word would Boston own in the mind? Market? A market sounds like a mini supermarket, not a fast-food restaurant.

Owning a word in the mind is a powerful driving force both inside and outside the company. It tells employees and customers what the company's primary focus is. A single, simple word is so much more powerful than the typical mission statements that companies spend endless hours dreaming up. Here's an example from the fast-food industry.

- To be the recognized leader in the fresh, convenient meals category.

- To provide our customers with continuously improving products and services that are responsive to their needs.

- To create and maintain an environment where responsible employees, area developers and franchisees can achieve their objectives.

- To allocate and focus corporate resources for maximization of long-term stockholder value.

- To respect, study and learn from our competition.

What company issued this mission statement? Do the five "missions" give you a clue? It's Boston Chicken, of course (now called Boston Market). With a mission statement like this one, it could be almost any type of restaurant chain serving almost any type of food.

Which, of course, is the idea. Top management doesn't want to be "locked in" to any particular direction. "We've got a box," says Vice Chairman Nadhir, "and that box will be what it has to be to be relevant to the consumer at this point in time. Unless you've got that attitude, you get ingrained in what you are doing." Translation: Whenever we see a better opportunity, we'll change the format.

In my opinion, the secret of success is "getting ingrained in what you are doing." Only by being ingrained in a narrow segment of the market can you hope to own a piece of the customer's mind. What drives success is not factories, facilities, products, or people. What drives success is owning a piece of the prospect's mind.

If the Rolex factory burned down tomorrow, the company wouldn't go out of business. They would turn to other suppliers to manufacture the watch cases and movements they need. While deliveries might be interrupted temporarily, the Rolex brand would continue to dominate the high end of the watch market.

(A shortage of Rolexes might actually benefit the company. Nothing creates demand as rapidly as scarcity of supply.)

On the other hand, if the Rolex brand did not exist, then a Swiss factory capable of producing expensive watches would be a worthless capital investment unless it could be sold to Piaget, Patek Philippe, or some other premium watchmaker.

As a matter of fact, many successful companies today manufacture nothing. They buy what they need on the open market, often in the Far East. Nike is a $3.8 billion company that sells one out of every three pairs of athletic shoes sold in the United States, but doesn't own a single shoe factory.

Nike does, however, spend $120 million a year on advertising. What Nike owns, and what the advertising is designed to protect, is a word in the mind.

What word does Nike own? Nike is the leader; Nike invented the category. But what is the category? Before the arrival of Phil Knight and his engineered running shoes, there were only Keds and other brands of casual shoes called "sneakers."

What Phil Knight invented was the amateur athletic shoe. (There were many professional brands of tennis and basketball shoes.) And then Nike turned the athletic shoe into a fashion statement with wild designs and high prices.

Both Nike and Reebok ($3.3 billion) are big, profitable athletic shoe companies that sell a full line. But the number three company, L.A. Gear, is neither big nor profitable. Nevertheless, L.A. Gear sells a full line of children's, women's, and men's athletic shoes. That's a mistake.

In five years L.A. Gear has racked up $186 million in losses on $2.7 billion in sales. Recently the company is beginning to see the light. "L.A. Gear will put more focus on its heritage as a women's athletic/lifestyle brand," says its management. Good move, but it may be too late.

When you're not the leading company, the only thing that ever seems to work is a narrow focus. Take the computer workstation, which got off to a flying start in 1980, the year Apollo Computer Inc. was founded. By 1984, Apollo had 60 percent of the market, three times as much as the number two player, Sun Microsystems.

But Sun had a focus, UNIX workstations, while Apollo sold equipment with its own proprietary operating system. As Sun's sales started to rise, Apollo decided to offer its customers a choice of either UNIX or the Apollo system. (Whatever you want, we got.)

It was a rout. By 1989, Apollo's share had plummeted to 14 percent of the market and the company was sold to Hewlett-Packard. Sun Microsystems, on the other hand, rose to the top, and today its UNIX workstations account for 36 percent of the market (in units), with Hewlett-Packard a distant second with 20 percent.

What Sun did with UNIX, Silicon Graphics did with 3-D. In 1981, James Clark left Stanford University to develop and market three-dimensional computer graphics technology. Today the company he founded, Silicon Graphics, is a $1.5 billion company, the leader in 3-D computing.

When you think of 3-D computing, you think of Silicon Graphics.

In the late eighties, StrataCom developed "frame relay," a complex data-routing technology for computer networks. Before frame relay, businesses usually connected computer networks in remote offices by leasing multiple lines. With frame relay, only a single line is needed.

StrataCom is booming. Sales have been doubling with no end in sight. When you think of frame relay, you think of StrataCom.

Sometimes the word that focuses a company is obvious, sometimes not. A decade ago, a small software company with less than

$500,000 in sales came to Jack Trout, my former partner, and myself with a product called "Act." But what does Act do? It wasn't obvious by the name.

"Everything," said Patrick Sullivan, the founder of a company called Conductor Software. "Too much," we said. "You need a focus."

After much discussion, we arrived at the concept of "contact" software. Sullivan, a former traveling salesman, had designed the software to handle all the chores a person needs to do on the road. Mailing lists, schedules, follow-up letters, etc.

Because the company had invented the concept, Act instantly became "the leading contact software." To reinforce the new focus, we suggested changing the name of the company to Contact Software International.

A focus can drive many management decisions. Who would use contact software? Obviously, owners of laptop or notebook computers. So the manufacturers of these machines were contacted to package Act with their computers.

And rather than advertise to everybody, Contact Software ran ads only in airline publications. (If you're doing contact work, chances are you are a frequent airline passenger, too.)

Eight years after the decision to focus the company and the product as "contact software," Patrick Sullivan sold the company to Symantec for $47 million. Today Act has about 850,000 users and 70 percent of the market.

When you see a company experiencing explosive growth, it's usually because that company is focused on a single word or concept. Sun Microsystems and UNIX workstations, Silicon Graphics and 3-D computing, StrataCom and frame relay.

Nor is focus a short-term phenomenon. A focus can last for exceptionally long periods of time. Back in 1957, Max Karl invented mortgage-guarantee insurance to allow low-down-payment buyers to obtain bank financing for home mortgages. (Private industry's answer to the FHA.)

Today, the company he founded, Mortgage Guaranty Insurance Corp., has over $100 billion of insurance in force and an investment portfolio of $1.3 billion. With 29 percent of the market, MGIC is still the largest company in the field.

Norman Gaut founded PictureTel in 1984 to pioneer the new field of videoconferencing. Today his company has $255 million in revenues and dominates the market, selling 49 percent of all videoconferencing equipment. You might think that equipment manufacturers like Sony, IBM, or Apple would capture this market. Or perhaps the television or cable networks. But they did not.

Power lies not in big brand names that mean everything but in the company with a narrow focus. A company that "owns" the videoconferencing word in the prospect's mind. PictureTel.

Sometimes your word can be a phone number. Jim McCann bought 1–800-FLOWERS in 1987 for $2 million plus the assumption of $7 million in debt. "It was a ridiculous price to pay for the rights to what was nothing more than a telephone operation," said McCann.

It was a bargain. Thanks to energetic promotion of the 1–800-FLOWERS number, McCann's company has blossomed. Annual sales are currently $200 million and growing rapidly. Next on the agenda is a telemarketing center in Europe.

Which brings up a good point. Companies hungry to grow often overlook international opportunities. Instead they introduce new products and services into the U.S. market, which often defocuses their operations. A better bet is to maintain a tight product focus and go global.

Alpine Lace is a twelve-year-old, $132 million-in-sales maker of low- and no-fat cheese. The company dominates the category in supermarket delis, with more than 50 percent of the market. So Alpine Lace tried to move into Kraft's territory, the dairy case, and got creamed. Overall sales declined 27 percent, and the company wound up losing money two years in a row.

A better direction for Alpine Lace would have been to take the deli strategy overseas. As trade barriers are lifted, what works in one country should work in another.

Another company that achieved success by being first is Guest Supply Inc. Thanks to their "guest amenity" program, you now find small bottles of shampoo, conditioner, body lotion, mouthwash, and other products in many better hotels and motels. In the process, Guest Supply became the leading manufacturer and marketer of hotel room supplies, with sales well in excess of $100 million a year.

Rocket Chemical, a three-person company that made lubricants for the aerospace industry, was asked to develop a formula to protect airplanes from rusting. After forty tries, the company came up with a formula it called WD-40. The formula was so successful that Rocket Chemical phased out its other products and changed its name.

Today the WD-40 Company owns the word "slippery" in the mind. Those little blue, yellow, and red aerosol cans can be found in 77 percent of American homes. What's so striking about a single-product company like WD-40 is its profitability.

In the past decade, WD-40 Company reported $864 million in total sales and $144 million in net income. This works out to an astonishing 17 percent of sales. (Net income of the *Fortune* 500 averages 5 percent of sales.)

Could you develop a more slippery product than WD-40? Probably. Could you successfully sell it? Probably not.

Invariably the leading company in a given field is the one that "invented the category." This is not the same thing as the first company to make the product. Remington Rand was the first company to manufacture and sell a commercial computer, the Univac I. But IBM was the company that invented the category. That is to say, IBM got into the mind early and dominated the category.

Who (or what company) actually invents something is irrelevant. What counts in business is the perception of who invented the category. That's why it's important to move rapidly and create the illusion that you or your company invented the category.

Who invented baby food? In the early 1900s, millions of parents "strained" their babies' food by hand. But it was Daniel Gerber who decided in 1928 to market a line of commercially strained baby foods. Gerber was first in the mind and never lost its leadership.

Leadership has multiple benefits. Leaders have time on their side. If a demonstrably better product hits the market, the leader usually has plenty of time to react. If a leader just copies the competitive development, it's usually good enough to maintain its leadership role.

Leaders can also hire better people. If you wanted to work for an athletic shoe company, wouldn't you try Nike first? If you wanted to work for a fast-food company, wouldn't you try McDonald's first?

If you wanted to work for a rent-a-car company, wouldn't your first thought be Hertz?

The evidence from colleges and universities suggests that leading companies tend to attract more and better prospective employees.

While it's easy for an outstanding prospect to slip through the hiring net, the truth is that leaders usually have the first crack at the best people. They may not always hire them, but they usually have the first crack.

Leaders also have the first crack at distribution. Whatever your distribution outlet, it's always much easier if you have the leading brand. What supermarket is not going to carry Coca-Cola, Campbell's soup, or Heinz ketchup? What drugstore is not going to carry Bayer aspirin, Tylenol, or Advil?

The same principle applies to industrial products sold by a company's own salesforce. What purchasing agent is going to refuse to see the Xerox copier representative?

Once you see that the power of leadership can be reduced to owning a word in the mind, then it's also easy to see what to do if you are not the leader. You have to do the same thing that made the leader successful.

If you're not the leader, you also have to own a word in the mind. The only restriction is, you can't own the category name, so you have to own a segment of the category.

Take the automobile industry. In the days of Henry, Ford owned the leadership position in the mind. Then, in a failure to "cover" the move into color and style, Ford lost its leadership to Chevrolet.

For six decades in a row, from the thirties to the eighties, Chevrolet was the largest selling automobile in America. Then, in a burst of models and a confusing collection of styles, Chevrolet lost its focus and its leadership to Ford.

At one point Chevrolet had fifty-one different car models and twelve different nameplates (Beretta, Camaro, Caprice, Cavalier, Celebrity, Chevette, Corsica, Corvette, Monte Carlo, Nova, Spectrum, and Sprint).

Those are just car models. Chevrolet also marketed 288 truck models and 12 different truck nameplates.

Why? Why in the world would one division of a large corporation like General Motors go to the trouble and expense of marketing so many different types of vehicles? The flaw in the Chevrolet strategy, the lunacy of leaders, is being all things to all people.

It happens all the time. When a company has a dominant brand, it thinks it can appeal to everybody. In the short term this works, but in the long term you lose your focus and often your leadership.

Some leaders use pricing to appeal to everybody. They practice a form of marketing "duage," where the entire market is divided into two categories: customers and noncustomers.

They charge their regular, loyal customers the full price and offer their noncustomers deals and incentives. They may pick up additional business that way, but only at the expense of alienating their regular customers.

The airline industry has specialized in this form of marketing duage for several decades. Advertising and promotional dollars are usually spent trying to attract the least profitable customers. No wonder regular customers are turned off.

The department store industry has developed the duage practice to a perfection. As recently as 1988, Sears sold an astonishing 55 percent of its goods at "sale" prices. Under pressure from "everyday low price" competitors like Wal-Mart and Toys "R" Us, Sears has moved in the direction of a single price strategy.

To be successful today you can't appeal to everyone on price, you can't appeal to everyone on features, you can't appeal to everyone on prestige. Some of the most successful automobile brands today are the ones that have learned how to focus. Especially those brands that "own a word in the prospect's mind."

Take Volvo. Ask any car owner what Volvo stands for and you'll usually get the reply "safety." This is not an accident of history, but a deliberate strategy of Volvo starting with its 1959 introduction of the world's first three-point lap-and-shoulder automotive seat belt.

At first Volvos were sold with a durability concept. "On Sweden's rugged roads, Volvos last an average of over thirteen years. Nine out of ten Volvos sold in the United States are still running." Gradually the shift was made to a safety theme, including the formation of a Volvo Saved My Life Club.

Today the boxy, old-fashioned-looking Volvo has become the largest selling imported European luxury car in America. Volvo has consistently outsold both BMW and Mercedes-Benz. In the past decade, for example, Volvo sold 880,000cars in the United States versus 750,000 for Mercedes and also 750,000 for BMW.

Meanwhile back in Sweden Volvo was driving in the opposite direction. In 1971, Pehr Gyllenhammar became Volvo's CEO and proceeded to diversify the company.

In 1981 Volvo bought Beijerinvest (energy, industrial products, food, finance, and trading) and White Motors' truck division. In 1984 Volvo launched a joint venture with Clark Equipment to create the world's third largest construction company. In 1988 Volvo acquired Leyland Bus in the UK.

During the eighties Volvo steadily increased its holdings in Pharmacia (drugs and biotechnology), Custos (investments), and Park Ridge. In 1990 the company consolidated its food and drug units with state-controlled holding company Procordia.

The straw that broke Gyllenhammar's back was the 1993 plan to merge with Renault, a move that shocked many managers and enraged stockholders because of the French automaker's poor performance and government ownership.

Within three months of the announcement, the plan was dead and the chairman had resigned. (It cost Volvo $170 million to back out of Renault's driveway, money well spent.)

Volvo recently announced plans to "refocus on its core businesses" and divest by 1996 all the other businesses it had accumulated during Gyllenhammar's twenty-two years of tenure, worth about $5.4 billion. Initial results are positive. Volvo emerged from the red with net earnings of $1.8 billion in 1994 after a loss of $471 million in 1993.

Conventional wisdom questions the logic of a narrow focus. "Volvo's chances would seem slim in a global car market where it has just a one percent share," said *Forbes* recently.

But a car maker with a 1 percent share and a strong focus (Volvo) might be better off than a car maker with a 16 percent share and dozen of brands with no focus (General Motors). Time will tell.

Even Volvo cannot resist the siren song of line extension. Volvo is investing $200 million in a joint venture with Tom Walkinshaw Racing, a British company that helped design Jaguars and the Aston Martin DB7. Objective: stylish, high-performance, convertible and coupe versions of Volvo's 850 series cars. Not a good move.

Aside from the British venture, Volvo has pretty much kept to its safety knitting. Over the years, the company has turned out a string of automotive safety features, including front-impact air bags, side-impact air bags, safety-cage construction, collapsible steering columns, and daytime running lights.

"Safety" as a driving force is as much as internal focus as an external focus. If you have only 1 percent of a market, it's helpful to have a focus for your design and manufacturing engineers. Instead of spreading their efforts over a wide range of automotive issues, they can concentrate on safety features.

Let others pioneer front-wheel drive, for example, and adopt the technology only after somebody else has spent billions proving its worth. It wasn't until 1991 that Volvo introduced its front-wheel-drive vehicles, the 800 series.

While Volvo has been the family car with a "safety" focus, the other two luxury European imports have each maintained their own individual focuses. Mercedes-Benz is the traditional "prestige" car, which is always a nice word to own.

How do you get to own the prestige position? Generally speaking, you have to be first and you have to charge high prices. That combination can be compelling.

Mercedes's parent, Daimler-Benz, was the world's first automobile company. As a matter of fact, Karl Benz invented the first three-wheeled car in 1885, and Gottlieb Daimler followed the next year with the first four-wheeled car.

They combined forces in 1926 and focused on the high end of the market. Their creation, the Mercedes-Benz, became famous around the world as a luxurious, prestigious motorcar.

BMW is different. A manufacturer of motorcycles and aircraft engines, Bayerische Motoren Werke didn't begin making cars until 1928. They weren't first, so BMW couldn't become successful just by charging high prices. They needed a focus.

It wasn't until 1961 that BMW found the formula that was to catapult the company into the top tier of automakers. One way to find a focus is to start with the leader and then do just the opposite.

Mercedes-Benz, the leader, made big luxury cars, so BMW focused on small luxury cars, or sports sedans. Mercedes was known for roominess and comfort (rolling davenports), so BMW focused on "driving." This focus was captured in one of the longest running U.S. advertising campaigns of all time, "The ultimate driving machine."

Serendipity played a role in the selection of BMW as the official car of the yuppie generation. What kind of car would a young, urban professional want to drive? Obviously a yuppie car had to be imported. (There's no cachet in Detroit iron.) It had to be expensive, but not too expensive. And it had to be fun to drive. What other choice can you think of besides BMW?

But both BMW and Mercedes-Benz were not content to rest their cases on "driving" and "prestige." In common with traditional thinking, both German automakers broadened their lines in the U.S. market. BMW with the larger, roomier, and more expensive 7 series and 8 series cars, which sell for as much as $69,900. And Mercedes-Benz with the smaller and cheaper 190 series cars (now replaced by the C series models, which go as low as $30,950).

Neither the big, expensive BMW nor the small, cheap Mercedes has been particularly successful. Currently only 17 percent of BMW sales in the U.S. market are the expensive cars. Only 35 percent of Mercedes sales in the U.S. market are the cheap series cars. (It's easier to sell a cheap version of an expensive product than an expensive version of a cheap product.)

What might have happened is always speculation. But it's my speculation that BMW would have been better off if they stayed focused on the relatively inexpensive "driving" machines and Mercedes-Benz better off if they stayed focused on the relatively expensive "prestige" machines.

Nothing dies harder than the perception that you need the full line to remain "competitive." American Motors labored under this misperception for years.

Formed by the merged remains of two renowned losers, Nash-Kelvinator and the Hudson Motor Car Company, American Motors didn't live as long as Amadeus Mozart. And unlike *Don Giovanni* and *The Marriage of Figaro,* American Motors produced such forgettable compositions as the Hornet, the Javelin, the Gremlin, and the Pacer.

From its formation in 1954 to its sale to Chrysler Corp. in 1987, American Motors had two golden opportunities, both of which it muffed.

One was in the early sixties, when American Motors' early lead in compact cars gave the company a head start. Unfortunately, the Big Three also jumped into the compact market and began to take business away from the Rambler Classic and other AMC compacts.

This was a crucial period for the company. The logical move was to focus on small cars. Instead AMC tried to become a full-line producer, offering the luxury Ambassador, various convertibles, and a variety of engine options. The full-line strategy was a major mistake.

The next opportunity occurred in the mid-seventies, thanks to

Jeep. In 1970, American Motors had bought manufacturing rights to the Jeep from Kaiser Industries. Sales started slowly, but by 1978 American Motors was selling more Jeeps in the United States than cars (163,000 versus 158,000).

Furthermore, the Jeep was profitable, the cars were not. That year American Motors lost an estimated $65 million on its conventional car business and still made a $37 million profit on total sales of $2.6 billion. Most of the black ink came from the sale of Jeeps.

That was the year to run up the Jeep flag and say American Motors is now a four-wheel-drive, off-the-road company. "Leave the highways to General Motors, Ford, and Chrysler, we'll take the rest of the country."

It was not to be. The previous year American Motors president Gerald Meyers told *Time* magazine that if American Motors stops making cars, the move would have to be forced over his dead body. According to *Time,* "It has long been AMC's claim that it needs to stay with cars to spread its total vehicle production costs and give its dealers more to offer the public."

What they should have done is so obvious it hardly seems worth mentioning. Dump the passenger car lines and concentrate on their leader product, the Jeep. In order to focus, you have to *subtract*, yet many managers want to *add* in order to spread the costs and increase sales. It rarely works.

(Sometime in the future Chrysler may find itself in the same position that American Motors was. They could be asking themselves the same kind of question that AMC should have asked. Should we dump our passenger cars to concentrate on Jeeps and minivans?)

In the late seventies, Renault made an investment in the company, and now American Motors was truly a mess. In addition to Concords, Eagles, and Jeeps, the company was also trying to sell Renault Alliances, Encores, and Fuegos. Not a happy situation.

By 1986, the only asset left at American Motors was a long history of losses. "The automaker may not have to pay taxes for the rest of the century," said the *Wall Street Journal.* "We are a $500 million tax shelter," bragged AMC's chief financial officer.

In 1987, Chrysler Corporation bought Renault's 46 percent stake in American Motors as well as the rest of the company. Chrysler promptly did what AMC should have done. They dropped everything except the Jeep (and the Eagle name, which they used on another series of cars developed by Renault).

The Jeep focus paid off. Jeep sales in the United States accelerated from 208,000 in 1987, the last year AMC owned the company, to 427,000 in 1995. With the exception of the year 1973, when AMC sold 460,000 cars and Jeeps in the United States, this was a better result than any other year in AMC's thirty-three-year history.

Just because you have fewer models to sell doesn't mean you sell fewer cars. It might be just the opposite. Fewer models usually means a much more powerful focus. And in business today, focus is what drives a company's success.

Volvo makes money selling 350,000 vehicles worldwide a year. Jeep sells more than 400,000 light trucks a year in the United States alone. Why couldn't Jeep stand alone as a company and a brand? As a matter of fact, Jeep would have been a more powerful brand if it hadn't been diluted by the Eagle passenger car models on the showroom floor. A focused approach is always more powerful than an unfocused one.

When Renault bought almost half of American Motors in 1978, it thought it was getting a distribution system to sell its LeCar, Fuego, and Sportwagon models. More than seven years later the American Motors/Renault combination had racked up losses of nearly $750 million.

When Chrysler bought American Motors, it had no such illusions. It promptly dropped the passengers cars to focus on Jeeps.

Unwisely, Chrysler made a deal with Renault to sell a new sedan the French company had developed. So it put the Eagle name on the car and threw it in the ring with the Jeep. Eagle has never made money for Chrysler and has sold relatively few cars in comparison with Jeep. In a recent year, Chrysler sold seven times as many Jeeps as Eagles.

Jeep is the premier name in the light-truck market. It's the only "generic" name in the category, right up there with Scotch tape, Kleenex, and Jell-O. Yet Jeep manages to sell only 7 percent of the six million light trucks sold in the United States every year.

You would think, would you not, that the primary objective would be to increase penetration in the light-truck market. Not to broaden the model base so that dealers would have more products to sell.

Less is more. The "narrowest" car line in America is Saturn. One platform, one model, one engine, one transmission. Your only choices are doors (two doors or four?), valves (eight valves or sixteen?) and type (sedan or station wagon?).

In terms of cars per dealer, Saturn has become the largest selling car brand in America. In a recent year the average Saturn dealer sold 960 cars. In second place was Honda with 651 cars per dealer, followed by Toyota with 569 cars per dealer. In other words, the average Saturn dealer sold nearly 50 percent more cars than the number two brand.

So what does General Motors plan to do with Saturn, the narrowest car brand in the country? They plan to "broaden" the line. On the drawing boards are a larger Saturn based on the Opel Vectra and a smaller Saturn based on the Opel Astra. In addition they plan an electric Saturn. Four lines instead of one.

Why not do the opposite? Narrow the focus even further. What about dropping the station wagon from the Saturn line? (Wagons account for only 5 percent of Saturn sales.)

When logic conflicts with reality, reality loses. Logic suggests that the more cars a dealer has to sell, the more cars a dealer sells. So the manufacturer broadens the line to give the dealer more cars and the customer more choice. But it doesn't work. The dealer with the narrow, focused line sells more cars than the dealer with the broad, less focused line. The logic is sound, but the focus is lost.

When you have a narrow, focused line, you stand for something. Your salespeople stand for something. Your service people stand for something. They get enthusiastic about the product. They believe in something.

When you walk into a Volvo showroom, the salesperson asks, "Do you have a family?" Translation: If you love your children, you'll protect them by buying a Volvo.

When you walk into a Chevrolet showroom, the salesperson asks, "What do you want to buy?" Translation: We don't stand for anything here.

We have $8,000 Geo hatchbacks, $16,000 Chevrolet sedans, $20,000 Chevrolet Blazers, and $40,000 Corvettes. And everything in between. Logic suggests that the full Chevrolet line would outsell the narrowly focused lines of its competitors. But logic loses.

This is the first fallacy of management, the tendency to act in ways that are logical rather than in ways that are supported by the facts.

But it gets worse. Companies continue to repeat their mistakes. If the logic is sound and the program is not working, *then the execution must be flawed.*

This is the second fallacy of management, the tendency to blame the execution rather than the strategy. *It can't be the strategy because the strategy is logically sound.*

This is at once the essence and the rationale for the concept of focus. It may not be totally logical, but focus works. The road to success, the route to increased sales, lies in narrowing the focus. If you make this concept an inherent aspect of your management approach, then you can become fabulously successful.

If focusing were totally logical, it would have no power. Everyone would be doing it and there would be no particular advantage to focusing your own business. You would still have to compete with a host of other focused companies.

Another barrier to accepting the focusing concept is industry history. Every industry has its own set of historical beliefs. To go against these beliefs you have to become a heretic. That's not easy to do. To get promoted, you have to be a conformist, not a heretic.

Which is why virtually every new CEO has the credentials of the previous CEO.

It's not very often that companies hire an outsider. Sometimes when they want to get new blood, new thinking in an industry, a board of directors will turn to an outsider. Why? To get someone who is ignorant of an industry's historical beliefs.

It's usually the outsider who truly understands the benefits of "leadership." If a business can achieve the perception of being the leader, its success is almost always guaranteed. Leadership alone is the most powerful perception. More powerful than a better product, a lower price, a more effective salesforce.

Why is leadership so powerful? It turns out that leaders own a word in the mind more powerful than leadership. Invariably the leading product or brand is perceived as the "real thing." Everything else is an imitation. If other factors are relatively the same, why wouldn't you want to buy the real thing rather than an imitation?

Coca-Cola is the real thing in cola, but the concept transcends the cola category. In every field, the leader has the perception of being the real thing.

AT&T is the real thing in long-distance telephone service. IBM is the real thing in mainframe computers. Hertz is the real thing in rent-a-cars. Hershey is the real thing in chocolate bars. Heinz is the real thing in ketchup. Hellmann's is the real thing in mayonnaise. Kleenex is the real thing in tissue. Scotch tape is the real thing in cellophane tape.

Everything else is an imitation.

"The real thing" was a Coca-Cola advertising slogan that touched a tender spot in the mind. Even though the slogan ran for just eighteen months in the late sixties and early seventies and for a few years in the forties, "the real thing" has become synonymous with "Coca-Cola."

Whenever possible, magazine and newspaper editors will use the words in headlines that talk about the product or the company.

Interestingly, Coca-Cola didn't put "the real thing" into the mind. It found those words there. "Those words kept coming up in our research," said Neil Gilliat, supervisor of the Coke account for advertising agency McCann-Erickson, "and so the campaign was changed to meet the times."

One strategy that helps reinforce a "real thing" perception is a visual difference. Coke's contour bottle, for example.

The watchband on a Rolex serves the same function. When you see a Seiko or a Citizen with a "Rolex" watchband, it strikes you as wrong. "That's not a Rolex," you think to yourself. "It's not the real thing."

Other leaders use similar visual differentiation strategies. Frank Perdue feeds his chickens marigold leaves to turn their skins bright yellow. Owens-Corning dyes its Fiberglas insulation products pink and then uses the Pink Panther character to create an unusual visual difference. (Back in 1987 Owens-Corning was the first company to trademark a color.)

Leadership is usually a domestic phenomenon, but that's changing. Arthur Andersen is the leader of the Big Six, the six largest U.S. accounting firms. But as the world of business goes global, there are opportunities to shift from a national to a global leadership strategy.

KPMG Peat Marwick is the fourth largest accounting firm in the United States (after Arthur Andersen, Ernst & Young, and Deloitte & Touche). But fortunately for KPMG, the company is the largest *global* accounting firm. Hence the company has begun a marketing program to establish itself as "the global leader."

Global business is a trend whose time has come. "If your business is global, you need a global accounting firm," is the essence of the KPMG message. (And in this day and age whose business is not global?)

"The global leader" is a concept that KPMG will have to earn, because it's not obvious. The obvious leader is Arthur Andersen because they lead in the United States. But as the trade barriers between countries come down, there will be a scramble to substitute worldwide words for purely domestic ones.

If you can move your products and services across borders, you can move your words, too. As a matter of fact, your words might be the most important "product" you can export.

If you're not the leader, then your job is more difficult, yet more clear-cut. You have to narrow your focus to own a segment of the category.

Take the airline business. The airline leaders (American, United, and Delta) serve all segments (business and pleasure), all price levels (coach, business, and first class), and all destinations (North America, South America, the Caribbean, Asia, and Europe). As a result, the airline industry is in trouble.

There is no clear-cut leader, and none of the big three own any words or concepts in the mind. The only big-three airline with a consistent approach has been United. "Fly the friendly skies of United." Does anyone with at least half a mind really believe that United's flight attendants are friendlier than American's or Delta's?

When everybody offers everything and nobody owns a word in the mind, how does a customer pick an airline? Easy. Just call a travel agent, tell them when and where you are flying to, and ask for the cheapest fare.

If you bought an automobile the same way you bought an airline ticket, you'd pick up a copy of a car-buyer's guide and select the cheapest four-cylinder car.

In four years, the U.S. airline industry lost $12.8 billion. Characteristically the industry blames the customers, the competition, the government, the airport operators, almost everybody but themselves.

"Unless the world changes," says Robert Crandall, CEO of AMR Corporation, the parent of American Airlines, "we will never buy another airplane. We won't replace the airplanes that wear out. We will never buy an airplane for growth. So if you look far enough down the road, when all the airplanes are worn out, the company simply won't be here anymore."

American is one of the world's largest airlines. Unfortunately, American is also hopelessly unfocused, a flying Sears, Roebuck, trying to appeal to everybody. You can't win an air war that way.

The industry rationalizes its predicament by citing how customers have changed. "People feel poorer," Crandall says. "People are therefore much more intent on finding value, whether it's with airlines, restaurants, hotels, products they buy, whatever. I think the world has changed."

All this will be forgotten once the airline business takes off again and the big three start making big money again. But the airline business is capital intensive, as are all cyclical businesses. When times are good the industry attracts additional capacity, but it takes a while to build a 747 and get it airborne. Sooner or later, the airline business levels off because of overcapacity, and the cycle starts again.

Crandall compares the airline business with the restaurant and hotel business, but does Lutèce or Bouley have rooms in the back where they serve cheap food to compete with McDonald's or Taco Bell? The airline industry does.

Does the Waldorf-Astoria or the Plaza have cheap rooms in the basement to compete with Holiday Inn or Motel 6? The airline industry does.

Furthermore, would Lutèce or Bouley march their tourist customers through the main restaurant dining rooms to get them to the cheaper tables in the back? The airline industry does.

But the airline industry is different, say airline industry experts. True, every industry is different; every industry has its own unique set of circumstances. As a result every industry develops its own unique way of operating.

"This is how we do it in the airline industry." Or the music industry. Or the supermarket industry. Or the pharmaceutical industry.

Then along comes an outsider with no commitment to the established ways of doing things, an outsider who just does the job in a straightforward way and is heralded as a genius. Deservedly so, for breaking the paradigm is no easy task.

Herb Kelleher founded Southwest as a one-class, one-price airline. Southwest's focus even extends to its choice of airplanes. The airline flies only Boeing 737s, which greatly simplifies training, scheduling, and maintenance.

As a result Southwest has a powerful focus. Southwest is the low-fare airline; it's the concept they own in the mind. Not the "lowest" fare, of course, because from time to time other airlines cut their fares temporarily to steal business from Southwest. But the airline's consistent low fares assure customers that they're not being ripped off.

While its larger competitors were drowning in red ink, Southwest has consistently made money. Southwest has been in business twenty-four years and has made money the last twenty-two years in a row, a record that no other major airline has come close to.

Southwest sells about 45 percent of its tickets directly to passengers, the highest percentage of any major airline, which sells, on average, only 15 percent of its tickets directly. Passengers trust Southwest because they don't play the fare "shell games" operated by most of the other airlines. "Now you see it, now you don't."

You read about a low fare in the newspaper, but by the time you call the travel agent: (a) the low-cost tickets are sold out, or (b) you don't qualify because you're flying the wrong day of the week, or (c) you don't want to spend Saturday night in Fargo, North Dakota.

Even more confusing from the passenger's point of view is the constant changing of fares. Their so-called yield management systems allow the airlines to change fares almost on an hourly basis. Each day, U.S. airlines make about 250,000 airfare changes. Some days up to a million.

Great for the airlines that use yield management to squeeze every ounce of revenue out of the marketplace. Bad for the passengers who try to cope with the situation. (And heaven forbid you want to change a ticket.)

As a result, the airline industry has a poor reputation with customers. In a survey of ten major service industries, scheduled airlines rated at the bottom in customer satisfaction, right down there with the U.S. Postal Service.

Nearly all air travelers get a big discount, including employees of large corporations that negotiate fares 30 to 55 percent off the full price. In fact, less than 1 percent of domestic flyers are paying full airline-ticket prices these days.

Whatever price you paid for your ticket, you can be sure that

someone else paid less. Not a comforting thought for an airline passenger. Not a very good way to run an airline.

"Do you know how much money it costs to go to New York?"
asks Jonah in the movie *Sleepless in Seattle*.

"Nobody knows," replies Maggie. "It changes practically every
day."

Southwest owns the low-cost position in most of the country, the
one noticeable exception being the eastern corridor from New York
to Miami. A number of start-ups have tried to use the Southwest
strategy in the East, including Kiwi International Air Lines. Started
in 1992 by a group of former pilots, Kiwi had a great strategy: low
fares, no restrictions, all seats one price.

A great strategy, but a bad name. (To make matters worse, the
kiwi is a *flightless* bird.) If the driving force in business is owning a
word in the mind, how can you succeed if you start out owning the
wrong word (New Zealand) instead of the one you want to own (low
fares)?

Actually the airline has had some success. It was honored as the
best domestic airline of 1994 by readers of *Condé Nast Traveler*, a
year in which Kiwi lost $16 million on revenues of $116 million.
The following year the Kiwi board ousted cofounder, chairman,
CEO, and president, Bob Iverson. Kiwi's future seems rotten.

Flying high with the same strategy as Kiwi, but with a much better name, is ValuJet. The low-fare airline was started a year after
Kiwi, but has consistently made money. Its 25 percent operating
profit margin is the highest in the domestic airline industry.

Like Southwest, ValuJet operates only one type of airplane (thirty-
nine DC-9-30 jets). "People ask us what we worry about," says
ValuJet president Lewis Jordan. "We worry that we'll lose our focus
or deviate from the game plan." Amen.

The airline industry has a reputation as a terrible business to be in.
But that's only true if you play the game the way everybody else
does. If you can find a focus, any business can be a barn burner,
including the airline industry.

In its first full year of operation, ValuJet earned $21 million on
revenues of $134 million. The second-year earnings and revenues
more than doubled. The stock is up 400 percent from its initial public offering.

What other areas are ripe for a Southwest strategy? Well, Southwest doesn't fly the northern tier, from Minneapolis to Seattle, but the traffic is relatively thin along the forty-ninth parallel.

The success of Southwest and ValuJet might send the wrong message to future airline start-ups. No-frills, one-class, coach seating, and low fares are only one way to focus an airline in the mind. When the available territories are used up, a would-be start-up has to look for other opportunities. What other possibilities might be available?

The obvious one is the "business" airline. Not only would a business airline promise better food and better service, it would also promise fewer crying babies and fewer crying-out-loud teenagers.

With seating and prices a compromise between first class and coach, a business airline might be very attractive to a segment that accounts for 45 percent of airline passengers and 60 percent of airline revenues.

One airline that has successfully tried this approach is Midwest Express, a unit of Kimberly-Clark. Midwest Express has no first-class or coach seats. Only business seats that are arranged in pairs so there's no middle seat. The airline spends $10 on each meal, compared to less than $5 for the major airlines.

And unlike the majors, Midwest Express has reported a profit each year since 1987. A recent *Consumer Reports* survey ranked the airline number one in service and comfort by a wide margin over eighteen other airlines.

When Jan Carlzon took over money-losing SAS Scandinavian Airlines System in 1981, he adopted a similar approach. He wanted to make SAS "the best airline in the world for the frequent business traveler."

His first step was to substitute an economy-rate business class for first-class service on European flights. SAS then began calling itself "the business airline." By the end of 1982 losses had turned into profits. The strategy worked brilliantly until Carlzon decided to broaden his horizon.

In April 1989 at a lavish, $2.5 million Copenhagen multimedia party complete with dancing girls and disco lights, Carlzon unveiled the new strategy. Instead of an airline, SAS would become a "global travel-services company."

According to Jan Carlzon, "There are limits to what you can develop in an aircraft cabin in terms of service. So we have to add services on the ground."

His goal was to double the profits from nonairline activities from a current 25 percent of the total to 50 percent by 1991. To this end Carlzon announced the purchase of a 40 percent interest in Intercontinental Hotels Corp.

The global travel-services company Carlzon put together included Diners Club Nordic and SAS Service Partner, Scandinavia's largest tour company. Carlzon also bought 9.9 percent of Texas Air and 42 percent of LanChile, as well as entering into a number of alliances with other airlines.

The combination never made money. By 1990 the ink turned red at SAS, and the global travel-services company continued to lose money (more than $200 million in total) until Carlzon was cast off in 1993.

The new CEO (Jan Stenberg) proceeded to shed noncore businesses and pare SAS back to an airline. By 1994 SAS was profitable again.

Others have tried similar strategies and failed. Richard Ferris, a former chairman of UAL Corp., once combined United Airlines, Hilton International, Westin Hotels & Resorts, and the Hertz Rent-A-Car business into a travel monstrosity named Allegis. Ferris was soon forced out, and new management kept the airline and sold the rest.

AMR Corp., parent of American Airlines, once tried the same thing with partners Marriott, Hilton Hotels, and Budget Rent a Car. The idea was to create a super reservations system, dubbed CONFIRM. The fiasco tarnished AMR's reputation as a technological leader as well as costing the company a $165 million write-off.

Will they ever learn? Recently AUA, the leading Austrian airline, bought Touropa, the leading Austrian travel agency, in an effort to fill its planes. Both will be less competitive in the future.

Any company, be it an airline or an automotive company, that tries to serve everybody with the same brand is asking for trouble. How long will it be before American, United, Delta, and the others learn this lesson?

Up till now, the major players in the airline business have tried to use their hub-and-spoke systems to create regional monopolies so they can charge high prices. But these never last. Any company that has the lion's share of a market *and* charges high prices is an obvious target for price-cutting by the majors and infiltration by the one-price, low-fare airlines.

In a competitive environment, monopolies never last. The only strategy that lasts is a strong focus.

Yet most companies are headed in the line-extension direction. The route taken by Carlzon at SAS is a well-beaten path. Virtually every major corporation sees success in one area as an opportunity to *broaden the base*, to get into other areas aligned to the initial successful product or service. They seldom look for opportunities to *deepen the ditch*, to turn their initial success into a company that dominates an industry for decades.

For every SAS that went down the line-extension road to financial failure, there are companies that refocused their way to financial success.

In a military war it's suicide to attack across a wide front. The only strategy that has a chance of success is an attack on a narrow front. "Deep penetration on a narrow front" is the mantra of a military mind. In a business war the same principles apply. In concentration there is strength. In diversification there is weakness.

Federal Express is one example of the power of concentration. When the company got off the ground in April 1973, it had its own planes and trucks and a unique hub-and-spoke distribution system with its hub in Memphis, Tennessee. Federal Express's strategy was to sell a better service at a cheaper price, primarily through direct selling to heavy users. The target was Emery Air Freight, the oldest, largest, most profitable company in the industry.

This approach produced three different product lines: "Priority One" (overnight delivery), "Priority Two" (two-day delivery), and "Priority Three" (three-day delivery) with correspondingly declining rates. The three services were lined up against the Emery offerings, all available from Federal Express at a lower price.

If you're not the leader, if you don't own the category in the mind, it's difficult to sell a better service at a cheaper price. In its first two years Federal Express lost $29 million.

Then Federal Express refocused the company around a new strategy emphasizing Priority One, the company's overnight service. (Priority Three was dropped and Priority Two was renamed "Standard Air Service.") At the same time a "Courier Pak" was introduced. Designed to hold up to two pounds of documents, the Courier Pak was the visual expression of the "overnight" idea.

The advertising was also refocused to reach executives rather than mailroom supervisors and shipping dock managers. The new theme: "When it absolutely, positively, has to be there overnight." There was no mention of being cheaper.

"Overnight" became the battle cry at Federal Express, and overnight the company turned around. It broke even in July 1975 and never looked back. Federal Express went public in April 1978 at $25 a share. Three years later, after two splits, that share was worth $180. By 1980 profits were over $50 million a year.

Not only did Federal Express move away from a "better and cheaper" strategy to an "overnight" strategy, it also let its prices drift higher than the competition's. This had two benefits. The company made more money and improved its reputation. If a service costs more, the customer thinks, it must be better.

The only question one has about the Federal Express strategy is "Why bother with Standard Air Service at all?" Fortunately for the company, many customers seemed to ignore the two-day service and thought FedEx meant "overnight" only.

Meanwhile back at Emery Air Freight, things were going from bad to worse. Federal Express's focus on small packages overnight had shifted Emery's business to the heavyweight side of the equation. In an attempt to recoup, Emery spent $313 million in April 1987 to buy Purolator Courier Corp., a specialist in overnight letter and document services.

The Purolator purchase was a "good fit," in the vernacular of the mergers and acquisitions crowd. Emery's strength was in big packages; Purolator's strength was in small packages. The combination of the two could handle *all* the needs of any customer.

But what looks good on paper doesn't always look good on the ground or in the air. Emery lost its focus and began to bleed badly. By December 1987 the board had forced out John Emery Jr., the strong-willed son of the company's founder.

In April 1989 Emery Air Freight was sold to Consolidated Freightways for $489 million. Things didn't get better; they got worse. By 1990 Emery Worldwide (the new name for the old Emery, which had been combined with CF Air Freight) had consumed all of Consolidated's cash and was losing money at a rate of almost $100 million a year. The CEO was fired and new management hired.

The answer to the Emery problem was focus. New management at Emery took the company out of the letter and small-package segments of the overnight delivery business and concentrated their resources on overnight delivery of mid- and heavyweight freight packages weighing over seventy pounds.

History repeats itself. This is exactly what Federal Express did, only in reverse. Emery established a heavyweight focus in contrast to FedEx's lightweight focus. Emery is now the dominant leader in the over-seventy-pound freight market, with a 24 percent share. Its nearest rival, Burlington Air Express, has a 13 percent share.

In a recent year Emery's operating profits were $77 million. Not bad, considering that Federal Express in the nineties has been averaging only $66 million a year in net income.

Then there's SonicAir, founded by Ray Thurston to pioneer the "same-day" air cargo business. After capturing 40 percent of the same-day market, Thurston sold his private company to United Parcel Service for $65 million.

"Do you know what the secret to life is?" asks Jack Palance in the 1991 movie *City Slickers*.

"No, what?" says Billy Crystal.

"One thing, just one thing. You stick to that and everything else don't mean shit."

"That's great, but what's the one thing?"

"That's what you've got to figure out."

NARROWING YOUR SCOPE

You don't have to invent something to own a word in the mind. Sometimes you can accomplish the same result just by narrowing your scope.

The biggest single barrier to the development of an effective corporate strategy is the strongly held belief that a company has to appeal to the entire market. More money has been wasted reaching out to a company's "noncustomers" than any other single endeavor.

"How can we grow, if we don't try to appeal to our noncustomers?" is a legitimate question. It's easy to see how broadening the base will increase your business and your profits; it's harder to see how narrowing the focus will do so.

To appreciate the power of narrowing rather than broadening the base, you should first consider the futility of appealing to the entire market. In truth, if reaching everyone were an effective approach, then there would be no need to consider the alternative.

In the face of competition, no brand, no company, no corporation can achieve 100 percent of any market. And it's not a benevolent government that defends an industry from incipient monopolies. It's the irascible mind of the customer.

There are two kinds of customers, and they vary by category. Some customers want to buy the same brand as everyone else; other customers want to buy a different brand than everyone else. This is not a function of personality, because within the mind of each individual, purchasing desires vary by category.

If I'm a man, I might want to wear a beard to be different from most other men who are clean-shaven. On the other hand, I might want to drink Coca-Cola because most other people do. My purchasing decisions vary from being different in certain categories to being the same in other categories.

Fortunately for the stability of the world, more people want to be the same as other people and fewer people want to be different. That's why the more popular brands, the more popular motion pictures, the more popular plays tend to continue to attract the larger share of the market while the less popular brands and attractions tend to appeal to the smaller share of the market.

Things are not what they seem to be on the surface, however. The rationale for buying the leading brand is the quality axiom. I.e., the better product will win. The rationale for not buying the better product is the urge to be different. Better or different is the choice that consumers make every day.

That's not quite it either. To justify their own positions, consumers with the urge to be different usually feel that the majority are misguided. That if they really evaluated the products fairly, they would not chose the leading brand. In other words, the better product didn't win, but it should have.

With these psychological factors stacked against you, it's impossible for one brand to capture 100 percent of a market.

Leaders attract people who want to do the same thing, who want to buy the same brands, as others. Leaders, on the other hand, repel those who want to be different. How can one brand, one company, one corporation appeal to everybody? It can't.

Loyalist or insurgent? Nationalist or rebel? Defender or challenger? Democrat or Republican? Coca-Cola or Pepsi-Cola? Life has a way of turning every situation, political or business, into a duality, where the leading institution faces a smaller institution challenging the leader for supremacy.

Perhaps the most popular president of the United States, Franklin D. Roosevelt, in his landslide victory of 1936 received only 61 percent of the popular vote. (Alf Landon, his Republican opponent, received 37 percent of the vote, with the remaining 2 percent shared by five other political parties.)

If Roosevelt, the only U.S. president ever elected for four terms, couldn't do better than 61 percent in his best year, what hope do you have of capturing 80 or 90 percent of a given market? No hope at all.

Abandon hope. Be prepared to give up a segment of the market. Deal with reality. All business is a niche business. The only difference is that the leader's niche is bigger than the niches owned by others, but it's still a niche.

The question is, what kind of a niche do you want to own? The quality niche? The price niche? The safety niche? The driving niche? The home delivery niche? The take-out niche?

No brand, no company, no corporation can achieve 100 percent of a market . . . in the face of competition. Once you accept this reality, finding a word to own in the mind is greatly simplified. You don't have to face those demons who keep telling you, "Let's not give up any part of the market."

Sacrifice is the essence of corporate strategy. Without sacrifice, there is no strategy. Without sacrifice a company or an institution becomes weak. Sears was unwilling to sacrifice any segment of the retail market, so they became progressively weaker and a juicy target for Wal-Mart and Home Depot at the low end and for a host of specialty chains at the high end (The Gap, Toys "R" Us, The Limited, Victoria's Secret, and others).

IBM refused to sacrifice anything in the computer field, so they became an attractive target for the PC specialists (Compaq, Packard Bell, Gateway, Dell, etc.), the workstation specialists (Sun, Hewlett-Packard, Silicon Graphics, etc.), and the software specialists (Microsoft, Oracle, Novell, Lotus, etc.).

Since you can't successfully appeal to everyone anyway, sacrifice is an easy concept to embrace. When you sacrifice you're not giving up anything at all; what you are doing is *defining* your position. And oftentimes a good way to define a position is by who you are not.

Who was Winston Churchill? The former English prime minister is best known as Adolf Hitler's most implacable foe. (And after the war, when there was no Hitler to fight, Churchill promptly lost his post. The Brits loved him for his foreign policy but didn't care for his domestic policies.)

In politics the principle of sacrifice is well established. If you state your own position and vigorously attack the opposition, prospective voters will know who you are and what you stand for. If you try to appeal to both sides, prospective voters will think you are wishy-washy and you will get few votes.

The art of politics consists of vigorously and publicly giving up the votes you know you aren't going to get anyway. That's the way you look like a decisive and forceful leader.

Companies could learn from political parties. Anytime you're *for* something you are automatically *against* something else. Without enemies you have no position in the marketplace. (The pro-life movement, for example, is focused against the "abortion" enemy.)

When Emery was in the letter and document business, as well as the heavyweight package business, it had no enemies and no position. It was just another company trying to survive in a business dominated by Federal Express and United Parcel Service.

When Emery refocused itself on the over-seventy-pound business, it had a nice convenient enemy in Federal Express. "Why do business with FedEx? They're good for documents and small packages, but we're the experts in handling the big stuff."

It's the specialist versus the generalist. Most of the time people prefer to do business with specialists, not generalists. If you have a heart problem, you see a cardiologist, not a general practitioner. If you want to buy a pair of shoes, you go to a shoe store, not a department store. If you want to buy toothpaste, you go to a drugstore, not a food supermarket. Most of the time.

But nothing is black or white in the field of consumer behavior. Sometimes, people will buy shoes at a department store and toothpaste at a supermarket. When convenience is an issue, people will often pay more and give up variety and choice to save time.

Witness the rise of 7-Eleven and other convenience stores. And why would you mix gasoline and food? Yet many gasoline stations are putting retail food outlets on their properties. Why? Convenience.

At the same time gas stations are adding food, they're also losing their oil-change business. Why? Specialization.

In a classic example of segmentation, the oil-change business is breaking apart from the gasoline stations and car dealers that used to do most of the business. Oil change is becoming a separate industry led by companies like Jiffy Lube, Auto Spa, and quite a few others.

The "ten-minute oil change" is the driving force behind the new oil-change industry. Not only is Jiffy Lube taking business away from service stations and car dealers, but the company is also taking business away from customers themselves. (More than half the oil changes are performed by car owners themselves.)

With the increase in the number of two-income households and a decline in the number of garages and gas stations with trained mechanics, the future of the fast oil-change business looks bright.

Whether you call it segmentation, specialization, or division, it's a fact of life in business today. Industries don't combine. They divide into separate industries with their own unique sets of leaders and followers.

The trick is to sense a coming division and then be the first to set up an operation or a company with a separate brand name that communicates the key word you want to own in the mind.

What's the key benefit of the oil-change specialists? Fast service. Market leader Jiffy Lube captures this concept perfectly.

Leaders sometimes think they can stop this division from happening. Perturbed by the loss of oil-change business at its dealers, Ford Motor Company announced its intention to open two thousand Fast Lube oil-change centers at Ford and Lincoln-Mercury dealerships by the year 1992.

Have you been to a Ford dealer lately? Have you seen a Fast Lube center in operation? It never happened.

Take the car-rental business, for example. Everybody knows Hertz is the leader, but who's the number two car-rental company?

Wrong. The number two car-rental company is not Avis, it's Enterprise Rent-A-Car. In 1994, for example, Hertz had $2.1 billion in revenues, Enterprise was second with $1.85 billion in revenues, and Avis was third with $1.7 billion.

Furthermore, Enterprise, with some 230,000 cars, has a bigger fleet than Hertz, with 215,000 cars, and more office locations (2,000 for Enterprise versus 1,175 for Hertz).

What's going on here? How can Enterprise be bigger than Avis in revenues and bigger than Hertz in cars? The answer is specialization. Enterprise specializes in the insurance-replacement market. More than two-thirds of its $1.85 billion revenues come from a market the airport giants don't go after: rentals to people whose cars have been wrecked or stolen.

This insurance-replacement focus allows Enterprise to limit its TV advertising and work the referral route. The company looks after the insurance agents and adjusters who point customers its way. It offers big discounts on personal rentals to the insurance trade, as well as sponsoring the occasional golf outing.

Enterprise also maintains close ties with local car dealers, body shops, and garages. It sometimes pays rent to maintain a booth on a car dealer's premises. Managers even deliver breakfast to referral sources. "One of our biggest sales methods is doughnuts," jokes CEO Andy Taylor.

Instead of expensive airport and downtown locations favored by Avis and Hertz, Enterprise works mostly from inexpensive storefronts and shopping strips. Instead of buying new cars every six months or so, Enterprise keeps its cars for about eighteen months before selling them.

Helped by such economies, Enterprise rates are up to 30 percent lower than its more visible competitors. In spite of its low rates, the company has posted a profit every month for the last twenty years. There's power in a focus.

There's another way of looking at the Enterprise numbers. It's a trap that happens over and over again. You see the insurance-replacement market that accounts for two-thirds of revenues and the conventional market that accounts for the rest. Where does opportunity lie?

Enterprise already gets the lion's share of the insurance-replacement market, but only a small fraction of the conventional market. If Enterprise could double its conventional market share, it would be bigger than Hertz.

The mathematics are sound, the reasoning is flawed. If Enterprise were to shift resources from its easy-to-get insurance-replacement business to the hard-to-get conventional business, its total revenues might suffer. Business is like a teeter-totter. You push down on one end; the other end goes up.

Business is also like politics. A move to the right loses votes on the left. A move to the left loses votes on the right.

A careful analysis of Enterprise's conventional business would probably show that it's related to its insurance-replacement business. There are hundreds of ways that one side of the business can drive the other. Friends, neighbors, relatives, and others could be influenced to search out Enterprise for conventional car rentals.

This is not just theory. Invariably when companies try to enlarge their market to do a better job with segments where their share is small, they lose focus and ultimately market share. It doesn't happen overnight. There's a delay factor.

It takes a while for the core customer to feel that somehow his or her interests have been neglected in favor of the broader market. It takes a while for new "focused" competition to move in and take away the core customers. Rome wasn't ruined in a day.

Another example of a highly focused company is LDDS Communications, the fourth largest long-distance telephone company. After forty-four acquisitions in the past five years, LDDS has $3.2 billion in revenues with 5 percent of the market.

Unlike AT&T, MCI, and Sprint, however, the company gets less than 5 percent of its revenues from residential service. Most of LDDS's business is with business. (You aren't likely to see any LDDS television spots attacking AT&T or MCI.)

The success of LDDS is based not just on segmenting the marketplace but also on verbalizing that segment. If you can't verbalize it in ways that are meaningful to customers and prospects, then you don't have a viable segment.

The word "business" has power when used by LDDS representatives. A business owner can appreciate the value of a long-distance carrier with a business orientation. Such a company could promise rates, services, and discounts tailored to the business customer, not the consumer.

On the other hand, if a company serves several states of the union, it generally can't treat them as a segment of the market. Where are the benefits to the buyer from such a segment? If there are no benefits, implied or otherwise, then there is no segment.

If you can verbalize the states, however, you can often create a segment that is powerful. Suppose you are selling a product in the Midwest only. By verbalizing your product as "the pride of the Midwest," you might be able to create a regional preference for the product.

Actually, a good candidate for this strategy might be the Royal Crown Cola Co. RC Cola (and its sugar-free sister Diet Rite cola) have about 3 percent of the national cola market. A Midwest-only strategy (where RC Cola is relatively stronger) might be an effective way to fight the power of Coke and Pepsi.

Narrowing your focus and being strong somewhere is a better approach than expanding your focus and winding up weak everywhere. Nor does it make much sense to sell RC Cola in fifty-three countries around the world, either. It might be profitable to do so, but at what cost in terms of management time and resources?

Another place to witness the power of a focus is the personal computer field. At first, all personal computers were "home" computers, and the leaders were Apple, Radio Shack, and Commodore Pet, brands with a strong consumer or home perception. But the market shifted. Executives were buying home personal computers and bringing them into the office, often in violation of corporate policies.

When IBM launched the PC in 1981, it had a narrow focus. It was the only "office" machine in a market served by companies that had spread their focus over both the home and business market. It was also a big success. By 1983, IBM was the number one brand, with 21 percent of the market.

What was IBM's next move? They launched the PCjr for the home market, which was stillborn. (History repeats itself. The largest selling office computer today is Compaq. What is Compaq's next move? They plan to launch a line of home personal computers.)

As a company, of course, IBM has a broad focus: everything from mainframes to software. Sooner or later this was going to hurt them in personal computers. But nobody loses business just because they have a broad focus. To lose business you have to run up against a competitor with a narrow focus.

Enter Compaq. Here was a company focused on just office personal computers. No workstations, no software, no home personal computers. At first, Compaq tried to become another Mercedes-Benz by selling at the high end of the market.

Good strategy in theory, but in practice nobody wanted to pay more for a higher quality machine because of the obsolescence factor. A car might be on the road for a decade or longer. A computer is unlikely to sit on a desk longer than three years before being replaced by a more powerful machine. Why waste money on expensive junk?

As soon as Compaq lowered its price, the company lowered the boom on IBM. In two years, Compaq zoomed from 5 percent to 14 percent of the personal computer market. In the process, Compaq became the leading brand.

So who's the fastest growing personal computer manufacturer today? Packard Bell. What Compaq did in the office, Packard Bell did in the home. By focusing exclusively on the home personal computer market, Packard Bell has dominated this market in a way that neither IBM nor Compaq has been able to achieve in the office market. Packard Bell has almost 50 percent of the home market.

If handled smartly, a narrow focus creates a powerful brand. Since you don't have to satisfy everyone, you don't have to compromise on design, packaging, pricing, and distribution.

Packard Bell packed its machines with features for home use. It was the first to sell personal computers with a built-in CD-ROM drive and speakers, allowing customers to run multimedia programs rich in sound and video. Its computers are loaded with preinstalled software, and its Navigator program has gotten good press for making personal computers less intimidating.

Although the nerd community pooh-poohed the Pentium chip for its propensity to make mathematical errors, Packard Bell jumped on the Pentium. (It's the only chip that home buyers have heard about.) About half of the company's sales are Pentium-based machines.

Packard Bell achieved its lofty market share with a less-than-lackluster reputation for reliability and service. A survey of ninety-six thousand buyers by *PC World* magazine rated the company's products of "average" reliability and "among the worst" of forty-two brands for customer service. Fortunately for Packard Bell, their primary market is general consumers and not the nerds who read the PC books.

What Packard Bell did in computers, Paychex does in payroll processing. While ADP (Automated Data Processing, Inc.) of Roseland, New Jersey, founded the industry and is the big gun with annual revenues of more than $2 billion, the rising star is Paychex of Rochester, New York.

Paychex's growth in the past decade has been averaging 20 percent a year, almost twice the growth rate of competitor ADP. Whereas ADP serves mostly large corporations, Paychex focuses on small companies.

The potential is enormous. Of the ten million businesses in America, 98 percent have fewer than two hundred employees. This is the market Paychex is targeting. Annual revenues are currently $224 million a year with net income of 12.5 percent.

Thanks to a cooperative government, the business is likely to continue to boom. In a recent year there were over four hundred changes to federal, state, and local tax laws. And employers are required to file as many as forty-two tax returns annually.

Focus works as well in a slow-growing business as it does in a fast-growing business like payroll processing. Take tires, for example. Traditional tire companies believe you have to sell at a loss to the car companies to build profitable replacement business through tire dealers.

Not Cooper Tire & Rubber. Cooper does not compete in the original equipment market at all. Yet the company has produced steadily increasing sales and profits. In the past decade, sales have increased 150 percent, and net income, as a percentage of sales, has more than doubled.

What you find in tires is typical of what you find in many industries. You have one or two full-line leaders (Goodyear and Michelin) and a number of profitable specialists like Cooper. In the mushy middle are marginally profitable companies like Bridgestone/Firestone.

What a company in the mushy middle ought to do is to focus on a segment of the market. But tradition dies hard. Once a company has been a full-line manufacturer, it's almost impossible to convert management to becoming a specialist. "What? Give up a part of our business?"

Yes. The secret of success in business starts with sacrifice. Start-up companies usually are quick to grasp the secret, but once a company has tasted the fruits of the full line, "focusing" seems to be a step backward.

Perhaps it's an ego problem. While existing management usually resists trimming the sales, new management often has the stomach to make the needed cutbacks.

The term "full line" may be a misnomer. What's needed for success is a focus, which sometimes can be achieved with a full line, but with sacrifices made in other areas. Distribution is one such area.

Two companies with significant shares of the personal computer market are Gateway 2000 and Dell Computer, each with about 5 percent of the market. Both offer full lines, but they sacrifice retail distribution and a direct salesforce. Their focus is direct marketing, and both companies have become very profitable indeed with a single distribution channel.

Dell was the first company to focus on direct marketing of computers. Dell uses commission salespeople to take orders over the company's toll-free telephone lines twenty-four hours a day. By eliminating the retail markup, Dell could sell its computers at about 40 percent of the price of an IBM PC. Sales took off.

But Dell has made a number of mistakes that have unfocused their operations. In 1988, the company added a salesforce to service larger customers. In 1990 Dell entered the retail market by allowing Soft Warehouse Superstores (now CompUSA) to sell its personal computers at mail-order prices.

The following year the company struck a similar deal with Staples, the office supply chain. In 1993 Dell began selling its personal computers through Best Buy's retail stores. The following year, Dell did an abrupt about-face, announcing it would no longer sell in retail stores.

While Dell dithered over its distribution strategy, Gateway kept its focus on the telephone. Today Gateway, with more than $2 billion in annual sales, is neck and neck with Dell.

What happens when the big guns (IBM, Compaq, Apple, and Digital Equipment) take to the telephones to sell personal computers? Not much. None of the big brands in the retail channel have made much of a mark in direct marketing. Currently Gateway and Dell have 47 percent of the mail-order business and as the business matures, their market share is likely to increase.

While a focus can start anywhere (mail order, for example), it soon becomes a driving force in the business itself. Because mail order is the preferred buying method for more knowledgeable customers, Gateway and Dell can focus their efforts on high-end computer models.

Furthermore, they can build to order rather than running up big inventories of finished systems that may or may not sell. (Dell carries 35 days of inventory versus 110 days for Compaq.)

What's often perceived as a negative (a single channel of distribution) is in reality the focus of these companies and the reason for their success. Without their powerful focus it's likely that both Dell and Gateway would have gone the way of hundreds of personal computer companies that have come and gone since 1975.

Another distribution-focused company is Amway, which makes an incredibly broad line of products: furniture, luggage, stereo systems, watches, encyclopedias, health and beauty aids, and home care products. This is the route to disaster, except for one thing. Amway has a powerful focus. The company was the pioneer in what is now known as "multilevel marketing."

Amway sells its products through more than two million independent representatives (called distributors) in nearly sixty countries. Distributors earn commissions not only on their own sales but also on sales of distributors they recruit.

Another distribution success is Snap-on Incorporated (formerly Snap-on Tools). Back in 1919 Joe Johnson invented interchangeable wrench handles and sockets. But it took two salesmen (Stanton Palmer and Newton Tarble) to put the company on the map.

The two developed a distribution business demonstrating Snap-on tool sets at customer sites. In 1921 Palmer and Tarble bought out Johnson's original supporters, and the company began to build its unique distribution system.

Today, more than five thousand Snap-on dealers and franchisees travel the highways of America with huge walk-in vans loaded with tools. Snap-on sales exceed $1 billion a year.

It's ironic, but successful companies can often benefit more from refocusing than unsuccessful ones. The successful company might be missing a big opportunity, while the unsuccessful company might be in a hopeless situation that no amount of reorganization is going to help.

Consider two miners. One is digging at the edge of a mother lode and making a good living. The other is digging in a barren territory and is going broke. Who can benefit the most from a refocusing strategy?

The successful miner, of course. With a little refocusing of his or her drilling efforts, the mother lode can be tapped and a fortune made. The situation for the unsuccessful miner is hopeless.

So, too, with many companies. With success, they feel they are doing everything right and need no help. With failure, they call in the marines and are disappointed that nothing seems to work.

Focusing will do more to propel a company into the stratosphere than any other single activity. But it's not easy. The temptation is to leave things alone when they are working and to fiddle with them when they're not.

What management needs to do is search for the one thing that is working and then focus the entire company behind that single effort.

Take Widmer Brewing of Portland, Oregon. The company is booming, its products are hot, and the company has been growing 50 and 60 percent a year. What else could you want?

A focus. Widmer brews eight different German-style beers plus draft root beer. But 70 percent of Widmer's sales are a wheat beer called "America's Original Hefeweizen." Golden in color, cloudy in appearance, and bursting with flavor, Widmer Hefeweizen is a Portland institution. Served with a slice of lemon, Hefeweizen looks different, tastes different, and is different. It's on the edge of a mother lode.

Widmer's logical next step is to drop the seven tagalong beers as well as the root beer and focus on Hefeweizen. Then roll out the barrels of Hefeweizen around the country.

In other words, trade in a broad focus in a small market in favor of a narrow focus in a large market. The bars, restaurants, and supermarkets of America can't possibly stock a wide range of German-style beers, but perhaps there is room for one unique and different "wheat beer."

Yet Widmer is unlikely to do so. What propels Widmer is what propels most of Corporate America. Growth before focus. Size before profits. Diversification before specialization.

Yet size does not equate with either success or profits. The largest "company" in the United States, in terms of number of employees, is the U.S. Postal Service, with about seven hundred thousand wage earners. In the past decade the Postal Service has had revenues of $368 billion, yet managed to lose more than $5 billion.

In addition to cheap capital, the Postal Service has the added advantage of being a monopoly. (If a free-enterprise monopolist like Bill Gates were running the Postal Service, he would probably make enough money to pay off a substantial part of the national debt.)

Yet a relentless push for size seems to grip the imaginations of chief executives everywhere. W. Michael Blumenthal, a former secretary of the Treasury, once headed up Burroughs Corporation, a $5 billion computer company. Not big enough.

"In any other field, Burroughs would be considered a Leviathan," Mr. Blumenthal said. "But in mainframes, we're a rabbit to an elephant." So he lusted after Sperry Corporation.

After an initial rejection, the two companies came together in June 1986. Shortly thereafter the merged company adopted the name Unisys Corporation.

Unisys is a good example of merger mathematics of the type "one plus one equals one-half." It's been nine years since the two companies have joined forces. In the premerger years, Burroughs had a strong position in the financial industry. Even today Unisys systems process half of the checks in the world for forty-one of the fifty largest banks.

In the nine premerger years, Burroughs had total sales of $29.5 billion and total net income of $1.9 billion.

In the nine postmerger years, Unisys (the Burroughs-Sperry combination) had sales of $72.9 billion. Not bad at all. But the company's total net income for these nine years was a minus $494 million. That's awful. That puts Unisys in the same category as the Postal Service.

What happened to Unisys also happened to International Harvester. Forty years ago, International Harvester was the 22nd largest industrial company in the country. Way ahead of Caterpillar (75th) and Deere & Co. (104th). But International Harvester was in three basic businesses: trucks, farm machinery, and construction equipment.

Its competitors were much more focused. Caterpillar in construction. Deere in farm equipment.

Today the narrowly focused companies are way ahead of International Harvester, now called Navistar. Caterpillar does $14 billion in sales. Deere, $9 billion. And Navistar, just $5 billion.

Furthermore, Navistar has lost $579 million in the past five years, while its competitors have been profitable.

It pays to stick to your knitting. Take Tyson Foods, the country's largest chicken producer, with 18 percent of the market. According to Chairman Don Tyson, about half of his customers will want a single supplier for what the industry calls "center of the plate" proteins: chicken, beef, pork, fish, turkey.

So in 1992 Tyson paid $243 million for Arctic Alaska, the country's largest publicly traded fishery.

Two years later Tyson wrote off $214 million in goodwill associated with the acquisition, which most seafood experts consider to be a disaster. Tyson is also trying to tap the pork market with some $100 million invested in hog-raising and processing facilities.

Yet three-fourths of Tyson's sales and virtually all its earnings come from its core chicken business. As a matter of fact, Tyson is going great guns in chicken. It sells 70 percent of all U.S. chicken exported to Japan. It developed Chicken McNuggets for McDonald's and Rotisserie Gold for KFC.

Specialized chicken products like these offer enormous potential as domestic fast-food operators move around the world. In the past few years, Tyson's gross margins have averaged 19 percent, roughly double the industry average.

Why not concentrate on chicken? It's that beguiling "center of the plate" strategy, which sounds terrific in the boardroom but may not seem so smart in the chicken coop. Customers often say they want to buy everything from a single supplier.

Yet somehow it never works out. Ask IBM why customers are not buying all their computer requirements from Big Blue. They might be hard pressed to explain why.

The truth is, when prospects say they want to buy everything from a single supplier, they usually add under their breath, "All things being equal."

But all things are never equal. The moment you become a full-line supplier, you are no longer a specialist. You are no longer "the expert." You lose much of your power.

Today Tyson is the chicken king, the recognized leader in quality, price, service, and innovation. But if Tyson succeeds in becoming a full-line center-of-the-plate supplier, they would lose much of this perception. They would be just another protein supplier with a mushy reputation.

It pays to narrow your focus. When Jorma Ollila took over as chief executive of Finnish conglomerate Nokia in 1992, the company made everything from television tubes to truck tires to toilet paper. It was also losing $140 million a year.

Ollila sold off the toilet paper and dozens of other products and focused on mobile phones. Nokia now ranks second in the world in mobile phones (behind Motorola) and is the market leader on its home turf in Europe. The future looks exceptionally bright for the former Finnish laggard.

Even the insurance industry is beginning to see the light. "Insurance giants no longer ask to be all things to all people," reports the *New York Times*. "There was a time when this company wanted to write every type of policy in all fifty states," said Walter Fitzgibbon, chief actuary of Aetna. "We just don't want to do that any longer."

In order to concentrate on health care and life insurance, Aetna recently announced the sale of its property and liability insurance businesses to Travelers Group for $4 billion.

Many successes in the insurance business have been achieved by narrowly focused companies. A.L. Williams in term insurance. SunAmerica in annuities. Progressive in car insurance.

Executives in other industries have also sensed the power of specialization. Bernard Taylor, who once headed the global pharmaceutical giant Glaxo PLC, left in 1990 to join Medeva PLC, a small four-year-old British firm. Taylor saw a chance to build a company by buying drugs and vaccines that larger companies no longer wanted because their sales were too low.

But not just any drugs. Taylor concentrates on buying products that treat a narrow range of ailments, especially bronchial conditions like influenza and asthma. "By targeting a few clinical areas," Taylor explains, "Medeva's salesmen can focus on doctors treating those conditions, and usually have more success with those doctors than salesmen promoting a wider range of drugs."

The strategy is working. Medeva's sales in 1994 rose by 30 percent from the previous year to about $400 million with pretax earnings of $90 million. "I saw Medeva," says Bernard Taylor, "as a new way to build a pharmaceutical company."

Or any company for that matter. The power in business doesn't derive from your products or your factories. It derives from your position in the mind. And a specialist, or focused company, is in a much stronger position than a generalist.

Salick Health Care focuses on cancer. The company operates twenty-four-hour cancer treatment centers located in hospitals. These centers allow people to schedule their treatments at their own convenience, even in the evenings and on weekends. Sales have been growing rapidly, reaching $132 million in 1994, with net income of $10 million.

Quantum Health Resources focuses on hemophilia. In five years the company grew from $4 million in sales to over $200 million, with net income averaging about 8 percent of sales.

Cerner digitizes medical information so that it can be called up on computer screens. Sales have tripled in the past five years to $155 million.

Opportunities are constantly being created by changes that take place in the market. The rise of the HMO has created a new kind of health care organization called a PPM, or physician practice management company. A PPM acts as a middleman between the doctor and the HMO, rendering services to the doctors and bargaining on their behalf with the HMOs.

One of the largest PPMs, seven-year-old PhyCor, does about $400 million in revenues. Yet there's plenty of room to grow. The nation's 650,000 physicians generate about $200 billion a year in revenues. So far the PPMs have captured only 2 percent of the market.

Even hospitals are specializing. Ten years ago, a community institution, St. Francis in Roslyn, New York, decided to promote itself as "the heart hospital." The results are remarkable. "Today, 75 percent of our work is cardiac related," said the president, Patrick Scollard. "Every bed is filled, every day. Last year, our official occupancy rate was 114 percent."

Nearby St. Charles Hospital in Port Jefferson, New York, is focusing on rehabilitation. "We knew managed care was coming to New York, and that would lead to a decrease in the number of general medical surgical beds," said the president, Barry Zeman. "We also knew there was a great need on Long Island for additional rehabilitation beds."

Today, St. Charles has the largest rehab program on Long Island. It is in the process of a $75 million expansion, which will add close to a hundred rehabilitation beds.

This same principle should be applied to education. Next to health care, it's one of the biggest businesses in America. With annual expenditures in the neighborhood of $270 billion, education alone accounts for 4 percent of the gross domestic product.

In the educational arena, you find few specialists. Virtually everybody is a generalist. Many college presidents, for example, can't wait to become chancellors by turning their institutions into universities. Yet a better direction might be to focus on a single field of study.

Only a handful of undergraduate institutions have specialized, notably Juilliard School in music, Rhode Island School of Design in design, Fashion Institute of Technology in fashion, and Babson College in entrepreneurship. Some have achieved a specialist reputation almost by accident, notably The Johns Hopkins University in medicine. (Only 29 percent of freshmen are premeds.)

Some graduate schools have also achieved world-class reputations as specialists, again mostly by accident—notably Wharton in finance and Kellogg in marketing.

What would work better, however, is for an educational institution to deliberately focus on a single field of study and then make an effort to achieve a world-class reputation. The spectacular success of INSEAD in Fontainebleau, France, is a good example of what can be achieved.

A thirty-five-year-old graduate school that focuses on turning out global business managers, INSEAD (European Institute of Business Administration) has a sterling reputation. It's the school most targeted by international corporate recruiters. Nearly two hundred visit the school annually, offering starting salaries averaging $75,000.

Here in the United States, the American Graduate School of International Management in Glendale, Arizona, is mining the same area. Known as "Thunderbird," the nonprofit school has enjoyed a 900 percent growth in revenues in the past five years.

Yet few American educational institutions specialize. Almost all of America's more than two thousand four-year colleges are generalists. So far, they have benefited from a steadily expanding market for their services.

But there's a limit. As the percentage of high school students going on to college levels off, the competition is going to get more intense. What you are likely to see is a shift toward educational specialization, which is exactly what has happened in the market for goods and services.

The legal profession is slowly moving in this direction. A law firm used to be a law firm; it handled every type of case. Except in small communities, law firms today generally specialize in accident, bankruptcy, business, criminal, employment, marital, social security, taxation, or one of the other legal specialties.

Invariably, legal power lies in being a specialist, not a generalist. When a specialist tries to broaden its base, it is asking for trouble.

Skadden, Arps, Slate, Meagher & Flom was the premier law firm in the go-go eighties. Led by senior partner Joseph Flom, the New York City law firm was involved in the biggest, splashiest takeovers of the decade. And the take-home pay was enormous, too. In the late eighties, profits per partner reached $1.2 million a year.

Mr. Flom says that he always "wanted to put the money into

becoming a full-service firm. I could be crazy, but that was my dream." So in pursuit of its dream, Skadden Arps moved into fifteen new cities and more than a dozen major practice areas. It opened nine foreign offices in four years alone. And, of course, it added bodies: from 526 lawyers in 1985 to about 1,000 by 1990.

As Skadden grew in size, its profits plummeted: from $1.2 million per partner in 1989 to just $690,000 per partner four years later.

What hurt Skadden Arps the most was the falloff in its mergers-and-acquisitions business. It's an example of the biggest problem in the planning process: one-dimensional thinking. This is the kind of thinking that says, "If I have two apples today and I go out and get an orange tomorrow, then I'll wind up with three pieces of fruit." It's not necessarily true.

Try on the mathematics for size. In the mid-eighties, Skadden had about five hundred lawyers and about 35 percent of the merger business. In the early nineties, the firm had almost twice as many lawyers. Question: What percentage of the merger business did the vastly expanded firm achieve?

Answer: somewhere between 20 and 22 percent. This is the mathematics of focus. When you expand to appeal to a larger number of markets, you often lose focus (and sales) in your core business. Two apples plus one orange often equals two pieces of fruit, not three.

The partners' pain at Skadden Arps was not alleviated by the success of their longtime rivals Wachtell Lipton Rosen & Katz. By keeping their focus on mergers and remaining small (103 lawyers in only two cities), Wachtell has kept its profits at much higher levels. The year profits per partner reached $690,000 at Skadden Arps, they were $1.35 million per partner at Wachtell.

What works on Wall Street also works in Hollywood. An actor or an actress who plays the same role over and over again often becomes a big star. If BMW is the ultimate driving machine, John Wayne was the ultimate macho cowboy. Marilyn Monroe was the ultimate sex symbol. And Clint Eastwood is the ultimate strong, silent type.

In essence, big Hollywood stars are focused. They play themselves, which simplifies their jobs and makes them a lot of money. As Sara Taylor once said to her daughter Elizabeth, "Actresses go hungry while movie stars have everything."

Humphrey Bogart always played Humphrey Bogart. Katharine

Hepburn played Katharine Hepburn. Ditto Cary Grant, Fred Astaire, and virtually every other superstar of the past. Focus got them to the top. Focus kept them there.

The next generation of superstars are following in the footprints of Wayne, Monroe, Bogart, Hepburn, Astaire, and Grant. They are becoming big stars by playing themselves. Sylvester Stallone and Arnold Schwarzenegger are the ultimate tough guys. Bruce Willis is the ultimate wise guy. Julia Roberts is the ultimate pretty woman.

What happens when a macho movie star plays against "type"? Did you see a pregnant Schwarzenegger in the movie *Junior*? Or a cowardly Stallone in the comedy *Stop! or My Mom Will Shoot*? Few people did.

As one radio talk show host said, "If he doesn't have an AK-47 in his hand, I don't want to see a Sylvester Stallone movie."

Not everyone sees it that way. In Hollywood, as in Corporate America, there's a deliberate attempt to "unfocus" their properties. To expand their acting horizons. To broaden their range. To avoid being typecast. So Mel Gibson does *Hamlet*.

Here's what Arnold Rifkin of the mighty William Morris Agency says about his client Bruce Willis: "The bad news is that he became categorized, he became positioned, and the visionaries of the industry would like nothing better than to keep him there." So Willis puts on a bunny suit and does *North*, a motion picture that took in all of $7.2 million.

According to Rifkin, Willis is prepared to work in certain films for a tiny fraction of his usual fee. The obvious objective is to broaden his range, to avoid being cast as just a tough wise guy. (Let's not get categorized as just a mergers and acquisition firm, Mr. Flom.)

In many other areas of life, developing and owning a focus can become a powerful force for success. In politics, Ronald Reagan became "the Great Communicator." In sports, Babe Ruth was "the Sultan of Swat" and Pete Rose is "the Hit King." In music, Mel Torme is "the Velvet Fog."

In business, Tom Peters owns "excellence." Michael Hammer owns "reengineering." Michael Porter owns "competitiveness." Philip Crosby owns "quality." Joel Stern owns "economic value added." And Joel Barker owns "paradigm shift."

Among corporate executives, Al Dunlap, the former CEO of Scott Paper, is a "turnaround specialist." In media stories and analyst reports, "doing a Dunlap" is shorthand for turning around a company at lightning speed.

Focus is the art of carefully selecting your category and then working diligently in order to get yourself categorized. It's not a trap to avoid; it's a goal to achieve. Don't let mindless criticism detract you from this goal.

If you're a Hollywood star, a Wall Street luminary, or a corporate executive, it's hard enough to burn your way into the mind with a single character. Why would you want to weigh yourself down with multiple personalities?

Nothing succeeds in life . . . or in business . . . like a carefully selected, carefully chiseled focus.

COPING WITH CHANGE

Sooner or later every corporate strategy is undermined by change: technological change, societal change, fashion change. The art of managing is to anticipate those changes and align your company with a new future.

This is not the same as change for change's sake. Virtually every large company that has gotten into trouble has been criticized for not changing rapidly enough. (IBM, Digital Equipment, and Sears are the classic examples.)

But their mistakes were not the speed of change, but the direction of change. They may have changed too rapidly, for example, and without enough thought given to the direction of change.

Technological change puts a company on the horns of a dilemma. Do you fight change or do you go with the flow?

Business books are filled with tales of companies that bit the dust because they fought change. Obviously, a company has to adjust its strategy to take advantage of change when change takes place. There are five basic ways to do so. Four are generally effective and one is not.

The five ways to react to change are: (1) A foot in both camps. (2) Both feet in the new camp. (3) Both feet in the old camp. (4) Both feet in the new camp with a new name. (5) Two separate camps, two separate names.

So which of the five is the least effective way of reacting to change? (Hint: It's also the most popular way to react to change.)

A FOOT IN BOTH CAMPS

This is the most popular and also the least effective way to react to change. It's easy to see why the "foot in both camps" approach is so popular. It's the time-honored way of dealing with change. "We'll just offer the new technology along with our existing line and let the customer decide."

Top management often sees variety or choice as a customer benefit. Furthermore, this full-line philosophy has a long history of management acceptance. In his classic 1960 "Marketing Myopia" article in the *Harvard Business Review,* Theodore Levitt eloquently explained the rationale behind the "foot in both camps" strategy.

"The railroads did not stop growing because the need for passenger and freight transportation declined. That grew. The railroads are in trouble today not because the need was filled by others (cars, trucks, airplanes, even telephones), but because it was *not* filled by the railroads themselves. They let others take customers away from them because they assumed themselves to be in the railroad business rather than in the transportation business. The reason they defined their industry wrong was because they were railroad-oriented instead of transportation-oriented."

Presumably the New York Central Rail Road, the largest railroad in the thirties and the bluest of the blue chips on the New York Stock Exchange, should have launched the New York Central Airline.

What is the net result of offering both rail and air service? Choice may be a benefit to the customer, but not to the company. The net result of offering both rail and air service is that it unfocuses the company.

But that doesn't happen right away. "The New York Central is a great company," thinks the prospect, "so their air service must be all right." But that holds true only in the short term.

In the long term, the prospect turns to the specialist. "American Airlines must know more about air service than a railroad company," thinks the prospect. And so the shift begins. From rail to air. From the New York Central Rail Road to American Airlines.

There's also a psychological component to change. When customers see a change in technology occurring, they feel more secure in changing companies or in changing brands.

When a family's income substantially increases and they want a larger home, they seldom buy or build one in the same neighborhood. They usually move to a "more expensive" neighborhood.

If they own a Chevrolet, they seldom trade up to a more expensive Chevrolet. They usually move to an Oldsmobile, a Buick, or a more expensive *brand*.

If the customer has a mental commitment to change, then that commitment is reinforced by changing the company that the customer normally buys from. This is especially true when technological change or economic change occurs.

The customer doesn't want to buy a computer from a copier company. A digital camera from a photographic company. An expensive watch from a cheap watch company.

Tragically, many companies try to straddle both the past and the future. They usually succeed in doing neither. It's not a product problem; it's a perception problem. This is an important distinction. Many companies believe the problem lies in developing a superior product or service, the quality axiom. They might actually win the quality battle and lose the mental battle.

Xerox was a powerhouse in copiers when they saw a mad rush to computers taking place. So they tried to get into the computer business, but with a copier name.

After spending billions of dollars, the company wisely retreated to the copier camp. This was a good move for Xerox unless they had the courage to use a new name for their computer products (which is strategy 5: Two separate camps, two separate names).

Xerox actually introduced a personal computer several months before IBM did, which should have given them an advantage. But the Xerox launch was buried in the blitz of PC publicity and the perception of Xerox as a copier company. What does a copier company know about computers?

Eastman Kodak is a powerhouse in photography, but the market is slowly going electronic. There used to be a substantial market for eight- and sixteen-millimeter motion picture film for amateur and documentary filmmakers. Today that market is almost all videotape.

Television commercials are routinely shot on photographic film and edited and distributed on videotape. Hollywood movies are shot on film but distributed to Blockbusters and other rental and sales outlets electronically on videotape. Some television programming is still shot on photographic film, but edited and broadcast using electronic videotape. Every year more and more programming originates and is broadcast using videotape only.

Mene, mene, tekel . . . silver halide photography. The handwriting on the wall says that the days of chemical photography are numbered.

The last major holdout is the thirty-five-millimeter still camera. Canon, Casio, Minolta, Kodak, and others have introduced digital electronic cameras that promise to make chemical photography obsolete. "Digital will grow quickly, but it will not replace traditional photography, at least in my career," says George Fisher, new CEO of Eastman Kodak, recruited from Motorola.

Fisher's first moves at Kodak were picture perfect. He sold off Sterling Winthrop (the drug company), L&F Products (Lysol, Mop & Glo, and other household products), and Kodak's Clinical Diagnostics division.

The company would "focus on profitable participation in the five links of the imaging chain: image capture, processing, storage, output, and delivery of images for people and machines anywhere in Kodak's worldwide market," said Mr. Fisher.

Later he sold Kodak's do-it-yourself products like Minwax wood stains, Thompson's water sealants, and Red Devil paints. And spun off Eastman Chemical to stockholders. In just a few short years the company was transformed from a highly unfocused conglomerate to a company tightly focused on imaging.

In 1992, Kodak was a $20 billion corporation with roughly half of its business represented by imaging products. Three years later Kodak is a $13 billion corporation with imaging products accounting for 80 percent. That's a pretty rapid turnaround for a company that was once number eighteen on the *Fortune* 500 list.

What could torpedo Kodak's efforts to become the major force in the emerging field of digital photography is the name "Kodak," which means photographic, not electronic or digital imaging.

Kodak, of course, recognizes the problem, which is why it recently unveiled a new brand to cover the electronic side of their business. The new brand: Kodak Digital Science.

Kodak Digital Science is not a new name for a new category. It's a generic name (digital science) weighted down by the name Kodak, which means just the opposite of digital.

When you try to keep a foot in both camps, you often wind up a winner in neither camp. It's like trying to jump a wide ditch. If you insist on keeping one foot on the near bank, you'll never jump the ditch to reach the far bank.

Kodak has to let go of the name that means "chemical analog photography" and choose a new name that means "digital electronic."

When Honda wanted to get into the luxury car market, it didn't call its expensive cars Honda Ultra or Honda Super or even Honda Automotive Science. It left the Honda name on the near bank and jumped the ditch with the "Acura" name. So did Toyota with the Lexus brand.

Wang Laboratories, on the other hand, thought it could carry its name across the ditch to the new field of computer imaging. "Wang, the imaging company," was the theme of the company's approach. But what was Wang? Wang was a word-processing company in the same way that Kodak is a photography company.

The handwriting was on the desk that day in August 1981 when IBM introduced the PC. Now there was a powerful, inexpensive, general-purpose personal computer that could do word processing and hundreds of other business tasks. *Mene, mene, tekel* . . . word processing.

Nothing happens overnight. But the future of word processing and a word-processing company was in doubt the day IBM launched the personal computer. That was the day that Wang management should have sat down with themselves and said, "What's next for Wang?" What "word" should we be working on to replace "word processing"?

But it's hard to prepare for the future when the present is going so well. And things were going well for Wang in the early eighties. The average annual increase in both sales and net profits exceeded 40 percent for the first half of the decade. What if someone had the nerve to mention that Wang needed a new word?

Mene, mene, tekel . . . getoutahere.

By the mid-eighties it was clear that Wang was in trouble. In 1985 sales went up 8 percent, but net income tumbled from 10 percent of sales to less than 1 percent. But Wang management continued to hang in there with their word-processing approach. Actually, they made it worse by trying to broaden their line.

Wang's strategy, according to the *New York Times,* was to "move out of the steno pool and into the executive suite with a new offering: state-of-the-art office-automation systems for managers that would feature computers, text editors, electronic mail systems, and graphic devices, all linked in a network enabling managers to summon and dispatch vast quantities of information with a single keystroke."

Bragged Wang's president, John Cunningham, "We have more pieces of the office than anyone else." But in a competitive environment, more is often less because with more you lose your focus.

In the next three years Wang limped along with minimal sales gains and net profits of less than 1 percent. Then in 1989 Wang banged the wall. Sales were flat and the company lost $424 million. They continued to lose money (more than $2 billion in total) and finally filed for bankruptcy in 1992.

Today Wang is a much different company. Hardware is gone. Wang is now a software and services company with under $1 billion in sales.

No company as big as Wang falls apart without a warning shot across the bow. Like a heart attack in your forties, the launch of the IBM PC was the warning shot that should have caused Wang to refocus itself. If not "word processing," then what?

Wang's response was to transform the company from an obsolete word-processing focus to no focus at all. To this end Wang dropped word processing as a flag and became "The Office Automation Computer People."

These are not just words, of course. They represented a large investment in design and manufacturing facilities to turn out a wide range of integrated products, including personal computers, a voice-mail system, and WangNet, a proprietary network that transmits data, text images, and voice signals from one office machine to another.

All for naught. As IBM learned later, when you try to sell everything in one big package, you wind up nowhere. A foot in both camps never works. What Wang needed was a new focus.

A new focus is also what Kodak needs. The warning shot has been fired. Yet Kodak's first response is identical to Wang's. "We will integrate the old focus with the new one." This kind of thinking resulted in the Kodak Photo CD, a method of electronically storing conventional photographic images. A flop as a consumer product, the Photo CD is finding some uses in business and industry.

Digital Equipment is another company that found itself in the same ditch as Wang. But it wasn't the launch of IBM PC that sent the message to Digital. It was the rise of the Apple II and the home personal computer in the late seventies.

Digital ignored the home personal computer because they owned another word, the minicomputer, a concept the company invented in 1965 with the launch of the PDP–8. One of the problems with inventing a concept is that you tend to fall in love with your prodigy. You never want to give it up.

According to Ken Olsen, Digital's founder and president, "There is no such thing as a personal computer." For years Digital people were not allowed to use the words "personal computer." Too bad. These were the words that were going to reach out and bite them.

According to Digital insiders, Ken Olsen turned down the opportunity to be first to launch a serious business personal computer eleven times before IBM introduced the PC. (I was there on one of those occasions, when Mr. Olsen said, "I don't want to be first. If IBM goes first, we can beat their specs.")

When Digital did get around to launching a personal computer (May 1982), they launched not one but three incompatible machines (Rainbow, Professional, and DECmate) that were doomed to failure. The lack of focus was obvious.

Business, as well as life, always gives you a warning signal. It's what scriptwriters call "foreshadowing." After the launch of the MITS Altair 8800 in January 1975, Digital Equipment had a six-and-a-half-year window of opportunity until IBM lowered the PC boom in August 1981.

But it takes a while for your mistakes to catch up with you. With its hot VAX line of minicomputers, Digital Equipment continued to prosper in the eighties. By 1990, with revenues of $13 billion, Digital managed to just about break even. In the next four years, however, on revenues that exceeded $55 billion, Digital lost almost $5 billion. But the basic mistake was not the loss of money but the loss of focus.

Another example of a company that tried to win with a foot in both camps is Atari. The pioneer in video games, Atari tried to broaden its product line into computers. "Atari's strength as a name also tends to be its weakness," said James Morgan, the ace Philip Morris marketer who became Atari's CEO in 1983. "It is synonymous with video games," so when buying a computer, "the consumer looks at that name and sees game."

That's the problem. What's the solution? Morgan said that Atari must redefine its image and broaden its business definition to that of "electronic consumer products." In other words, a foot in both camps. It never works.

The eighties were a disaster for Atari. By 1992, Atari lost $74 million on sales of $127 million. In 1993, Atari lost $49 million on sales of only $29 million. Things couldn't continue.

How could a company compete with Compaq, Apple, and IBM in computers and Sega and Nintendo in video games? Both at the same time. It was time to refocus.

"Due to intense competition from larger competitors and shrinking margins in computer products," said Atari in its 1994 annual report, "the company decided to exit this line of products and to refocus itself as an interactive media entertainment company. In an effort to ensure its competitive advantage, the company developed a 64-bit system called Jaguar. The Jaguar was launched in the fourth quarter of 1993 and is the only 64-bit interactive media entertainment system in the market today." (The media refers to Jaguar as a thirty-two-bit system, creating a credibility problem for Atari.)

Finally Atari is back to a single focus. But it may be too late with the momentum achieved by Sega and Nintendo. One can only speculate what might have been possible if Atari had maintained its video game focus and did not "broaden out" into computers.

Porsche is another example of the power of a focus. The Porsche 911 is unique, the only six-cylinder air-cooled rear-engine car on the market. So naturally, Porsche decided to put a foot in the front-engine water-cooled camp with its 924, 944, and 968 four-cylinder models and its 928 eight-cylinder car.

Initially the water-cooled models were a big success, especially the relatively inexpensive 924 and 944 models.

If Sir Thomas Gresham were a management consultant, he might have said that cheap products drive out expensive ones, and that's exactly what happened to Porsche. By 1986, high-water mark for Porsche in the United States, 64 percent of Porsche's sales were the less expensive 924 and 944 models. Why spend $63,295 for a 911 Turbo coupe when you can get a 924S for $23,910?

But Gresham's law only works in the short term. In the long term, the word gets around. A cheap Porsche isn't the real thing.

What's a Porsche? A rear-engine, air-cooled, "bat out of hell" sports car best exemplified by the 356 Speedster of the fifties, the predecessor of today's 911 models. (Would James Dean have driven a 944?)

Over the years Porsche buyers did what the Porsche company failed to do. They focused on the real thing, the 911. Today 77 percent of Porsche's sales in the United States are the expensive 911 models. Which leads one to ask the obvious question: Why doesn't Porsche refocus on the 911?

The answer to questions of this type is always the same: We can't give up the 23 percent of sales that are in the other camp.

Carry this kind of thinking to its obvious conclusion. No company can afford to give up any part of its business, and therefore, sooner or later, every company is going to make everything. We have reached the ultimate in unfocusing.

To refocus a car or a company, you have to be willing to sacrifice. Look at Porsche again. Back in 1986, Porsche sold more than eight thousand copies of its core car, the 911, in the United States. Even though this was only 27 percent of total Porsche sales, it may have made sense to focus on the 911 model only.

If Porsche had done so, how many 911 cars would they have sold in 1986? Certainly some of the 22,387 buyers of other Porsche models would have bought 911s. Maybe two thousand, three thousand, four thousand? If they had focused on the 911 only, perhaps Porsche would have sold twelve thousand cars in the United States.

Now turn to today. Prices are up because the mark is up and the dollar is down. (The 911 Turbo coupe is now $99,000.) How many cars would Porsche have sold if it had maintained its focus on its core vehicle, the 911? My strong belief is that Porsche's 911 sales would be more than double the 4,471 cars they actually sold. And, of course, greatly exceed the 5,819 total Porsche sales.

No one knows for sure. But there is plenty of evidence that when you narrow your focus, sales decrease in the short term and increase in the long term.

When you broaden your focus, sales increase in the short term but decrease in the long term.

This is the heart of the focusing argument. It's also why focusing is so difficult. Nobody wants to reduce current sales even though the long-term effect is positive and powerful.

Decision time for many companies occurs when there is a sharp break in technology. When the battery business was in transition from zinc-carbon to longer lasting alkaline batteries, Eveready tried to keep a foot in both camps. Eveready flashlight batteries (zinc-carbon) and Eveready alkaline batteries.

PR Mallory, on the other hand, launched a line of alkaline batteries only. Called "Duracell," the new product had a narrower focus and a more powerful name.

(The two are related. The narrower the focus, the more opportunities there are to select a powerful name. A name that has to cover a variety of products, in general, will be much weaker.)

Trying to cover both camps with the single Eveready name proved to be impossible. So Eveready introduced Energizer, its line of alkaline batteries. But it was too little and too late. Today, the Duracell line of alkaline batteries outsells both Eveready zinc-carbon and Energizer alkaline batteries combined.

Rapid technological changes are undermining many companies today. Their instinctive reaction is to have a foot in both camps. They become overextended and lose focus. It's so easy, so natural, and so wrong.

In the computer software field, for example, most of the mainframe software companies are moving into client-server using the same name and the same staff. A potential problem if specialist competition develops.

Convergence is often used as an excuse for getting into two different businesses. "It may be two camps today, but it's going to be one camp tomorrow."

Based on the notion of convergence, any company in the computer, communications, telephone, cable, entertainment, or media business can justify buying almost anything that uses electronics. For all the talk, there has been remarkably little action. Name two industries that have come together?

None, that I know of. Do you know of any?

BOTH FEET IN THE NEW CAMP

This is the second way to react to change. Why not? If you are sure that a new technological development is bound to replace the old in the near future, why not jump in with both feet?

One reason to adopt this strategy is to focus the attention of your own people. It's very difficult to communicate excitement about a new product line if you keep the old one around, "just in case." Employees will keep looking over their shoulders to see if they should be retreating.

When Hernan Cortés landed on the Yucatán coast of Mexico in 1519 in preparation for the march inland to assault Montezuma's Aztec capital, he first burned his boats. Without the possibility of retreat, he was sure his men would fight all the harder. When you put both feet in the new camp, you send a similar message to your own people.

Philip Morris introduced Marlboro in 1937 as a cigarette for women. "Ivory tip, protect the lip" and "Mild as May" said the advertisements. Seventeen years later the brand had less than one-tenth of 1 percent of the market. So in 1954 Philip Morris sent Marlboro to Leo Burnett in Chicago for a sex change operation. Women were out, from now on the brand would be for men only.

The first ad featured a cowboy, although the research company hired by Philip Morris came back with the alarming report that there were only three thousand full-time cowboys in America. In spite of the shortage of cowboys, the campaign worked.

In the first year the newly minted masculine Marlboro brand captured 2 percent of the market. The second year, 4 percent. From then on, the brand slowly climbed the cigarette ladder until 1976, when it beat out Winston to become the largest selling cigarette brand in the country.

Bell Sports was once the country's biggest maker of motorcycle helmets. No more. In 1991 Bell got out of motorcycle helmets and moved full-time into bicycle helmets.

Says Bell Sports chairman Terry Lee: "We had to laser-focus on spending the scarce resources we had in the most effective way." Both sales and profits are up substantially. With 50 percent of the market, Bell's net profits in 1994 were $10.5 million on $116 million in revenues.

The Gap, a retailer of clothing for the younger crowd, went from a schlocky, pile-them-high, sell-them-cheap retailer of jeans and related items to a trendy, value-priced outlet for fashion basics.

One thing they didn't change was their target audience. The Gap is still focused on the younger crowd, but also sells a lot of merchandise to older people who want to dress young. The Gap has had ten straight years of revenue increases and today does $3.3 billion in sales. Over the past decade, net income has averaged 7.3 percent of sales, a spectacular result for a retailer.

When opportunity arises, the key question to ask yourself is, "Do we stick to our knitting or do we take up weaving?" Yet too many companies procrastinate. They stick their toe in the new camp's water without leaving the security of the old camp. This usually results in the worst of all possible worlds. They don't make a big splash in the new business and they also lose credibility in the old business.

One company that did make a bold move from one camp to another is Intel. Back in 1985, Intel made a strategic shift from memory chips to microprocessors, a market the company now dominates. You can't find many examples of companies like Intel jumping from one camp to another.

That's not too surprising. You don't find many examples of companies making bold moves of any kind. In one way it's a good thing, or the torrent of lawsuits would increase at an even faster rate. Any strategic change spells opportunity for a lawyer to drag a company into court for a little legal blackmail.

BOTH FEET IN THE OLD CAMP

This is the third way to react to change. One of the myths of management is the notion that rapid change is desirable. Who says a company has to constantly change?

One way to develop a unique position, to stand out from the pack, is to resist change. You may end up with an old-fashioned product, but that can sometimes be an advantage: Jack Daniel's bourbon, Levi's 501 jeans, Zippo lighters.

Witness the power in the fashion field of traditional materials like cotton, wool, and silk versus the newer fabrics like nylon, rayon, and Dacron. One of the powerful appeals in business today is "We still make 'em like we used to."

What's a Zippo? It's the original windproof lighter invented in 1932 by George Blaisdell of Bradford, Pennsylvania. Three hundred million lighters later, Zippos are still manufactured in Bradford by the Blaisdell family and they still come with the same lifetime guarantee. "If any Zippo lighter ever fails to work, we'll fix it free."

There are no plastic Zippos, silver Zippos, solid-gold Zippos, designer Zippos. Nor did Zippo jump on the hot trend to butane lighters. "In a constantly changing world," said a recent Zippo advertisement, "we don't. Why change the most durable lighter ever made?"

This consistency hasn't seemed to hurt Zippo sales. In the last eight years, for example, the average annual sales increase at Zippo Manufacturing Company has exceeded 20 percent.

The Zippo of hamburgers is White Castle. Founded in 1921 by Walter Anderson and Billy Ingram, the company is still run by an Ingram, E. W. Ingram III, grandson of the cofounder. White Castle hamburgers are still cooked the Walter Anderson way, steamed over a bed of onions.

Known affectionately as "sliders," a White Castle burger is square (so that more of them fit on the griddle) with five holes (so that the steam can cook both sides at once, making it unnecessary to turn the burger over).

The White Castle focus extends to the franchising system. There are no franchised operators. All restaurants are wholly owned. In a recent year the 290 White Castle units in twelve states did $307 million in sales, more than a million dollars per unit. That's higher than Hardee's, Wendy's, or Taco Bell. (Among sandwich chains, only McDonald's and Burger King rank higher in sales per unit.)

Instead of focusing on the tried-and-true and perfecting it (like Zippo and White Castle), business has a bent for the new and different. Companies tend to invest immense resources in wild bets on the future rather than cultivating the cash cows they already own. They worship change for change's sake. They buy into the consultant's cry for innovation, innovation, innovation and change. This is the kind of thinking that results in New Coke, Apple's Newton, and other man-made disasters.

Coors made the same mistake. For most of its formative years, Coors was a one-brand beer company. The brand was Coors Banquet, brewed in one plant in Golden, Colorado, and distributed in only eleven western states.

The brand had a product difference (draft) and a unique ingredient (Rocky Mountain spring water). It even had a potential focus. Proudly printed on every can were the words "America's Fine Light Beer."

By 1975 Coors Banquet was the best-selling beer in ten of the eleven states it was sold in. (The exception was Texas, where it wasn't available in every area.) Although distributed only in the West, Coors was the fourth largest beer in the country (behind Budweiser, Schlitz, and Pabst).

"The most chic brew in the country," raved the *New York Times*. Celebrities like Clint Eastwood and Paul Newman drank the stuff.

Then Coors rapidly became unfocused as the brand was extended in all possible directions. First came geographic extension as the Coors brand was rolled out into all fifty states. Then came product extension as new brands came rolling out of the brewery with such names as Killian, Keystone, and Shulers.

Then came line extension as Coors cooked up flavor after flavor. They got into light beer, ice beer, dry beer, red beer, extra-gold beer, nonalcoholic beer. If there was a fad in beer, there was a Coors brand there to greet it.

In addition, there was production extension as Coors branched out from Golden, Colorado. In 1987, Coors opened a packaging plant in Elkton, Virginia, that added water to concentrate from Colorado, an unfortunate move since it meant that Virginia water had to be substituted for the real thing. In 1990, Coors bought Stroh's Memphis brewery.

Today, Coors is no longer the number one beer in those ten western states. Nor is Coors the leading brand in any state of the Union. What crippled the Coors brand were all those extensions: geographic, product, line, and production. In other words, a lack of focus crushed Coors.

Coors couda been a contenda. Twenty years ago, when Miller launched the Lite Revolution, Coors was already a light beer. (Coors Banquet had fewer calories than Michelob Light.) When they wanted a Coors, locals used to ask the bartender for a "Colorado Kool-Aid."

Coors had mystique. Coors had momentum. Coors had Henry Kissinger, who used to lug the stuff back east on the plane from Denver. The only thing Coors didn't have was a focus to take advantage of the situation.

Coors couda fought for the championship. That focus, handed to them on a silver platter by Miller Brewing, was "light." Coors was the original light beer and could have shifted its marketing programs to take advantage of this fact.

Coors couda been the best-selling beer in America. If Coors had concentrated on one brand, the original "light" product, it would be the number one beer in the country today. That's the promise of the focus concept.

Most companies have to struggle to find their word. Other companies have to struggle to get their word accepted in the minds of their prospects. Sometimes it's difficult, sometimes it's easy.

Sometimes it seems too easy and companies reject the obvious word like Coors did. That can prove to be a costly mistake.

BOTH FEET IN THE NEW CAMP WITH A NEW NAME

This is the fourth way to react to change.

The classic example of this type of change is the Haloid Company, a small manufacturer of photographic paper in Rochester, New York, that bought the rights to Chester Carlson's "electrophotography" invention. In 1958, the company changed its name to Haloid Xerox, Inc., in preparation for the launch of the 914, the first plain-paper copier. In 1961, the company changed its name again, to Xerox Corp.

This three-step name change, from Haloid to Haloid Xerox to Xerox, could have been accomplished easier and cheaper in two steps. Yet many companies hate to give up the security of an established name for the unknown prospects of a new one. (Haloid was founded in 1906.)

Yet the principles of focus strongly suggest that the transition name is not only unnecessary, it also blurs a company's reputation. Better to either stay where you are or make the leap to the new name. "Hanging in midair" benefits no one and confuses everyone.

Today's parallel to Xerox is Powersoft Corporation. Founded in 1974 by Mitchell Kertzman as Computer Solutions, the company was a consulting company that also developed bookkeeping packages for the Hewlett-Packard HP 3000 computer.

When HP phased out the HP 3000 in 1987, the company looked around for a new focus. With David Litwack (now president), CEO Kertzman decided to concentrate on client-server software tools.

In 1990 Computer Solutions changed its name to Powersoft in preparation for the launch of its first client-server application tool, PowerBuilder. Strong demand for its products prompted the company to go public in 1993.

In 1994, Sybase Inc. bought Powersoft Corporation for stock valued at $904 million. Not a bad reward for a shift in strategy.

There is a blind spot in management's eye when it comes to changing a name. Most managers believe a name change is difficult to accomplish. Yet when executed correctly, a name change can easily be accomplished and the results can be astonishing.

In October 1971 at the Mark Hopkins Hotel in San Francisco, Werner Erhard gave the first in a series of seminars he called "est" (for Erhard Seminars Training). Soon thereafter est became the hottest movement in the sensitivity field.

Five years later, eighty-three thousand est graduates had each spent sixty hours (and $250) experiencing Erhard's method of "transforming your life."

Est came to an end in the early nineties when critical stories began appearing in the Bay Area. These newspaper reports detailed Erhard's violent temper and included charges that he beat his wife and molested his children. The low point was a March 3, 1991, segment on the CBS program *60 Minutes* that interviewed three of his daughters about the alleged abuse. (Erhard denied it.)

After an hour of *60 Minutes,* Erhard was as dead as Audi. One might have thought that Werner Erhard, the company, was beyond saving. Not true. The name was destroyed, but not the company. Before the CBS program ran, but with knowledge of what it would likely say, Erhard sold the assets of Werner Erhard & Associates to his former employees and moved to Costa Rica.

The new name: Landmark Education Corporation. Today Landmark is a thriving company with forty offices around the world and some $40 million in annual revenues. Each year sixty thousand people participate in its programs. Landmark is bigger than Erhard ever was. You can change a name successfully. In fact, a name change may be the only practical solution to a serious public relations problem.

When a company tries to change its focus without changing its name, however, it often runs into problems.

A good example is National Cash Register Company, which once had 90 percent of the cash register business. But cash registers went the way of the typewriter. More and more they became miniature computers. So National Cash Register went into the computer business, changing its name in 1974 to NCR Corp.

Changing your name to initials is like not changing your name at all. People said "NCR" but thought "National Cash Register." NCR needed a name that said "computers." (One simple possibility was National Computer Company, or NCC.) Like Wang, NCR was in never-never land with an obsolete product perception and an obsolete name.

NCR continued to make money by finding niche markets like automatic teller machines and a large overseas market (half of NCR's sales). But the company wisely got out of the mainframe business. Without a focus and without a defining name, the future looked dim. "National Crash" was its nickname before AT&T rashly bought the company in 1990.

TWO SEPARATE CAMPS, TWO SEPARATE NAMES

This is the fifth way to react to change. If a company can't or doesn't want to give up its existing business and still wants a foot in a new camp, the best way to do so is with a separate name.

Levi Strauss is the world's largest producer of brand-name clothing, with annual sales in excess of $5 billion. Its mission statement proclaims its dependence on the Levi's name. "The mission of Levi Strauss & Co. is to sustain profitable and responsible commercial success by marketing jeans and selected casual apparel under the Levi's brand."

Yet Levi's biggest recent success is the 1986 introduction of the Dockers line of casual wear. Currently, Dockers sales in the United States alone are more than $1 billion (wholesale).

What created this opportunity for Levi Strauss was the trend toward casual clothing in the workplace. Almost 90 percent of consumers wear casual clothing to work some days, reports NPD Group, a retail consulting firm. Seventy-four percent of employers allow casual dress, with dress-down Fridays the most popular policy in the office.

The company had a lot of evidence that Levi's, as a name, belonged in the blue jeans camp and would never make it in the casual camp. In 1979, Levi Strauss boasted that it would become a major athletic apparel manufacturer with a new line of Levi's Activewear, including skiwear and warm-up suits. Three years after its introduction, the new line generated only $9 million in sales.

Then there was the mid-eighties launch of the Levi's name in the men's suit business. "Levi's Action Suits" didn't generate much action and the line was soon withdrawn. There was also Levi's shoes, hats, and luggage. "Top management," said *Business Week,* "seriously overestimated the power of Levi's name."

Names have power, but only in the camp in which they have credentials. When they get out of their camp, when they lose focus, they also lose their power. The more products and services you hang on a name, the less focused and less powerful it becomes.

When Rolex decided to market a relatively inexpensive watch, they didn't call the product the Rolex Jr. They called the new product Tudor.

IBM is the most powerful computer name in the world. But Big Blue has no power in the home. Even though IBM has spent millions promoting their home personal computers, the products have gone nowhere. The office is one camp, the home is another.

Apple Computer had a powerful position in the home with the Apple II line of computers, but the market shifted to the office. So Apple introduced the Macintosh. Apple is for the home camp. Macintosh is for the office camp.

Two separate camps need two separate names.

DIVIDE AND CONQUER

Decades of mergers, acquisitions, hostile takeovers, and alliances have created scores of hydra-headed corporate monsters. How do you focus one of these mastodons?

In concept, it's easy. You just spin off some of the heads. Divide and conquer. Easier said than done.

The problem is what's in the heads of the company's top officers. To most corporate managers, size equals importance, power, and psychic satisfaction.

Even when IBM was losing billions of dollars, John Akers was still the CEO of a $60 billion computer corporation, not the CEO of a minus $8 billion company. The year they lost $23 billion General Motors was still number one on the *Fortune* 500 list of the largest U.S. industrial corporations.

In theory, spin-offs are just another management tool, useful in some situations and not in others. But in practice, there is a strong resistance to their use. How many CEOs will voluntarily give up half of their job, half of their power, half of their psychic satisfaction? Not too many. In spite of all the talk about profits, most of the financial measurements, most of the lists, revolve around sales.

In truth, most companies are run by their inside managers, not by their outside boards of directors. Until the CEO truly becomes a hired gun under the direction of an independent board, management is going to go for size, not for profit. Management knows which side its bread is buttered on.

But the resistance to spin-offs is changing. "Corporate spin-offs are gathering momentum," reported the *Wall Street Journal* in its June 15, 1995, issue, "fueled by investor pressure to unlock hidden values, compelling tax advantages, and evidence that stocks of both the parents and the new companies outperform the overall market."

What triggered the *Journal*'s spin-off story was an announcement that had occurred two days earlier. This was one of those watershed events in corporate history, the day chairman Rand Araskog announced that ITT Corporation planned to split into three separate companies. Analysts were calling the move the largest spin-off of corporate assets since the 1984 breakup of American Telephone and Telegraph.

The ITT spin-off is just one deal in a year that saw a record $30 billion in corporate spin-offs. As a matter of fact, each of the last three years has seen a record number of corporate spin-offs. (In 1993, there were $17 billion. In 1994, $27 billion.)

Under the acquisitive leadership of Harold Geneen, ITT was the prototypical conglomerate, buying companies at the rate of one a week at one point. At its apex, ITT Corporation comprised more than 250 companies.

The theory was that the whole is worth more than the sum of its parts and that diversification would provide a more dependable stream of earnings. That theory didn't hold water. From 1979 to 1991, for example, shares of ITT trailed the Standard & Poor's 500 index by 36 percent.

The spin-off represented a major shift in strategy. In his 1989 book *The ITT Wars,* Rand Araskog denounced those who would break up conglomerates as seeking to profit from "tearing down and destroying what had already been built." They had, he said, "no positive program, no vision of a better, more productive, or more fruitful economy."

The new ITT will consist of three separate companies: ITT Hartford Group, an insurance company; ITT Industries, an automotive, military, and electronics concern; and ITT Destinations, a hotel, gambling, entertainment, and information-services business. (Sounds like a positive program with the hope of a better, more productive economy.)

Three months later came the AT&T announcement. AT&T would divide into three separate companies: one focused on communications, one on communications hardware, and one on computers. "AT&T's restructuring is not about size," said the company, "it's about focus, speed, and enormous opportunity."

In commenting on the AT&T announcement, Michael Porter said: "What we keep learning over and over again is that focus is better than diversity and complexity."

Four months later came the Dun & Bradstreet deal. The $5 billion information giant would divide itself into three publicly traded companies. "We believe the winning paradigm as we head into the next century is focus and speed," said CEO Robert Weissman.

Spin-offs tend to do well on the market. A J.P. Morgan study of seventy-seven spin-offs from 1985 through 1995 shows that they outperform the stock market by more than 20 percent on average during the first eighteen months after the transaction.

Another high-profile spin-off announcement was General Motors' decision to let Electronic Data Systems go its separate way.

EDS was a great buy when General Motors bought it from Ross Perot in 1984. For one thing EDS had few competitors and the market was booming. Today is different. There are hordes of competitors, including IBM, Digital Equipment, Unisys, and Computer Sciences.

Furthermore, the computer-services industry is facing the technological challenge of moving from mainframes to client-servers. As an independent company, EDS would be in much better shape to cope with the transition.

With conglomerates rushing to spin off their incompatible divisions, the question naturally arises: Can a conglomerate ever work?

Sure, even a flawed strategy will work if combined with superb execution and the expenditure of prodigious amounts of energy. Even ITT was successful in its early years. But as a conglomerate grows it falls victim to the flywheel effect. The larger the wheel, the faster the speed at the periphery and the greater the chances of problems developing.

Compare ITT Corporation (number 23 on the *Fortune* 500 list, with 1994 sales of $24 billion) with Dover Corp. (number 361 on the list, with sales of $3 billion). Dover has fifty-four operating companies engaged in more than seventy diverse businesses, from elevators and garbage trucks to valves and welding torches.

Dover is a classic conglomerate. Yet the company has consistently produced returns on shareholders' equity in the high teens and average annual total return to stockholders of nearly 14 percent over the last decade.

It worked in the past, but will it work in the future? Unlikely. As Dover grows, the flies are going to start coming off the wheel.

The Dovers of this world also benefit from their concentration on yesterday's businesses when diversification and the resultant conglomerization were the standard way of operating. What works in elevators and garbage trucks won't necessarily work in computers and software.

When you look at companies like Dover, you find that most of their competitors are also conglomerates. If every competitor in a category is a conglomerate, then the winning company is sure to be a conglomerate.

Only when a specialist has a chance to compete with a generalist can you see the value of being a specialist. If there are no specialists, then all the winning companies will be generalists.

Winning conglomerates are also likely to put great emphasis on cutting costs and operating with lean staffs. Even though Dover has twenty-two thousand employees, the company has a headquarters staff of just twenty-two people.

In other words, winning conglomerates emphasize execution, which is the only way to differentiate their companies from their conglomerate competitors.

This leads to the mistaken notion that winning is all about execution rather than strategy. That you can turn any company, any situation, around with discipline, teamwork, TQM, and effort.

"Only the most productive companies are going to win," says General Electric's Jack Welch. "If you can't sell a top-quality product at the world's lowest price, you're going to be out of the game."

GE is the world's most successful conglomerate, number five on the *Fortune* 500 list with sales of $64.7 billion and profits of $4.7 billion. General Electric is also one of the most emulated companies in the world, with its management practices eagerly studied by consultants and corporate leaders.

But GE has two things going for it that are hard to duplicate. First of all, the company was founded in 1878. And the GE brand name is one of the country's best known and most admired. (The two are related. It takes a while for a brand to become an institution.)

So for a new company with a relatively unknown brand name, the only things left to emulate are the benchmarking, the workouts, and the other management techniques advocated by General Electric. Not nearly enough to make a company successful.

Furthermore, most of the companies GE competes with are also conglomerates. In aircraft jet engines, GE competes with United Technologies, a conglomerate that owns Pratt & Whitney as well as Otis elevators, Carrier air-conditioning, and other divisions. In diesel-electric locomotives, GE competes with General Motors. In power equipment, GE competes with Westinghouse.

Although GE has been successful in the past, there is doubt about the future. Can the company continue to move up the *Fortune* 500 ladder? My feeling is that GE has peaked and has only one way to go. Down.

While General Electric may well be one of the last companies to resort to spin-offs to achieve better focus, it could happen sooner than you think. One prime candidate is GE Capital, a $20 billion operation that is light-years away from the company's traditional manufacturing base.

Spin-offs, as a focusing tool, have been accelerating. To the investment community, companies with divisions that can easily be spun off are tempting "tangerines." Recently many tangerines have been taken apart.

Marriott Corp. has split into two companies: Host Marriott Corp., which owns and trades hotel real estate but does not manage hotels, and Marriott International, Inc., which manages hotels but does not own them.

The divorce has been a smashing success. When the split was announced in October 1992, the market valued the common shares of Marriott Corp. at about $2 billion. Today the two companies combined are valued at about $6 billion.

The focusing process is continuing. Since the split, Host Marriott has shed most of its cheaper hotels as well as fourteen retirement homes that reaped a reported $320 million. It has sold off 114 Fairfield Inns and 21 of its 54 Courtyard by Marriott hotels, most of which the other Marriott continues to manage. Recently it announced that it will spin off its airport and toll-road concession business.

The objective of all these Host Marriott moves is to focus on the strategy of buying luxury hotels. It should prove to be a winning strategy. The only missing ingredient is a new name to help differentiate one Marriott from the other.

Also in the hotel field, The Promus Companies split in two by spinning off its hotels into a separate corporation called Promus Hotel Corp. The gambling casinos would remain in a company to be called Harrah's Entertainment Inc. (The market liked the move. In less than three months, Promus shares rose 50 percent.)

The split makes a lot of sense. Promus becomes the parent company of four hotel chains: Embassy Suites, Hampton Inn, Homewood Suites, and Hampton Inn and Suites. Harrah's Entertainment becomes the parent company of the country's largest chain of gaming establishments.

The Harrah's half of the deal is the exciting part. While other gaming companies are building real estate, Harrah's is building a brand name. As states slowly wake up to the fact that people like to gamble, the gaming business is becoming a national industry.

The scope of Harrah's U.S. operations might surprise you. The company has eight hotel-casinos in Nevada, New Jersey, and Colorado. There are also four Harrah's riverboat casinos in Illinois, Louisiana, and Mississippi. In addition, there are development deals with Indian tribes in Minnesota, Alabama, Maine, and Arizona.

More than five million people now have Harrah's Gold Cards, and the company is adding more than half a million new customers a year. Now that hotel-casino operations are focused in a single company, the Harrah's brand has a particularly bright future.

As the dominant brand in the category, Harrah's has both the financial and political power to assure seizing the lion's share of an escalating market.

There's no better formula for success than to get in early, become the leading player in the category, and then ride the rocket to the stratosphere as the category takes off. What Hertz did in rent-a-cars, what Charles Schwab did in discount brokerage, and what H&R Block did in income tax is exactly what Harrah's is doing in the gaming industry. The sky's the limit.

Following in the footsteps of Promus is the $1.5 billion Hilton Hotels Corporation. In May 1995, Hilton announced it would split its hotel and gambling operations into two separate companies. It makes eminent sense. Hotels provide Hilton with 41 percent of revenue and hotel-casinos provide 59 percent. Where's the focus?

Furthermore, a hotel and a hotel-casino may look the same, but they operate differently. A hotel hopes to break even on food and other services in order to make money on rooms. A hotel-casino hopes to break even on rooms and food in order to make money on slot machines and table games.

This is an enormous difference between the two that can frustrate attempts to manage operations and transfer employees from one site to another.

Another corporation in the hotel-casino field that has announced plans to spin off a major portion of its business is Bally Entertainment. Bally is the country's leading fitness club operator, with about 340 centers, as well as a major hotel-casino operator with three hotel-casinos and one riverside gaming facility.

Revenues are split almost evenly between the fitness centers and the hotel-casinos, a surefire recipe for problems. (What is Bally trying to do? Give your wallet a workout as well as your body?)

And Bally has had a bellyful of problems. Bally's Grand, Inc., the operating company for Bally's Las Vegas resort, has been in and out of bankruptcy. Over the years Bally has bought and sold its theme-park businesses and its amusement game manufacturing company.

A schizophrenic company seldom has a healthy bottom line. Over the past decade, Bally Entertainment Corporation has had total revenues of $15.8 billion. Not a bad take. Yet profits were nonexistent. As a matter of fact, Bally lost $265 million in the ten-year period.

Soon there will be a Bally's Health & Tennis Corporation as well as a Bally Entertainment Corporation.

Compare Circus Circus Enterprises with Bally. In 1974, William Bennett and William Pennington bought the Circus Circus hotel-casino in Las Vegas. When the two partners took over, the hotel-casino lacked focus. The hotel rented over half its rooms to tour groups that seldom gambled, while the casino tried to attract serious gamblers despite a carnival atmosphere on the gaming floor that included an elephant that played the slot machines.

Bennett and Pennington shifted the company's direction by appealing to value-minded families. (This was the first Las Vegas hotel-casino to narrow its approach to the low end of the market.) They offered reasonably priced rooms and food, did away with credit in the casino, and lessened the reliance of the company on tour groups. They also reduced the use of "comps," free rooms, food, and drinks for high rollers.

This approach was so successful the company opened a second Circus Circus in Reno. Today Circus Circus operates six hotel-casinos, all in Nevada, and two smaller casinos, both in Las Vegas. This tight focus should pay off on the bottom line, and it does.

Whereas Bally lost $265 million on revenues of $15.8 billion in a decade, Circus Circus made $730 million on revenues of just $5.7 billion. What's the difference between Circus Circus and Bally? In a word, focus.

In addition to casino spin-offs, there has been a profusion of chemical spin-offs. Chemicals, often petroleum based, are "intermediates," used in the production of a wide range of other products. The temptation to vertically integrate chemicals with oil and gas production, on the one hand, and finished products, on the other hand, has been too alluring for many companies to resist.

DuPont's ill-conceived 1981 acquisition of Conoco Oil Company for $7.8 billion is a case in point (known internally as "DuPonoco"). Many financial analysts have called for DuPont, the country's largest chemical company, to spin off Conoco, so far without success. Yet the logic is inescapable. Strategically, oil and chemicals don't mix.

Nor do photographic film and chemicals. On the last day of 1993 Eastman Kodak Company spun off its $4 billion chemicals business as Eastman Chemical Company. Formed in 1920 to serve as Kodak's captive chemical provider, Eastman Chemical had in recent years become more important to its debt-heavy parent as a supplier of cash rather than chemicals.

"It became apparent we could add more value to Kodak shareholders" as an independent concern, says Earnest Deavenport Jr., now Eastman Chemical's CEO. Nor should the spin-off hurt Eastman Chemical's business. Kodak accounts for just 7 percent of the company's sales.

Deavenport was right. Since the spin-off Eastman Chemical has posted two back-to-back yearly earnings gains of more than 60 percent.

The next logical step is a name change. Since Eastman now means "chemicals," Eastman Kodak Company should change its name to Kodak Corporation.

Dow Chemical Company, the country's second largest chemical

company, is also doing a little spinning off of its own. In 1992, Dow sold its share in an oil-field-services venture to its partner, Schlumberger. In 1993 Dow sold its Freeport, Texas, oil refinery to Phibro Energy for $200 million. But Dow's biggest divestiture was its prescription-drug and over-the-counter health care business (Marion Merrell Dow, 72 percent owned).

Purchased by Dow in 1989 for $7.7 billion, Marion Merrell Dow was sold to Hoechst AG, the world's largest chemical company, who promptly changed their name to Hoechst Marion Roussel. Why would a chemical company want to buy a drug company? If it didn't work for Dow, why would it work for Hoechst?

Another chemical company going back to its beakers is W.R. Grace. The world's largest specialty chemicals manufacturer, W.R. Grace also had a foot (actually a kidney) in the medical business with its National Medical Care subsidiary, the nation's largest kidney-dialysis provider. In June 1995 W.R. Grace announced plans to spin off the $1.9 billion subsidiary, which accounted for 37 percent of its revenues and 43 percent of its profits.

Following the National Medical Care spin-off, the company said, Grace will be stronger "strategically, operationally, and financially."

Very true, but it was a long time coming. Founded in 1854 in Peru by William R. Grace to charter ships for trading guano, the company has been involved in everything from aviation to banking to coal to cocoa to oil and gas to sporting goods to Mexican food. Finally, 141 years later, Grace has a focus.

The spin-off would be a tax-free transaction. Grace considered selling National Medical Care, but the sale could have saddled the company with a huge capital-gains tax, estimated at almost $1 billion. (In a tax-free spin-off, the parent company distributes at least 80 percent of the stock to shareholders as a dividend. Neither the shareholders nor the company has to pay taxes.)

Tax laws encourage companies to spin off winners and sell off losers. The spin-off of a winner can be tax free and the sell-off of a loser can generate a capital loss that can be used to offset future capital gains. Which also makes sense from the stockholder's point of view because it reflects the most basic law of investing: Keep the winners and sell the losers.

Meanwhile in the United Kingdom, another chemical company decided to cut itself in half. Imperial Chemical Industries (ICI) spun off its pharmaceuticals and specialty chemical divisions into a new company called Zeneca.

The Zeneca spin-off, or what the English call a demerger, marks a major milestone in ICI history. For sixty-six years ICI grew like a classic conglomerate until it was (by some measures) Britain's biggest firm and the world's fourth largest chemical company.

But profits were thin and the company's stock lagged. Between 1980 and early 1991, for example, ICI's share price rose by 230 percent compared with the all-share index of London equities, which rose by 420 percent.

The market applauded the Zeneca spin-off. In eighteen months, the combined valuation for the two companies, adjusted for the proceeds of a stock issue, increased by 57 percent, compared with a 25 percent increase for the *Financial Times* Stock Exchange 100 index.

While chemical companies are spinning off their drug and medical operations, drug companies are spinning off chemical operations. Sandoz AG, one of Switzerland's three big pharmaceutical groups (Ciba-Geigy and Roche are the other two), recently announced plans to spin off its $2 billion chemical division.

Sandoz said it would become primarily a drug firm with annual sales in the vicinity of $12 billion. Unfortunately, their actions are not always consistent with their words. Sandoz recently purchased Gerber Products for $3.7 billion, which dilutes their drug focus with baby food.

Spin-offs are a logical reaction to the large number of unwieldy, inefficient, unmanageable companies in the marketplace today. But what made them that way in the first place? One factor is the search for the easy sale.

Call it synergy or vertical integration or diversification, the acquisition of a captive customer is just too enticing a proposition for many companies to pass up.

Which is why Ford invested in Hertz, General Motors invested in Avis and bought majority control of National Car Rental, and Chrysler acquired Thrifty Rent-A-Car and Dollar Systems. These are big, juicy, captive customers indeed.

The average General Motors dealer, for example, buys just 345 vehicles a year. A large car rental company buys hundreds of thousands of cars a year. (Hertz has 215,000 vehicles in its fleet and turns them over every six or seven months.)

In 1991, for example, General Motors sold more than eight hundred thousand cars to rental fleets, roughly a quarter of its total car sales. When the deep discounts and the losses on resale were added up, GM often wound up losing more than $1,000 on every rental car it sold.

Then there's the management problem. Making cars and renting cars are two different businesses. It's hard to find managers who can easily make the transition between the two.

National Car Rental System, which General Motors bought in 1987, is a case in point. In 1992 GM took a $744 million charge related to losses and the write-off of goodwill. In 1993 National was losing so much money that GM considered liquidating it. In 1995 General Motors sold National Car Rental to an investor group led by William Lobeck, a former owner of Thrifty Rent-A-Car.

The only answer to a corporate hodgepodge is to sell or spin off the operations that don't fit. When Bruce Atwater retired as chief executive of General Mills in May 1995, he completed a fourteen-year project of turning the company into two clearly defined and sharply focused businesses.

In 1981 General Mills was a company loaded down with odds and ends like Monet costume jewelry, Ship 'n Shore blouses, Kenner toys, Parker Brothers board games, Izod and Eddie Bauer apparel, a footwear unit, a chemical company, and Wallpapers to Go. Today all are gone.

"Our growth rates expanded," says Bruce Atwater, "every time we tightened our focus."

In his last major focusing move, Mr. Atwater spun off the Red Lobster and Olive Garden chains into Darden Restaurants Inc. Named for William Darden, founder of Red Lobster, the $3.2 billion Darden corporation immediately became the world's largest casual-dining company. General Mills Inc. became a $5.5 billion company specializing in breakfast cereals like Cheerios and other packaged foods.

Now General Mills can concentrate on the real strategic issue: how to overtake Kellogg in the cereal market. With 27 percent of the U.S. market, General Mills is within striking distance of Kellogg with 36 percent. When managers know they have only one battle to fight, it concentrates their minds wonderfully.

One reason Kmart got rid of its books, sporting goods, office supplies, and other specialty stores was to concentrate on their real problem, Wal-Mart.

Another reason was to conserve its financial resources. (During the buying binge, Kmart was often called "the Bank of Troy" in reference to their headquarters in Troy, Michigan, and their willingness to generously finance the expansion plans of their subsidiaries.)

Many spin-offs and sell-offs are taking place in the financial arena. One reason is the number of institutions that fell victim to the financial services hype that filled the media. "Ultimately the consumer will be able to deal with one corporate giant to fill his banking, insurance, investment, and credit card needs," gushed the *Wall Street Journal* in a 1981 editorial.

But will they want to? Apparently not. Which is why Metropolitan Life, the country's largest life insurer, has sold its Century 21 subsidiary, the world's largest real estate franchise sales organization. Just because a family buys a home from you doesn't necessarily mean they will buy their life and casualty insurance from you. People like to deal with specialists, not generalists.

And just because they buy their socks from you doesn't necessarily mean they will buy their stocks from you. In June 1993 Sears spun off its 80 percent stake in Dean Witter, Discover & Co. to its shareholders.

And just because they buy their car batteries from you doesn't necessarily mean they will buy their car insurance from you. In June 1995 Sears spun off its 80 percent stake in the Allstate Corporation to its shareholders.

As a stand-alone insurance company Allstate should do very well. It has a focus (car insurance) and a well-known name, a powerful combination.

No company got hooked on the financial services line as deeply as American Express. In addition to credit and charge cards, the company sells life and property/casualty insurance, annuities, investment funds, and financial advisory services. It also owns a bank, American Express Bank, with eighty-one offices in thirty-seven countries. "Cross selling" became the mantra at American Express.

The centerpiece of Amex's financial supermarket strategy was Shearson Lehman Brothers, an amalgamation of two brokerage firms (Shearson Loeb Rhoades and E.F. Hutton) and an investment bank (Lehman Brothers).

It didn't work. Shearson Lehman ate up $4 billion in capital before being sold in 1994. The retail brokerage operations went to Primerica Corporation (now Travelers), and Lehman Brothers was spun off as an independent investment bank.

As might be expected, the financial turmoil at American Express kept management's eye off the charge card ball. As the number three player in the credit and charge card industry (behind Visa and MasterCard), Amex is in a difficult spot. Its market share has steadily fallen from 25 percent in 1990 to 16 percent today. The road back up charge card mountain is going to be long and tedious.

Another victim of the financial services follies is Prudential Insurance Company of America. The closest thing to a cradle-to-grave provider of financial services, Prudential is the nation's largest life insurer, the second largest mortgage lender, the third largest medical care insurance provider, the fourth largest securities firm, and the sixth largest insurer of homes. It's a bundle of financial services with very few synergies.

Perhaps even some negative synergies. A 1993 scandal at Prudential Securities may cost the company more than $1 billion in customer settlements. Some analysts think the scandal was behind the 20 percent drop in new 1994 sales at Prudential's core insurance business.

Prudential is the Rock of Gibraltar, the biggest and best-known life insurance company in the country. Would Prudential and its policyholders (Prudential is a mutual company) have been better off if "the Rock" had focused on life insurance only?

I think so. The dominant company in any field ought to be able to produce big, stable, long-term profits, which Prudential clearly has not. "Hardly any part of the company is earning up to its potential," said David Havens, a life insurance analyst at Standard & Poor's.

What happened at the Pru is typical. A company takes its eyes off the main chance in order to dabble in a lot of related businesses, looking for synergies that never happen. Then it turns around and finds its core business in trouble. The trumpets sound and the word goes out, "back to basics."

Wouldn't it make more sense to stay focused on the core business in the first place so it wouldn't need fixing in the second place?

It always happens. The minute management takes its eyes off the

core business and starts chasing synergies and secondary opportunities, the company starts to go downhill. It may not be immediately
obvious. Problems usually fester for some time before they become
visible.

The CEO is often quick to blame the manager running the core
operation. "I turn my back and you let the operation go to hell." So
it's off with his or her head and on to the next executive in line.

A focus problem often looks like a people problem. You can't
solve a focus problem by changing managers. You solve a focus
problem by refocusing the company on the core concept. You need
to put the power of the corporation behind the main line of attack.

If business was just a question of picking the right people to manage each of a company's operations, then you would see an economy
dominated by conglomerates. Nothing could be further from the
truth. Except for General Electric, the largest conglomerate on the
Fortune 500 list is ITT at number twenty-three. And ITT is being
broken up.

Where you do see economies dominated by conglomerates is in
Japan, Korea, Malaysia, Indonesia, and other countries where governments tamper with free-enterprise systems in the name of efficiency or national objectives. As trade barriers between countries
dissolve, you are also likely to see the dissolution of many of these
conglomerates. A focused company is so powerful that no conglomerate can stand up to one in a fair fight.

A wide range of companies from The Limited to US West have
announced plans to spin off major pieces of business.

US West plans to break into two pieces: US West Communications
Group, which will be the regulated telephone company, and US West
Media Group, which will have the cable, cellular, entertainment, and
other nonregulated businesses.

The split is designed to boost stock prices, but that is not a valid
objective. A split should be designed to improve the focus of the
individual business units. If it does this, increased stock prices will
follow.

Furthermore, to create a successful spin-off, you need to create
separate identities for each company. US West Communications and
US West Media are confusing. Which one is the phone company?
Aren't media a form of communications? Two US Wests aren't necessarily better than one.

Another company planning a major spin-off is Leslie Wexner's The Limited, Inc. Current plans call for three separate companies.

There will be a women's apparel group, consisting of The Limited, Express, Lerner, Henri Bendel, and Lane Bryant stores. This group will be spun off, with the parent company retaining 85 percent of the stock.

There will be an intimate apparel group, consisting of Victoria's Secret stores and catalog, Cacique, Bath & Body Works, and Penhaligon's. This group will also be spun off, with the parent company again retaining 85 percent of the stock.

The parent company keeps everything else, including Abercrombie & Fitch, Structure, and The Limited Too. Wexner isn't letting go. He will remain chairman of all three companies. But clearly this is the first step in bringing some degree of focus to The Limited's sprawling retail operations. (At one point Leslie Wexner had twenty-four executives reporting directly to him, a situation that was inherently unsound.)

Another retailer that recently announced its intention to split into three companies is Melville. An $11-billion-dollar company with 117,000 employees, Melville is just too big and unwieldy to be manageable anymore.

The company proposes to spin off Kay-Bee as a toy company, Thom McAn as a shoe company, and keep the CVS drugstore chain as its core operation. Other assets and retail chains will be divided between the three companies.

Even healthy companies are turning to spin-offs to improve their financial performance. Signet Banking Corp., the largest bank headquartered in Virginia, spun off its credit card operations under the name Capital One Financial Corp. Signet, the country's thirty-eighth largest bank holding company with revenues of $1.4 billion, is in very good financial shape. Dividends on common stock have been paid continuously since 1963.

Here is a case where two very similar businesses (banking and credit cards) are being divided in order to create two more powerfully focused companies. (American Express, please take note.) In Signet's case, the credit card division was generating two-thirds of the parent company's profits. Yet it was consuming resources needed by the bank to grow and prosper.

"The card was growing so fast," said Chairman Robert Freeman, "we were throwing every human and financial resource at the card." The King Solomon solution to cut the bank in half helps both halves.

Capital One, one of the nation's largest credit card issuers, could take advantage of its rapid growth and presumably high stock price to tap the financial markets for additional capital. Signet Banking could concentrate on its core banking business without the distractions, financial and human, of its card business.

The success of spin-offs like Signet is encouraging astute investors to press for similar moves at other banks. Mutual fund manager Michael Price, for example, bought 6 percent of Chase Manhattan Bank stock and immediately suggested that Chase's pieces might be more valuable than the whole.

As a money-center bank Chase Manhattan has been falling behind its big-city competitors. Ten years ago Chase was the third largest banking company in the country. Today it has dropped to sixth place.

Chase Manhattan assets grew by 40 percent in the past decade, which meant that Chase had not even kept up with the Consumer Price Index, which grew 42 percent over the same period. Michael Price had a point. Chase might make more progress if it spun off some of its operations.

"The whole is greater than the sum of the parts," was the reflex reaction of Arjun Mathrani, Chase's chief financial officer. Maybe, just maybe, that's not true. Maybe all these years banks have been operating under a fallacious philosophy.

Maybe money-center banks like Chase should stop chasing everyone from the smallest depositor to the largest corporation while pursuing a variety of other businesses ranging from currency trading to securities safekeeping.

After a decade of poor performance, Chase Manhattan was recently taken over by Chemical Bank. Combined, the two banks are bigger (in assets) than Citicorp, the former leader. But that's only temporary.

Citicorp is a much more focused bank and should be able to reclaim its leadership position. Citicorp is focused on its consumer banking business. Twenty years ago, Citicorp (and its Citibank subsidiary) was 80 percent corporate and 20 percent consumer. Today, Citicorp is 30 percent corporate and 70 percent consumer.

Citicorp is also rapidly building its consumer banking franchise

on the worldwide scene. So far Citicorp has branches in ninety countries, including a strong penetration in developing countries. As a
matter of fact, Citicorp is virtually the only U.S. bank trying to build
a worldwide brand name.

Developing a narrow focus and then going global is one of the
most effective strategies in the world of business today.

Amid signs that banks are becoming more focused, Congress is
finally getting around to repealing the Glass-Steagall Act, which
separates investment banking from commercial banking. Maybe
Congress had it right the first time. Maybe a bank can be more successful if it focuses on one or the other but not both.

(Citicorp would not buy an investment bank, said chairman John
Reed, even if the laws were changed to permit it. A wise decision.)

One classic way of unfocusing a company is for a manufacturer
to become a retailer of the company's products. Or vice versa.
"Nobody knows more about our products than we do," is the mind-
set of most manufacturing companies. "Therefore, we should also
retail our products."

IBM, Digital Equipment, Xerox, and other computer manufacturers tried to set up company stores. They all failed. Many retailers have also tried to become manufacturers. Tandy Corporation
(through its Radio Shack outlets) was a major retailer of computers. So logically Tandy turned to manufacturing. It was a major
mistake.

(A $100 investment in Tandy at the beginning of 1986, when the
stock was still robust, would have been worth $105 eight years later.
A similar investment in Compaq Computer or retail rival Best Buy
would have been worth $1,600 or $1,200, respectively.)

What toppled Tandy was not lack of success, it was lack of focus.
Tandy had an abundance of success on the manufacturing side. It
produced the first popular home computer, the Radio Shack TRS-80,
and one of the first laptops ever.

During the early eighties, Tandy was both the nation's largest personal computer maker and the nation's largest personal computer
retailer. As late as 1986 Tandy was second only to IBM in personal
computer market share.

The notion that you can't do both dies hard. "Tandy once was
king of personal computer retailing and manufacturing," said the
Wall Street Journal in October 1994, "and some observers believe it

squandered a unique opportunity to dominate both ends of the personal computer market."

Not this observer. This observer believes that Tandy squandered the opportunity to dominate either end of the market. If Tandy couldn't decide what end to focus on, perhaps they should have flipped a coin.

In 1993, as part of a focusing shift, Tandy sold its manufacturing operations. Tandy, Victor, and GRiD personal computer manufacturing operations were sold to AST Research for $200 million. Memtek Products was sold to a Japanese company for $128 million. And O'Sullivan Industries Holdings was sold through an initial public offering that raised $350 million.

The decks were cleared. Tandy was now a pure "retail" operator. Even its core operation, Radio Shack, has retreated from the computer business to return to its original focus, cut-rate electronic gadgets like "lightweight titanium digital stereo headphones" that sell for $19.99.

Tandy finally recognized the fact that its lightweight Radio Shack stores were not considered serious computer outlets. To take their place in the huge personal computer market, Tandy has built Computer City SuperCenters to compete with CompUSA for the personal computer market and Incredible Universe stores, which sell a huge assortment of computers, electronics, and home entertainment products.

The stores are incredible. At 185,000 square feet, an Incredible Universe is seventy-five times the size of an average Radio Shack outlet and costs $21 million to build and stock. By the end of 1995, Tandy will have seventeen of these gigastores in operation. Plans call for fifty by the end of the decade.

Tandy has also announced a further sharpening of its focus by closing 233 Video Concepts stores and 60 of its 93 McDuff electronics stores. Tandy's future is now focused on Radio Shack, Computer City, and Incredible Universe, which may be one chain too far.

From a strategic point of view, the 6,700 Radio Shack stores are the holding operation, the retail chain that provides the cash flow to finance the future. But what's the future?

What might make more sense is to focus the future on either Computer City or Incredible Universe, but not both. If Tandy can't decide which chain has the greater potential, why not flip a coin?

You see the Tandy problem reflected at Woolworth Corporation.

An eclectic collection of more than eight thousand stores doing almost $10 billion in sales, Woolworth has a serious schizophrenic streak.

On the one hand are the specialty stores led by market leader Foot Locker, which does some $1.5 billion in annual sales. On the other hand are the general merchandise stores led by Woolworth and various line extensions. "Basically, Woolworth is a kennel club," said one analyst. "Most of them are dogs."

Following a terrible 1994, a year in which Woolworth lost $495 million and endured an accounting scandal, the company brought in a new chief executive, Roger Farah, and a new president, Dale Hilpert. Mr. Farah says he will evaluate Woolworth's operations "format by format."

This is a typical financial approach. Evaluate each of the retail formats, then keep the winners and fix or sell the losers. Not a good strategic approach.

You cannot develop a powerful strategy by focusing on the financials. If this were so, most American corporations would be robust performers. Woolworth needs a focus and possibly a new name.

If the focus is to be on specialty stores like Foot Locker, then the thing to do is to spin off or sell off the variety stores, *regardless of whether they are profitable or not.* If the focus is to be on general merchandise or variety stores, then Woolworth should spin off Foot Locker and the other specialty stores.

First things first. First, find a focus, even if that focus is unprofitable. Then make it profitable. If you develop a powerful, narrowly focused corporation, then the job of making it profitable is greatly simplified.

If you take an unrelated collection of profitable businesses and try to build them into an organization, you are asking for problems. Sooner or later you are bound to run the corporation off the road.

Back in 1981, Harley-Davidson was a subsidiary of AMF Corporation. An unprofitable subsidiary with a scant 3 percent of the American motorcycle market. So AMF put the company up for sale, but there were no buyers.

Finally AMF accepted an offer from thirteen Harley executives, who took over the business in an $81.5 million leveraged buyout. (Today Harley has 20 percent of the U.S. motorcycle market and a stock market value in excess of $2 billion.)

Often referred to as "one of the greatest comebacks in U.S. history," the Harley story has been repeated over and over again. The story, as normally presented, is one of Japanese management principles, updated manufacturing methods, improved quality control systems, and a modernized model line. All of these things are undoubtedly true, but why didn't AMF do them?

First things first. The Harley success story is one of focus. First, focus on motorcycles, and then do what it takes to become a motorcycle success.

Back in 1992, Dresser Industries spun off its industrial products and equipment operations as Indresco. Industrial products and equipment? You couldn't find a more old-fashioned business if you tried. Yet Indresco has become a hot stock, with 28 percent annual returns ever since it was spun off.

The typical divisional spin-off in a leveraged buyout by managers is usually profitable. Sometimes enormously so. There are three reasons for this: (1) The managers know the business, (2) they have an immense incentive to succeed, and (3) they have a focus. Knowledge plus incentive plus focus is a powerful combination.

It's hard to find that combination in a big company today. The one or two people at the top have the incentive to succeed, but often lack the knowledge. The people down the line with the knowledge often lack the incentives.

Obviously divisional managers do have incentives, often expressed as *percentages* of their base salaries. But top management often earns *multiples* of their base salaries. You almost never heard of someone down the line receiving a big check for a job well done. "Nice job, kid. Here's $10 million." On Wall Street maybe, but it never happens in real life.

On the other hand many CEOs have been richly rewarded for their achievements.

- Jim Manzi, CEO of Lotus Development Corporation, earned $26 million in salary and stock options in 1987.

- Craig McCaw, CEO of McCaw Cellular, earned $54 million in pay and stock options in 1989.

- Roberto Goizueta, CEO of The Coca-Cola Company, received one million shares of stock worth $81 million in 1992.

- Michael Eisner, CEO of The Walt Disney Company, received $203 million in salary and stock options in 1993.

Spin-offs create more people at the top. More people at the top mean more incentives to perform. Which is one reason why it's hard to find a company that hasn't profited by a spin-off. Take the Adolph Coors Company. One way that Coors survived Prohibition was by entering the cement and ceramics businesses. Good for survival, bad for focus.

Over the years Coors collected an assortment of businesses, many of which were only vaguely related to their core brewing business. While Coors was making a lot of products, they weren't making very much money. In 1991, for example, the company did more than $2 billion in sales, yet netted only $18 million in profits, a dismal 1 percent of sales.

So in 1992 all the nonbeer assets, including high-tech ceramics, aluminum, and packaging, were spun off to Coors shareholders as stock in ACX Technologies. Adolph Coors was now a beer company. Period.

Not only were there too many products at Coors, there were also too many Coorses. After the split, Peter Coors got the beer business to run and Joe and Jeffrey Coors were made copresidents of ACX Technologies.

"The Coors family decided on a corporate divorce." said *Forbes* magazine about the great-grandsons of Adolph. "Where there was once one big disgruntled company, there are now two happy ones."

By 1994 the two companies together did $2.4 billion in sales and netted $70 million, or 3 percent of sales. A big improvement.

Shareholders were also happier. Since the split, ACX stock has risen from 16 to a recent 42. The stock is serving as a powerful incentive for managers. "When we were with the brewery," says ceramics president Jim Wade, "I never cared much about the stock price. Now I check it four times a day."

Coors stock, on the other hand, has gone flat. Right after the spin-off, Adolph Coors sold at $16 a share. Today it still sells for $16 a share. The reason is the usual one, a lack of focus.

Coors makes everything. Coors Regular, Coors Light, Coors Extra Gold, Coors Extra Gold Light, Coors Dry, Coors Red Light, Coors Cutter, and Coors Artic Ice are some of their permutations. There was even Coors Rocky Mountain sparkling water.

The fact that the beer company's problems were caused by line extensions is a conclusion not shared by most observers. As a matter of fact, Coors's spate of product introductions brought nothing but plaudits.

One noted industry analyst said, "That's why Anheuser-Busch has been so successful: Anything you want, from cheap to expensive, they've got. To survive, you've got to have a full range of products to compete with them."

To survive, maybe. But to make progress against the King of Beers, you've got to focus.

Perhaps the most unfocusing move of all was Coors's decision to launch Zima, the first clear malt beverage.

When you're the leader, a second brand can protect your core brand and provide some insurance for the future. But when you're in third place in the beer business, like Coors, you need to concentrate your resources on overtaking the leader. It's wasteful to start looking for other businesses to invest money in.

If you're Anheuser-Busch, you can take a chance and invest some of your resources in a new product that could replace your cash cow. But if you're not the category leader, you need to focus all your resources on the main event. Coors needs to keep an eye on Budweiser and look for an opening to close the gap.

The same is true of Kmart Corp., which recently fired its CEO, Joseph Antonini. Back in 1987, when Antonini took over the company, Kmart actually outsold Wal-Mart $26 billion to $16 billion. But the warning signs were there to see. Wal-Mart was closing the net income gap rapidly. By the following year Wal-Mart was making more money than Kmart. By 1990 Wal-Mart was the sales leader.

Meanwhile Kmart was diversifying into books, sporting goods, office supplies, drugstores, and warehouse clubs. One billion dollars raised in a 1991 equity offering was frittered away on the specialty stores rather than on the core discount store operation. Many Kmart stores were shabby and depressing, earning Kmart a reputation as the home of blue-light specials and schlocky merchandise.

Wal-Mart whipped right by Kmart on the discounting front. Currently Wal-Mart has almost twice the market share of its blue-light rival. By one estimate Wal-Mart has 42 percent of the market versus 23 percent for Kmart. In eight years Wal-Mart stock quadrupled while Kmart stock stood still.

Nor were the specialty stores setting the world on fire. By 1993, the specialty stores were contributing 30 percent of Kmart Corp. sales but only 15 percent of operating profit.

As military commanders as diverse as Napoléon Bonaparte and Adolf Hitler have learned, it's almost impossible to successfully fight a two-front war.

Whether you are a corporate chief executive or a country's chief executive, it pays to keep a single focus on your main enemy. Which is why Kmart threw in the towel on the specialty front.

The company expects to raise about $3 billion to fight the Wal-Mart war. In 1994 the company raised $896 million in public offerings of its Sports Authority and OfficeMax chains. It also sold its 22 percent stake in Coles Myer, an Australian retailer, for $928 million. Its Pace Warehouse Clubs and PayLess Drugs went for close to $900 million.

In 1995 Kmart received more than $500 million in a stock offering of its Borders Group (the book and music store chain, which also owns Walden Book Company). Still to go is Builders Square, a home-improvement retailer.

Wal-Mart is a tough competitor. Even a slimmed-down Kmart will have its hands full competing with the Discount King. But at least a single-focus retail strategy will allow the company to concentrate its efforts. A similar strategy seems to be working for Sears. With a new CEO (Floyd Hall) it could also work for Kmart.

All those years Kmart was diversifying, Greyhound Corporation was going in the opposite direction. When John Teets took over as chairman in 1982, Greyhound was a classic conglomerate.

Greyhound was into everything: buses, bus manufacturing, meatpacking, turkey and chicken raising, needlecraft, financial services, and consumer products like Dial soap. (Reminds one of the Bob Newhart routine "The Grace L. Ferguson Airline and Storm Door Co." or the cartoon depicting a business whose sign reads "Fill Dirt and Croissants.")

By 1995 Greyhound had completed its transformation to a company focused on consumer products and travel-related services. Gone were the buses, the bus-manufacturing operation, the pizza chain, and the 80 percent stake in Premier Cruise Lines. GFC Financial was spun off and the Armour meatpacking business was sold off.

The company went through a series of name changes to reflect its new focus. From Greyhound to Greyhound Dial to Dial Corporation.

Along the way Dial bought some decent brands to reinforce its new consumer focus. Among them: Purex in 1985, Breck in 1990, and Renuzit in 1993. Today Dial is a healthy corporation. Profits are up, the stock is up, expectations are up.

Dial, however, is still not a totally focused company by any definition of the word. It still has one foot in consumer products and one foot in services.

It could benefit by splitting the company in half with the three hundred different consumer products in the Dial Corp. The service company (under a new name) could include Travelers Express, the nation's largest seller of money orders, and Dobbs International, the nation's largest airline caterer.

Tenneco Inc. is another company that has profited by a spin-off. Best known for its highly profitable gas pipelines, Tenneco has been saddled with its J.I. Case division, a manufacturer of farm and construction machinery. From 1982 to 1992 Case lost money eight out of ten years. In 1991 Case took a pretax charge of $461 million to cover restructuring and a second charge of $920 million the following year.

It helped. Case earned $39 million in 1993 and $131 million in 1994. But restructurings are like taking drugs. In time, the effects wear off. With an exquisite sense of timing, Tenneco spun off 56 percent of Case in 1994, with presumably the rest to follow. So far, so good. The stock is up one-third in the first year.

Tenneco has been trimming other operations as well. In the nineties it sold its natural gas liquids business to Enron, its pulp chemicals business to Sterling Chemicals, and a soda ash plant to Solvay. Total proceeds: $1.3 billion.

Tenneco also took Albright & Wilson, its UK-based chemical company, public for about $670 million. The next shoe to drop is probably Tenneco's Newport News Shipbuilding and Dry Dock Co., the nation's largest privately owned shipbuilder.

The focusing process feeds on itself. Every dose tends to encourage a company to speed up the process because they see the benefits. It's not so much the benefit of getting rid of the losing operation; it's more the benefit of improving the remaining operations.

The effective business, observes Peter Drucker, focuses on opportunities rather than problems. When a company spins off or sells off a loser, it begins to see how much management time has been wasted on problems. When this time is devoted to the remaining opportunities, it generally shows up in the results obtained. No business runs itself. A business always needs to be run.

Spin-offs and sell-offs are becoming very popular. Some recent examples:

• IBM spun off its $2 billion printer and typewriter division in a leveraged buyout by investment firm Clayton, Dubilier & Rice. Renamed Lexmark International, the company has exceeded profit expectations and has won praise for its entrepreneurial management style. "We're just much faster as a company than we were under IBM," says Marvin Mann, Lexmark CEO.

• Kimberly-Clark announced that the company would spin off its Midwest Express Airlines unit and its $400 million cigarette-paper and tobacco business. "If [Chairman] Wayne Sanders spends 5 percent of his time on tobacco paper," said one analyst, "that's 5 percent of his time that should be spent on consumer products, where the payoff is bigger."

• Ralston Purina spun off its cereals, baby food, and ski resorts as Ralcorp Holdings. It also set up its $2 billion Continental Baking subsidiary as a separate company, distributing 55 percent of its stock to shareholders. Then it swapped its controlling interest in Continental for a one-third stake in Interstate Bakeries Company, a transaction valued at $584 million.

Some analysts think Ralston will divest its Interstate stake and exit the baking business altogether. If so, Ralston will become a two-focus company: pet foods and Eveready batteries. Next logical step: split the company in two.

• Anheuser-Busch announced plans to spin off Campbell Taggart, its $1.4 billion baking subsidiary, and its $400 million Eagle Snacks unit. Number two to Frito-Lay, Eagle hasn't made a dime in its fifteen-year history. The company also plans to sell its St. Louis Cardinals baseball team and Busch Stadium. "We are focusing on what we know best," says August Busch III.

• Dole Food Company is planning to spin off its growing real estate business from its produce operations.

• RJR Nabisco spun off 19 percent of Nabisco Holdings Corporation in an initial public offering in 1995. Presumably the remaining shares will eventually be distributed to RJR Nabisco shareholders, effectively splitting the corporate into a tobacco company and a food company.

• Humana spun off its hospitals into a separate company called Galen Health Care (which later become part of Columbia/HCA). Today, Humana is a managed health care company, focused on HMOs, PPOs, and Medicare supplement insurance.

• Eli Lilly spun off Guidant Corporation, its medical devices and diagnostic equipment company, in order to focus on its drug business. (Technically, this $1.26 billion transaction was a split-off, since share owners were given the option of exchanging their Lilly stock for Guidant shares.)

• Both Sprint and Pacific Telesis are spinning off their cellular businesses into separate companies.

• Thermo Electron has become a fast-growing billion-dollar company using a spin-off strategy. Starting in 1983 with the spin-off of Thermedics Inc., the company has spun off nine public subsidiaries in which it retains a majority interest ranging from 52 to 81 percent. The company has increased both sales and net income ten years in a row. "Thermo Electron is a money machine," said one financial analyst.

Most of the spin-off activity has taken place in the United States, where companies have begun to value the concept of focus. In the Far East and South America, old-style conglomerates are still the rule. In Japan and Korea, the *keiretsu* and *chaebol* systems are a barrier to breaking up the conglomerates. In Europe, however, spin-offs are stirring.

In addition to previously mentioned spin-offs at Imperial Chemical Industries, Sandoz, and Volvo, UK-based Pearson PLC recently spun off its Royal Doulton china division to focus on publishing.

Both Royal Dutch/Shell and British Petroleum have sold off most of their nonoil businesses. And Thorn EMI PLC has announced plans to spin off EMI, its $4.3 billion music company, from Thorn, its $2.5 billion furniture-rental unit.

As competition heats up in the European Union, you can expect to see much more of the same.

One exception might be France, where the pattern of interlocking corporate stakes creates the same problem as the *keiretsus* and *chaebols* of the Far East. Since the privatizations of the eighties, French firms have been fitted out with *"noyaux durs,"* or hard nuts, of presumably friendly corporate shareholders. With many cross-shareholdings there is little incentive to create value by breaking a company into its logical pieces.

In addition to the general benefits of a narrow focus, spin-offs also improve a company's performance in three important ways: (1) Spin-offs reduce the span of management control. (2) Spin-offs create chief executives. (3) Spin-offs reduce the problem of "competing with your customers."

SPIN-OFFS REDUCE THE SPAN OF MANAGEMENT CONTROL

If you're the chief executive of a company with two major product lines and one of your competitors has just one, then you're at a disadvantage. Your competitor's CEO can give full attention to the problems at hand. You have only one-half of a CEO to run things.

Many multiple-product companies are obviously doing well, but not necessarily because they are more efficient. It's usually because they start with an inherent advantage, normally product leadership. Ralston Purina didn't build Eveready into the number one appliance battery brand. It already was number one, with 52 percent of the market when Ralston bought the battery brand in 1986 from Union Carbide.

"You can't sell batteries like you sell dog food," one analyst warned Ralston Purina shortly after the Eveready purchase. They tried, but they couldn't. Today Eveready has 43 percent of the U.S. battery market and is no longer the leader.

Duracell is the number one battery now. One reason is that Duracell International Inc. is a single-product company. Spun off from Kraft in a 1988 leveraged buyout, Duracell went public in 1991 at $15 a share. (Today the stock is over $50 a share.)

SPIN-OFFS CREATE CHIEF EXECUTIVES

This fact alone accounts for much of the success of the spin-offs that have already taken place.

"The buck stops here," read the sign on Harry Truman's desk. When you are chief executive, you are at the end of the line. This is a powerful motivating force for the ego-driven people who aspire to a CEO's chair. It's not just the money, it's the power, too. When you're in charge, you are driven to succeed. When you're the leader, you are the focus of attention both inside and outside the company.

What company has received the most media attention in the past few years? It's either Microsoft or IBM. I'll bet you know that Bill Gates is CEO of Microsoft and Lou Gerstner is CEO of IBM. But who is second-in-command at Microsoft? Second-in-command at IBM? Unless you work for one of these companies, you probably don't know.

When you're second in charge, or even further down the chain of command, it's not the same as being the CEO. It's never your fault when things go wrong, nor do you get to take the credit when things go right. Nor is the money there either.

A survey of three hundred large companies shows that, on average, the CEO makes 54 percent more in salary and bonuses than his or her second-in-command. And that's before stock options, which tend to skew toward the top even more.

When you're the CEO, the bucks also stop there.

SPIN-OFFS REDUCE THE PROBLEM OF "COMPETING WITH YOUR CUSTOMERS"

When GM owned National, it was hard to sell General Motors cars to Hertz, Avis, and Alamo.

One of the biggest problems a diversified company faces is competing with its own customers. Few customers want to talk about this problem because they don't want to foster the illusion that they can be so petty in their buying decisions.

Unless you have a monopoly, "competing with your customers" is usually a serious strategic mistake. What looks like synergy often turns to be antisynergetic. Which is why PepsiCo does so poorly in the fountain trade, yet is neck and neck with Coca-Cola in the supermarkets.

When you own Pizza Hut, Taco Bell, and KFC, it's hard to sell Pepsi-Cola to Little Caesars, Del Taco, and Popeyes Famous Fried Chicken.

Ask your salesforce. Whenever they try to sell to a customer that one of your other divisions competes with, they run into serious obstacles. Put yourself in the shoes of a PepsiCo salesperson trying to sell soft drinks to Domino's Pizza. He may not say it, but you can be sure that Tom Monaghan would never buy his cola from the owner of his archrival, Pizza Hut.

When AT&T announced its entry into the computer services business in 1995, Electronic Data Systems, one of AT&T's largest customers, threatened to take its telephone business elsewhere. "AT&T keeps on making it more difficult for us to continue being a large customer of theirs," said Gary Fernandes, an EDS senior vice president.

Now that Walt Disney owns the ABC television network, they will find it difficult to sell programming to NBC and CBS. And if they dump dismal Disney programming on ABC, both will suffer.

The recent trend of manufacturers like Sony, Montblanc, Liz Claiborne, Nike, Levi's, and Speedo to open their own retail stores is potentially dangerous. It takes a while, but these things often boomerang. At first the manufacturers' stores sell at full list price, with no end-of-season sales and no markdowns.

Their regular dealers are happy because they can discount the famous brands. "Pick out what you want at the big Sony store on Madison Avenue," a dealer might say, "and then come back and I'll sell you the same merchandise at a discount."

At some point the manufacturers also start discounting, and it gets ugly. Your customers don't mind competing with you when you are losing, but they hate it when you are drawing their customers away from them with discounts. When it comes to the cost of the merchandise, the manufacturer has what the dealer considers an unfair advantage.

Yet the "retail temptation" is always there. It's just one of the many temptations that cause companies to become unfocused. "If we break even on the stores, we'll get a lot of free advertising and display value that's bound to impress both customers and dealers."

The logic is almost always on the side of broadening the scope of a company's operations. The logic is almost never on the side of narrowing the focus of a company's operations.

In the many hundreds of corporate meetings in which I have participated, I have heard many arguments for expansions: in product line, in distribution types and outlets, in flavors, in sizes. But, with few exceptions, almost no arguments for contractions.

The only time companies want to narrow the focus is when their expansions start losing money. By then it's usually too late. The core operation has started to go south, too.

Spin-offs are one of the easiest, quickest ways to narrow a company's focus. It's surprising there haven't been more of them. Many companies are Siamese twins, yearning to be separated. Some of my personal spin-off candidates include . . .

• CompuServe. When H&R Block bought the company in 1980, CompuServe was the leading computer on-line service. Today CompuServe has fallen behind the new leader, America Online, which has 2.3 million U.S. subscribers to CompuServe's 1.8 million.

Granted, CompuServe was a good buy for H&R Block at $23 million. Today the company is worth $1 billion, according to some analysts. But it might be worth a lot more if it could recapture the on-line leadership from America Online. As an independent company, it would have the resources and the motivation to do so.

• Prodigy. This CompuServe competitor has consumed some $1 billion in capital supplied by its Sears and IBM parents. With the Internet poised to provide stiff competition for the on-line services, Prodigy needs a miracle to survive. What it doesn't need are two out-of-touch owners arguing about the direction the company should take.

• Eveready. Same story as CompuServe. When Ralston Purina acquired the Eveready battery business from Union Carbide, the brand was number one in the United States. Today it has fallen behind Duracell, itself a spin-off. Eveready lost its leadership in the transition from zinc-carbon to alkaline batteries. Technology transition points are always difficult for leaders to cope with.

• Claris, the applications software division of Apple Computer. With its market share declining, Apple is in a life-or-death battle with its "Wintel" competition. Apple management doesn't need the distraction of running both a hardware company and a software company. (Several years ago, John Sculley planned to spin off Claris, then apparently changed his mind.)

• Holiday Rambler. Bought by Harley-Davidson in 1986, this maker of premium-priced recreational vehicles couldn't be more different from its parent company. Motorcycles are small, high-powered, sporty vehicles designed for the younger crowd. RVs are big, low-powered, practical vehicles designed for older folks. Harley executives should remember how they prospered when they were cut loose from AMF and should do the same for Holiday Rambler.

• Hughes Electronics Corporation and General Motors Locomotive Group. Now that General Motors has announced the planned spin-off of EDS, they should let the other shoes drop. By spinning off Hughes and the Locomotive Group, GM would revert to being a "pure" automobile company.

• Burger King. A fast-food company buried in a traditional food company (Pillsbury) owned by an English conglomerate (Grand Metropolitan), Burger King needs to be unleashed from its master in order to focus on its mortal enemy, McDonald's.

History has shown that number one companies can often muddle through as part of a conglomerate because they have the power of leadership. But number two companies like Burger King almost never do well in the same environment.

Number two companies need their independence. To compete with an entrenched leader like McDonald's, you need to be quick, bold, nimble, and aggressive, all qualities that conglomerates seem to squeeze out of an organization.

• American Express Financial Advisors (formerly IDS), American Express Bank, and American Express Financial Services Direct. Spinning off these three operations would allow the company to concentrate on its credit card business.

• Weight Watchers. America is the fattest country in the world and yet the diet division of $7 billion H. J. Heinz Company has been losing members. Instead of a predicted $3.3 billion from class fees and sales of food in 1994, revenues at Weight Watchers reached just $1.6 billion.

Worse still, Weight Watchers went from a $45 million profit in 1992 to a $50 million loss in 1994. There are a number of critical issues for Weight Watchers to face, including how to avoid competing with itself by marketing a line of frozen foods through supermarket distribution.

• Hill's Pet Nutrition. Makers of the $800 million Science Diet, a hot product distributed through veterinarians and pet stores, Hill's is coming under attack by a number of new brands. As an independent company, freed from its Colgate-Palmolive parent, Hill's would be in much better shape to blunt the attacks and consolidate its leadership in the premium pet-food category.

• Braun, Oral-B, stationery products, and toiletries. Gillette gets 39 percent of its sales (and 69 percent of its profits) from razors and blades. Gillette should focus on wet shaving and spin off the other four operations.

• Sara Lee. An $18 billion corporation, Sara Lee gets about half of its sales from personal products and half of its sales from food products. Sara Lee should split itself in two.

• Miller Brewing and Kraft General Foods. Michael Miles, the first nonsmoking CEO of Philip Morris, was eased out in 1994 after he suggested splitting the company into separate tobacco and food entities. (The same split that RJR Nabisco has already started.)

I would go one step further and also spin off Miller Brewing as a separate company. Same problem as Burger King and Pepsi-Cola. Miller is a number two brand, buried in a conglomerate, and forced to compete with an independent, well-entrenched leader, Anheuser-Busch.

The new Philip Morris CEO, Geoffrey Bible, is strongly opposed to spin-offs: "Our management and board were convinced (and remain convinced) that splitting the company would have diminished, not increased, shareholder value over the long term." The company, he says, enjoys "tremendous and powerful synergy" from marrying its food and tobacco businesses.

Maybe so. But it's hard to be objective about the wisdom of cutting the company into three parts when (1) you're fifty-six years old, and (2) you've just been appointed CEO after a long career with Philip Morris.

- Burson-Marsteller, Hill and Knowlton. The two largest public relations agencies are owned by Young & Rubicam and WPP Group, respectively. Both should be spun off, along with most other public relations operations acquired by advertising agencies.

The promised synergies between public relations and advertising agencies have never developed. The public relations units operate separately and have a separate list of clients. They would do better on their own.

Furthermore, public relations and advertising are natural competitors. When both are housed in the same company, they sometimes resolve their conflicts internally and thus deprive their clients of objective advice.

One often overlooked problem of spin-offs is the name issue. The objective of a spin-off is to create a separate company with a separate identity. When two companies have similar names their identities become blurred. Some examples:

- Host Marriott and Marriott International. Which one manages hotels and which one owns and trades hotels? Forever will they be confused.

- US West Communications and US West Media. Help, which one is the phone company?

- ITT Hartford Group, ITT Industries, and ITT Destinations. Three multibillion-dollar companies with the same name. Total confusion.

- Indresco and Dresser Industries. Indresco sounds like the international operations of Dresser, not a separate company. Forget cleverness (*In*dustrial products of *Dres*ser *Co*mpany). Give the new company a new name.

- Bally's Health & Tennis and Bally Entertainment. What's a Bally? Is it a casino or a fitness center?

Spin-offs are not without their problems, such as the name issue. But they are one of the surest signs that Corporate America is refocusing itself.

The surge of spin-offs and sell-offs is proof positive that the age of diversification and the age of conglomerization are finally over.

We have entered the age of focus.

BUILDING A
MULTISTEP FOCUS

In some cases, a company should consider building a multiple-step focus rather than using a single focus.

General Motors is the best example.

When Alfred Sloan took over the company back in 1921, General Motors was a general mess. The product line was all over the map.

- Chevrolet: $795 to $2,075.

- Oakland: $1,395 to $2,065.

- Oldsmobile: $1,445 to $3,300.

- Scripps-Booth: $1,545 to $2,295.

- Sheridan: $1,685.

- Buick: $1,795 to $3,295.

- Cadillac: $3,790 to $5,690.

Furthermore, the country had just entered a recession, which encouraged the competition to cut prices. The basic price of the Ford Model T was cut to $360, the runabout to $395, and the top-of-the-line sedan to $795. No wonder Ford with one brand had more than 50 percent of the U.S. market while General Motors with seven brands had only 12 percent.

What should Sloan have done?

The usual management response is to cut staff, rationalize parts and services, sell off assets, and, of course, cut prices. In other words, attack the problem from an operational point of view. But like most situations, then as well as today, General Motors was not an operational problem, it was a focus problem.

When a company is unfocused, you can't dramatically improve results by doing the same things, only better. It's like a photograph that's not in focus. You can enlarge it, increase the contrast, color it, and print it on better paper, but you're not going to dramatically improve the result until you get the picture in focus.

In his icy, emotionally detached way, Alfred Sloan developed a single-focus strategy with multiple steps. To compete with Ford, General Motors would develop a phalanx of brands that would span the market. That way the customer could move up the automobile ladder to any height his financial situation permitted. ("A car for every purse and purpose.")

Sloan selected the brands and the price points he felt were needed to dominate the automotive industry. Those that didn't fit the scheme were discarded. Here is his 1921 master plan with the Oakland Motor Car Company of Pontiac, Michigan, renamed as "Pontiac."

- Chevrolet: $450 to $600.

- Pontiac: $600 to $900.

- Oldsmobile: $900 to $1,200.

- Buick: $1,200 to $1,700.

- Cadillac: $1,700 to $2,500.

In the Sloan scheme, there were no price overlaps. No division competed directly against another, except to serve as the next step in the customer's climb up the ladder to Cadillac at the top. At General Motors they had a saying: "Chevrolet is for the hoi polloi, Pontiac for the poor but proud, Oldsmobile for the comfortable but discreet, Buick for the striving, and Cadillac for the rich."

Along with the plan came a general office to coordinate and supervise the divisions and a system to provide accurate, uniform data. As a result, General Motors was transformed from an agglomeration of many businesses into a single, coordinated enterprise. In other words, a company with a multistep focus.

But success didn't happen overnight. Ford continued to make gains. In 1923, a year in which Henry Ford celebrated his sixtieth birthday, Ford sold more than two million cars, good enough for 57 percent of the American market and 50 percent of the world market. But that was the high-water mark. Never again was Ford going to dominate the industry, not even when they introduced the six-cylinder Model A in 1928.

It takes time for a focus to take hold. It takes time for prospects to learn the new brands and what they stand for. It takes time for "word of mouth" to make the rounds. Car buyers have to hear the messages from a number of different sources before the words actually sink in.

It wasn't until 1931 that General Motors, with 31 percent of the U.S. market, finally passed Ford, with 28 percent. But from then on, the Sloan juggernaut could not be stopped. For more than fifty years, General Motors' share of the market approached 50 percent (and even more in the fifties and sixties).

Without iron-fisted control from the top, however, a company will soon lose focus. Slowly each division began to deviate from the plan. Chevrolet and Pontiac began to introduce expensive models; Oldsmobile, Buick, and Cadillac began to introduce inexpensive models. Instead of maintaining their narrow focus, each General Motors division headed for the middle of the market where the volume was.

And instead of coordinating and supervising the divisions, top management divorced themselves from the automobile business altogether. "General Motors is not in the business of making cars," said chairman Thomas Murphy at the time, "General Motors is in the business of making money."

Today, there are no clear-cut separations between the divisions. In fact, there is enormous overlap. Here are current passenger car base prices for the six General Motors brands.

- Saturn: $9,995 to $12,995.

- Chevrolet: $8,085 to $68,043.

- Pontiac: $11,074 to $27,139.

- Oldsmobile: $13,500 to $31,370.

- Buick: $13,700 to $33,084.

- Cadillac: $34,990 to $45,935.

Notice something? General Motors has gone right back to 1921 with the same pattern of overlapping car prices.

Notice something else? The two divisions with the most focused pricing are Saturn and Cadillac. These two are also GM's most successful divisions.

Compare the price ranges. The highest priced Saturn model is 30 percent more than the cheapest Saturn. For Cadillac, the difference is 31 percent.

The highest priced Oldsmobile, on the other hand, is 132 percent more than the cheapest. For Buick, the difference is 141 percent. For Pontiac, 145 percent, and for Chevrolet, an astounding 742 percent.

What's a Chevrolet? A large, small, cheap, expensive, domestic, imported car. In other words, a brand that has lost its focus.

In the past decade, annual Chevrolet car sales in the United States declined 36 percent, from almost 1.6 million a year to barely over 1 million. General Motors' share of the total market also fell, from 44 percent of the domestic market to 33 percent today.

A limited line doesn't necessarily limit sales. The average Saturn dealer sells almost a thousand cars a year. With a much broader line, the average Chevrolet dealer sold only 226 passenger cars during a recent year. (Even with light trucks added, the Chevy dealer moved only 553 vehicles out the door.)

The success of Saturn may be a mixed benefit for General Motors. What's good for Saturn may not be good for General Motors.

Chevrolet used to be GM's entry-level car, the first choice of most first-time car buyers. Now Saturn has moved into the entry-level position. Every Saturn sale is to a customer who is also a prime prospect for Chevrolet. Alfred Sloan must be turning over in his grave. (General Motors has been trying to prop up Oldsmobile as the place where Saturn buyers would go next.)

The success of Cadillac is also not what it seems to be. A Cadillac used to be . . . well, a "Cadillac," the top of the line, the best car you could buy (within reasonable limits). That's no longer true. Yesterday's Cadillac owner is now driving a Mercedes-Benz or a BMW. The truth is, Cadillac cars are too cheap; they are not occupying the high-priced slot as originally planned by Sloan.

In order to increase volume, Cadillac abandoned its traditional role at the high end and went downmarket. What's good for Cadillac isn't necessarily good for General Motors. Inexpensive Cadillacs leave no room on the ladder for Oldsmobile and Buick, which are getting crushed between expensive Chevrolets and Pontiacs, on the one hand, and cheap Cadillacs on the other.

It goes without saying that Cadillac can't move up the car ladder just by increasing the prices of their existing models. What they would have to do is to build more expensive cars with better performance and more features. Actually, they could give their existing cars to Buick, which would open up space for Oldsmobile, etc.

Meanwhile at Chrysler and Ford, confusion reigns. Both companies try to make one name serve two functions: as a corporate name and as a brand name. Car buyers accept a General Motors Cadillac, but what's a Ford Lincoln? If you tell your friends you bought a Ford Lincoln, they're going to question your sanity.

A new corporate name would help to clarify the steps in the Ford focus, but Chrysler is a more difficult problem. The company is entangled with brand names like a bowl of spaghetti.

At the dealer level, the inexpensive brand (Plymouth) is dualed with the expensive brand (Chrysler). Dodge is theoretically in the middle, but it sells both the small Plymouth Neon (as the Dodge Neon) and the large Chrysler Concorde (as the Dodge Intrepid). To further mix up matters, Dodge is one-third cars and two-thirds light trucks and minivans.

What's a Dodge? A small, large, cheap, expensive car, truck, minivan. Dodge marketing people used to brag that Dodge sold vehicles in categories that accounted for 85 percent of the total U.S. market. "Whatever you want to buy, we've got it."

That's the road that leads nowhere in the long run. What saves a brand like Dodge in the short term is the booming market for minivans and light trucks.

Then there's Neon, which has become very successful since its 1994 launch. In its first year, 178,960 Neons were sold. If Neon were a brand, it would rank as the seventeenth largest selling car brand in the country, right behind Lincoln (179,000) and Chrysler (197,000).

By comparison, Saturn sold only 74,493 cars in its first full year without, of course, the huge dealer network enjoyed by Neon. But unlike Neon, Saturn has created a high visibility profile among car buyers because it is a strong brand, not a model.

What a waste. All the effort put into Neon, the model, should have been put into Neon, the brand, or one of the company's other brands. But that strategy would first require a straightening out of the spaghetti strands at Chrysler Corporation.

The average buyer looks at three different brands before choosing a car. Marketing a wide variety of models with a wide variety of messages is bound to confuse shoppers, not help them. In truth, most car buyers are more impressed with what their friends drive than what they see on television or read in the papers.

Automotive demand is created on the street. "What kind of a car is that?" is the first question you get when you arrive in a good-looking new model.

"Neon," you might say.

And the second question is, "Who makes the Neon?"

There are 632 car and light-truck models on the market. And those are domestics only. Imports add another 277 models. It's this proliferation that causes confusion on the streets and in the mind and seriously undermines the ability of a car manufacturer to create a powerful brand.

Are car makers worried? They don't seem to be. As one General Motors executive said recently, "If the customers want your product, they will find you!"

But will they? Who can remember more than a small fraction of those 909 model names, let alone connect the model name to the name of the manufacturer? It's hard enough to remember the names of the thirty-five major automotive brands on the market.

Contrast Neon with Acura. When Honda decided to go upmarket, it didn't put its more expensive cars into its existing Honda dealer organization, even though this would have been the less expensive way to launch the new model. No, it set up a separate Acura dealer organization. This had two advantages.

One, it maintained Honda's focus as an inexpensive Japanese car. (Relatively inexpensive, that is.) And two, it allowed Acura to be established as the expensive, or luxury, Japanese car brand.

Now Honda has a single-focus strategy with two steps instead of one. Because Acura was first to establish the luxury Japanese car in the United States, it became the largest-selling brand in its category. In a recent year Acura sold 97,000 cars in the United States compared to 79,000 for Lexus, the second brand in the category, and 59,000 for Infiniti, the third brand.

But Honda didn't have the courage of its convictions. It made a mistake that will eventually cost them their luxury-car leadership. Believing that Acura dealers couldn't live on the expensive six-cylinder Legend model alone, Honda allowed them to sell the cheaper four-cylinder Integra model. This had two disadvantages.

One, it undermined Acura's focus. Is Acura a luxury car like the Legend, which sells for $36,000 to $44,000, or is Acura a middle-of-the-road car like the Integra, which sells for $16,000 to $21,000? As you might expect, Integras outsell Legends almost two to one. Acura is selling cars, but Acura is not building a focus.

Two, it almost certainly will allow Lexus to ultimately capture leadership in the imported luxury-car category. Lexus sells only six- and eight-cylinder cars in the $32,000 to $51,000 price range. In luxury cars only, Lexus outsells Acura more than two to one. It will only be a matter of time before the more focused Lexus brand will overtake the less focused Acura brand.

Compounding Acura's problems was the launch of the NSX sports car, a critical success but a financial failure. Acura sells some 900 NSX cars a year in America. Not enough cars to make money, but plenty of cars to undermine their focus. Why did Honda introduce the NSX?

"Mainly to create an image," said Kenichi Koyama, general manager of Honda's North American sales division. This is faulty thinking.

For many years, the traditional wisdom in Detroit was that every brand needed three things: (1) An inexpensive "entry-level" car. (2) An "image" car. And (3) a full line of mainstream models. One car to get the prospect in the door, one car to impress them, and one car to sell them.

Chevrolet had the Chevette and the Corvette. Pontiac had the LeMans and the Fiero. Buick had the Skylark and the Reatta. Even crusty Cadillac tried the entry-level Cimarron and the image Allanté, both no longer with us.

The fundamental mistake that car makers make is to treat each individual brand as an entity in itself and not as a single step in an overall corporate focus.

While entry-level and image cars may be bad for Chevrolet, Pontiac, Oldsmobile, Buick, and Cadillac, oddly enough, they may be good for General Motors. General Motors does need an entry-level brand.

GM's problem is they need only one entry-level brand and they have two: Chevrolet and Saturn. In order to focus the company, they need to decide which of the two brands should serve as the entry-level brand and how to refocus the other.

Maybe General Motors also needs an "image" brand. If so, it should be handled by a separate dealer organization. A separate step in the General Motors ladder.

In order to maintain a single focus, companies should consider adding new steps on the ladder instead of broadening the product offering on a single step.

Can you have too many steps in a multistep focus? Of course, but most companies have not reached that stage yet.

Consider Subaru of America. In the eighties the company was cooking along as the fifth largest importer of cars in America (after Honda, Toyota, Nissan, and Mazda). Subaru sales during the decade averaged 160,000 cars a year.

Even more important, Subaru had a focus. The cars were cheap. Or as the advertising said: "Inexpensive and built to stay that way."

Actually, Subaru had a secondary focus, four-wheel drive. By the middle of the decade, Subaru was selling half the four-wheel-drive passenger cars retailed in the country. Even so, this amounted to only about a third of the Subarus sold in America. What to do?

It's not unusual for a company to have two focuses, both valid and both potentially effective. A company will often shift back and forth from one focus to the other, confusing both its customers and its employees. What a company needs to do is to make a choice and deliberately emphasize one focus and de-emphasize the other.

In Subaru's case, the two focuses were particularly confusing since they were inconsistent. How can an inexpensive car have four-wheel drive? Four-wheel-drive cars should be more expensive than two-wheel-drive cars.

Instead of dealing with the real focusing issue (inexpensive versus four-wheel-drive), Subaru chose to move up the automobile ladder. Subaru asked their supplier, Fuji Heavy Industries, to build a sports car, which the company christened the XT.

With its flying-wedge shape and its vibrant colors, the XT looked like everything a Subaru was not. In one of the most famous advertising commercials of all time, a farmer tells his son to buy a Subaru. When the son barrels back to the ranch in an XT, the father frowns and says, "I thought we agreed you'd buy a Subaru."

"But, Dad, I did."

Tom Gibson, Subaru of America's president, called it his favorite automobile advertisement of all time. "It was the transition from cheap-and-ugly to upscale." Dealers loved the ad and so did the advertising industry, which gave "Dad, I did" a Clio Award as the best automobile commercial of the year.

And so did car buyers . . . at first. Although the XT was almost twice as expensive as the average Subaru, the company sold twenty-seven thousand the first year, after which sales steadily declined until the car disappeared.

It's a common phenomenon. Whenever a company introduces a product totally different from its normal product line, the "shock" value creates an initial burst of interest. After the shock wears off, so do sales.

From the Subaru XT to the Acura NSX to Crystal Pepsi, you see the same phenomenon. The first month it was on sale in test markets Crystal Pepsi had 4 percent of the soft-drink market. A year later it was dead.

The first year the Acura NSX was available, twenty-six hundred cars were sold. Currently, sales are less than a thousand cars a year and declining.

The 1985–86 launch of the XT sports car coincided with the high-water mark for Subaru sales in the United States. From then on things went downhill. By unfocusing the Subaru line, the XT contributed to its decline, from 183,000 cars in 1986 to a current volume of about 100,000 a year.

In 1991, Subaru tried again. This time the sports car was called the SVX, and like the XT it was almost twice as expensive as the average Subaru. The automobile press was ecstatic.

"If its banzai assault on the heavily defended luxocoupe market is even half successful," said *Car & Driver* magazine, "it will not only change what the word Subaru means, it will raise the all-around performance ante for subsequent similar cars." After an initial burst, sales dropped in half, repeating the XT pattern.

You can't change what the word Subaru means. You can't change what any word in the mind of a customer or prospect means. The only thing you can change is the word Subaru itself. Which actually might have been a good idea.

Because the name ends with a *u*, Subaru is a bad-sounding name. And a bad-sounding name is difficult to associate with an upscale concept like sports car. To most people, a Subaru sports car is an oxymoron.

With a bad name like Subaru, an inexpensive focus is a good choice. When things are cheap, prospects ask themselves, "What will I have to give up to get the low price?" Volkswagen was very successful when they were selling the Beetle, a bad-looking car at a low price.

"The 1970 VW will stay ugly longer" was one particularly effective message. The disadvantage of being ugly also had a benefit. The car will last longer.

In its day Volkswagen had a powerful focus. Small, reliable, inexpensive, ugly cars. In 1968, for example, Volkswagen sold 564,000 cars in the United States, an incredible 57 percent of the imported car market. But VW was drifting away from its focus.

In 1971, the company introduced the 412 model. "Volkswagen announces a new kind of Volkswagen. Big," said the advertisements. First small, then big?

In 1976, the company introduced the Dasher. "With great pride, VW enters the luxury car field. Dasher, The Elegant Volkswagen," said the advertisements. First ugly, then big, then elegant?

The loss of focus coincided with a loss of market share as Volkswagen continued to drive downhill. Virtually every year in the seventies and eighties Volkswagen lost market share. Today the company is down to 7 percent of the imported car market, or about 114,000 cars a year, roughly the same as Subaru.

Many, many companies have lived a life similar to Volkswagen. The saga starts with a hot product that puts the company on the map, like the original Beetle. But nothing stays hot forever. Sooner or later, sales start to slide. What should Volkswagen have done?

At this stage of the game, Volkswagen had three choices: (1) Follow the market with larger, more expensive Volkwagens, (2) hang in there with the original focus, or (3) launch new brands to capture the changing market.

FOLLOW THE MARKET WITH LARGER, MORE EXPENSIVE VOLKSWAGENS

This is the strategy VW pursued with tragic results. The overall theme: "Different Volks for different folks."

What destroyed the brand was the unfocusing effect of trying to market cars that were inconsistent with Volkswagen's perception in the mind. This is the critical point.

Many businesspeople believe it's the inherent quality of the product itself that determines success or failure. The quality axiom runs rampant at companies like Volkswagen.

A properly focused brand will have the illusion of quality, regardless of reality. An unfocused brand will have the illusion of somehow not being right, again regardless of the quality of the product. A prospect looks at the big and relatively expensive Volkswagen and thinks, "That's not a Volkswagen." The car on the showroom floor doesn't match the perception in the mind.

HANG IN THERE WITH THE ORIGINAL FOCUS

This is not a bad strategy. Hanging in there, or doing nothing, has kept White Castle, Zippo, and other companies consistently profitable. Furthermore, products come and go. In Volkswagen's case, there is a strong trend today toward the kind of car represented by the original Beetle. Small, practical, inexpensive, fun to drive.

In the United States, the Neon is a good example of this trend. Neon has been outselling the seven current Volkswagen models (Cabriolet, Corrado, Jetta, Golf, Passat, Cabrio, and Fox) almost two to one. The Geo Metro sold by Chevrolet dealers is another, selling about 80,000 cars a year.

In Europe, the Renault Twingo and Fiat Cinquecento are examples of the trend. The two models are selling about 350,000 cars a year. Ford has announced plans to introduce a similar car, tentatively called the "Ka."

But what really should have shook up the folks at Volkswagen was the rave reception given to their Concept One car. A reincarnation, if there ever was one, of the original Beetle, the car has been the hit of auto shows around the world.

If Coca-Cola was able to bring back its original formula after the failure of New Coke, why can't Volkswagen? A classic VW might be almost as popular as Classic Coke.

LAUNCH NEW BRANDS TO CAPTURE
THE CHANGING MARKET

Instead of introducing its larger, more expensive cars under the Volkswagen name, the company could have used one or more new brand names. This, of course, is the successful strategy followed by Honda with Acura and Toyota with Lexus.

What Volkswagen could have tried to do is to become a German General Motors with a brand in each price range. VW may have thought they had a brand in each category with Golf, Jetta, and Passat, their three major lines.

But there's an enormous difference between a brand like Volkswagen and models like Golf, Jetta, and Passat. Not so much in the dictionary but in the mind. When a prospect sees a strange automobile, the first question is "What kind of a car is that?"

If the answer is "Passat," the next question is "Who makes the Passat?"

"Volkswagen makes the Passat." A brand is the name of the company that makes the product. A model is the name used to differentiate between similar products made by the same company. Prospects tend to see models from the same company as similar and brands as different because they are made by different companies.

What about General Motors? Specifically, who makes the Cadillac? Strange as it may seem, General Motors has created the perception that it's the Cadillac Motor Car Division, a separate company owned by GM, that makes the Cadillac.

If General Motors tried to turn out Chevrolets and Cadillacs on the same production line and prospects found out about it, there would be hell to pay! (You might remember the scandal that occurred when General Motors put Chevrolet engines into Oldsmobiles and Buicks. "If I paid for a Buick," said the Buick owner, "I want a Buick, engine and all.")

Who makes the Audi? Actually Volkswagen makes the Audi, but in a separate subsidiary, which allows them to establish Audi as a separate brand with its own manufacturing facilities and its own dealer organization. But Audi, like Subaru, is a weak name, so it is not all that helpful in building a multistep focus for Volkswagen.

Furthermore, the name Audi was virtually destroyed by a 1986

CBS *60 Minutes* broadcast entitled "Out of Control." The show supposedly documented "sudden acceleration" in the Audi 5000. (After years of investigation, the evidence points to driver error.)

Perception is more important than reality. Audi sales nose-dived, from seventy-four thousand the year before the program ran to a current eighteen thousand a year.

If "Audi" were a "better" name like Mercedes-Benz, for example, the damage would not have been nearly as great. By better I don't mean a better known or more prestigious name, I mean a better sounding name. A good-sounding name will shed problems like water off a duck's back. A bad-sounding name will absorb them.

Time marches on. At some point in any company's life cycle, it will face the Volkswagen problem. Do we: (1) Follow the market with new models, (2) hang in there, or (3) launch new brands?

One is a losing strategy because it undermines a company's focus. Most companies follow this losing strategy because they believe it's more important to chase the market than to maintain a focus.

Two can be a winning strategy because it maintains a company's original focus. And three can also be a winner because it establishes a multistep focus.

Having said that, don't underestimate the difficulty and expense of launching a new brand. New models come and go, but new brands should be launched only rarely. But companies should keep in mind that the road to success is paved with brands, not models. New brands are expensive to be sure, but who ever said you could nickel-and-dime your way to success?

One question that comes up repeatedly is whether or not a company should put its corporate name on a brand. Should General Motors puts its name on Chevrolet, for example? From the customer's point of view, probably not. Because you want to keep the illusion that Chevrolet is the manufacturer of the brand.

This is why Saturn was introduced as "A different kind of company. A different kind of car." General Motors wanted to create the illusion that Saturn was a car company, not a division of GM like Chevrolet.

Did the public buy this idea? Yes, partially. Although they knew that Saturn was a part of GM, they felt that it "operated as a separate company."

But from the point of view of many other interested people, including shareholders, financial analysts, bankers, and reporters, including the corporate name can be helpful. A good compromise is to feature the brand name in large type and use the corporate name in much smaller type.

The average buyer of a box of Tide detergent would have trouble finding the Procter & Gamble corporate name, but it's on the box somewhere. Tide is a brand name and needs a separate identity.

There's nothing wrong with buying a brand to fit into a multistep focus. Too many acquisition-minded companies look for a "fit" rather than a "step." If the proposed acquisition is everything the acquiring company is not, then the fit is deemed to be right.

In 1989, Ford bought Jaguar for $2.6 billion in a transaction that was described as a perfect fit. Jaguar cars were small, sporty, and expensive, unlike anything built by the Ford Motor Company. But where did Jaguar fit in the Ford lineup? Ford, Mercury, Lincoln, Jaguar? Not a very likely ladder.

A Lincoln owner is more likely to step up to a big car like a Mercedes-Benz, not a small car like a Jaguar.

Nor has the merger been a financial success. In the five years that Ford has owned the company, Jaguar has lost about $1.3 billion. Furthermore, Ford was forced to pour millions more into the company to modernize facilities.

By the end of 1996, Ford will have spent $1.6 billion for new product, production line modernizations, and workforce reductions. That's a gigantic investment for almost no return. So would Ford buy Jaguar again?

"It's a tough question," says Ford CEO Alexander Trotman. Translation: No, but I'm not going to admit that we made a mistake.

If your company wants to maintain its focus, don't buy a brand. Buy a "step" in your single-focus strategy.

BMW made a similar mistake in its $1.2 billion purchase of Rover Group Holdings from British Aerospace.

BMW bought itself two problems. Rover itself is an unfocused company, making both passenger cars and sports-utility vehicles under the Rover name. Furthermore the expensive sports-utility vehicle (Land Rover/Range Rover) is widely confused with the less expensive Land Rover/Discovery. Prognosis: another Jaguar.

Bernd Pischetsrieder, chairman of Bayerische Motoren Werke, sees the Rover passenger car as his lower priced entrée into such markets as Latin America, Indonesia, India, China, and the Philippines.

That's highly unlikely. Unlike Fiat, Renault, and Volkswagen, Rover is not known for low-cost "econobox" vehicles. Nor does a low-cost basic car provide a logical first step in a single-focus BMW strategy.

What's a BMW? It's a driving machine. Small, powerful, maneuverable, expensive, and German. Should BMW move up the car ladder or down? If they move down, they will go head-to-head with Volkswagen, Fiat, and Renault. Not an attractive prospect given BMW's heritage. Moving up, on the other hand, pits them against Mercedes-Benz.

But there's always room for two brands in any category. Coca-Cola and Pepsi-Cola. McDonald's and Burger King. Chevrolet and Ford. Cadillac and Lincoln. At the high end, Mercedes-Benz is unique. There are no alternatives.

Actually, BMW has had some success with its 7-series cars, selling about fifteen thousand a year in the U.S. market at a base price of $58,000. What BMW could use is a high-end brand name that would put them on an equal footing with Mercedes.

Putting a second brand name on the 7-series cars would serve two purposes. It would refocus BMW on smaller, pure driving machines and it would give the company a luxury brand to compete with Mercedes-Benz.

The magazine business is a good template for building a multistep focus. Time Inc., perhaps the world's most successful magazine publisher in its day, did not introduce its second magazine as *Time for Business*. Instead it was called *Fortune*.

Life magazine wasn't called *Time for Pictures*. Nor was *Sports Illustrated* called *Time for Sports*. *Money* wasn't called *Time for Finance*. Nor was *People* called *Time for Celebrities*. And *Entertainment Weekly* wasn't called *Time for Entertainment*.

Time, Fortune, Life, Sports Illustrated, Money, People, Entertainment Weekly. Multiple steps in a corporate strategy with a single focus: news.

News of the world, news about business, news in pictures, news about sports, news about personal finance, news about celebrities, and news about entertainment. *Life* was tripped up by television, but the other six remain powerful, profitable publications.

Like the old Time Inc., a company can have a single focus with brands that have their own individual identities.

When you sacrifice these individual identities in order to emphasize the corporate connection, you are asking for problems. Back in the early seventies, *Saturday Review* decided to publish four separate magazines using the corporate connection to give credibility to the individual publications.

- *Saturday Review: The Arts.*

- *Saturday Review: Education.*

- *Saturday Review: The Society.*

- *Saturday Review: The Sciences.*

It was an unmitigated disaster. A little over a year later, Saturday Reviewed its situation and decided to call it a day, losing a reported $17 million in the process. And that was when $17 million was a lot of money.

The opposite approach was taken by Pat McGovern when he started International Data Group in 1967. His first publication, *Computerworld,* has been joined by some 235 others (each with different names), which are published in twenty-four languages in sixty-seven countries around the world. Total revenues exceed $1 billion, and they have been growing at the rate of 15 percent a year.

All of IDG's publications are computer based. "We've maintained our focus—information technology—and as the industry has grown, we've grown, too," says Mr. McGovern. One key to the company's success is the global scope of its operations. IDG went to Japan in 1971, Germany in 1975, and Brazil in 1976.

Companies that are anxious to grow often expand their product line domestically when they would be much better off using the same resources to go global.

A narrowly focused product line in the international arena is a much more successful approach than a broad line in the domestic market. A global strategy allows a company to grow without losing its focus.

Darden Restaurants, the General Mills spin-off, is a highly focused company with multiple steps. The world's largest casual-dining company, Darden has two steps, both focused on different cuisines: Red Lobster and Olive Garden.

Darden can now expand in two directions without losing its focus. It can add additional steps in the form of different cuisines and it can expand internationally.

Perhaps the classic example of a multistep focus is Wm. Wrigley, Jr. Co. For more than a hundred years, Wrigley has had a single focus: chewing gum.

For most of its lifetime, the company sold just three brands of chewing gum: Juicy Fruit, Spearmint, and Doublemint. As the market changed, the gum giant added Big Red to capitalize on the cinnamon trend, Extra to jump on the sugar-free trend, and Freedent to ride the "stick-free" trend. The latest brand is Winterfresh, a breath-freshener product.

Wrigley's performance over the past decade has been astonishing. Sales have risen every year, from $590 million in 1984 to $1.6 billion in 1994. Even more astonishing is the fact that net profit margins have steadily increased, from 7 percent of sales in 1984 to 14 percent today. (This is chewing gum we're talking about, folks, not computer chips.)

Half of all Americans chew gum, and Wrigley has half of the gum market. Already, Wrigley gets half of its income from outside North America, and this percentage should substantially increase in the near future. This intense focus on a single product has numerous advantages.

Wrigley has continually lowered its cost of production, which allows the company to keep its prices low and keep its competitors out. (The private-label gum business is practically nonexistent.) Low production costs also allow lots of room for big advertising budgets. Wrigley spends 7 percent of sales, or $120 million a year, on advertising without hurting the bottom line.

In the future, a company with a narrow focus like Wrigley will use a "high/low" strategy to dominate its market. High volume and high advertising expenditures combined with low production costs and low prices.

In retail, this combination is called a "category killer." In manufacturing, the combination doesn't have a name, but four of its disciples are Intel, Compaq, Coca-Cola, and Wrigley.

When you dominate a market like Wrigley does, you can afford to spend money to increase the size of the market and not just on your brands. Wrigley's "When you can't smoke" campaign is widely credited with substantial gains in chewing gum sales.

Wrigley's multistep focus translates into a long-term consistency in everything they do. For example, the Doublemint "twins" advertising started back in the sixties. Not only is Doublemint Wrigley's largest seller, but the twins look like they will continue to chew Doublemint forever.

As one financial analyst said, "Wrigley is the opposite of two guys from New York wearing $3,000 suits trying to decide how to carve up the world."

On the surface there are a lot of similarities between what Wrigley has done with gum and what Hallmark has done with greeting cards. On the surface only.

Like Wrigley's approach in gum, Hallmark also has multiple steps in its strategy: the classic Hallmark line, the Ambassador line for discounters, the Pet Love line for pet owners, and the Shoebox line of humorous cards. It has worked. Like Wrigley, Hallmark accounts for almost half of its market, too.

But unlike Wrigley, Hallmark doesn't have a single-focus strategy. Over the years Hallmark has bought and sold a jewelry company (Trifari), a picture-frame company (Burnes of Boston), an investment in a Spanish-language television operation (Univision), and a $1 billion investment in a cable company.

Yet Hallmark remains hopelessly diversified with Binney & Smith (Crayola crayons), a printing company (Litho-Krome), the recent $365 million purchase of a TV production company, and extensive real estate holdings.

"Can Hallmark get well soon?" said the headline of a recent article in *Business Week*. "Bogged down by its specialty shops, the card giant is sagging," added the publication. Return on equity of the privately held corporation was estimated at 8 percent. (Wrigley's is 37 percent.)

It's hard to tell just how bad things are at Hallmark. But *Business Week* reports that profit-sharing contributions for the twenty-one thousand Hallmark employees, who own a third of the company, have dropped from 10 percent of salaries in 1990 to 6.5 percent in 1994.

The need to refocus the company on greeting cards seems to have escaped Hallmark management, who are still enamored of the glamour of the Hallmark brand and its many possible line extensions. "We could start a family of mutual funds, and people would buy it," boasts Hallmark's CEO. "That's the power of the brand."

Hogwash. Brands have power only when they are focused around a single product or concept. Cars, computer magazines, casual restaurants, chewing gum. These are just some of the products that companies have built a focus around.

But a focus doesn't always have to be built around a single product. Some companies have built a successful multistep focus around an attribute. An attribute common to many different products.

Luxury, for example. The Vendome Luxury Group is dedicated to developing and acquiring brands that meet its definition of luxury: "quality, identity, and authenticity."

The company's brands include Cartier jewelry, Alfred Dunhill men's products, Montblanc pens, Piaget and Baume & Mercier watches, Sulka ties, Karl Lagerfeld designs, and others. An impressive list.

The impressive performance of Montblanc alone is worth mentioning. Its cigar-shaped pens have taken over the high end of the market from its cigarette-shaped competitors like A.T. Cross and Gillette's Waterman and Parker pens, which are scrambling to catch up.

Profits at Vendome have been impressive, too. The company does about $2 billion in sales, with net profits in the 13 percent range. (Vendome Luxury Group is actually two companies, one incorporated in Luxembourg and the other in the UK, locked together in a twined share arrangement. Shareholders own Vendome units, which consist of one share of each company.)

Simple corporate concepts like "luxury" are the wave of the future. If a company can define and own a single word like gum, or driving, or safety, or luxury, it can build a powerful worldwide organization that can dominate an industry, a category, or an aspect of a market.

A narrow focus becomes a driving force that can sweep away competition and establish the company as the dominant player in its selected market. Focus is not a luxury; it's an essential element of the business organization of the future. That is, if the organization wants to have a profitable future.

The multistep approach has had some surprising successes. Take Levi's blue jeans, for example. Here is a brand name admired around the world. A brand right up there in the same category as Coca-Cola, McDonald's, and Marlboro.

You might think that Levi Strauss (Levi's owner) would be the largest U.S. seller of jeans, but they're not.

The largest U.S. seller of jeans is VF Corp. of Wyomissing, Pennsylvania. VF has two major blue jean brands (Lee and Wrangler) that in total outsell Levi's. Two brands allow VF to appeal to two separate markets. In addition, two brands give VF flexibility to handle retailer demands for exclusivity.

Furthermore, VF maintains each brand's individual identity by having separate headquarters. The Lee Apparel Co. is located in Merriam, Kansas. Wrangler Co. is located in Greensboro, North Carolina.

Could VF save money by merging the two headquarters in one location? Of course. Is this a good idea? Of course not.

But Levi is learning. A year after Levi Strauss launched its Dockers line of casual wear, the company acquired Brittania, which it turned into a value-price line for discounters.

Levi Strauss now has three steps in its clothing ladder: Brittania, Levi's, and Dockers. These three powerful brands should help Levi Strauss maintain its role as the world's largest producer of brand-name clothing at least in the short term.

In the long run, Levi Strauss is vulnerable at the bottom of the age ladder. When people grow up, they tend to stick with the same brands they fell in love with when they were young.

People in their thirties and forties, according to a recent survey, selected Levi's as the number one brand "they most closely associate with their generation." (Coke was second and Macintosh was third.) This is both good news and bad news for Levi Strauss.

The bad news is that young people today are wearing the baggy, hip-hop look. They're not into 501s. Children don't want to listen to the same music and wear the same clothes their parents did. They want their own thing and their own brands. Except for a few fringe, urban brands, there are no clothing brands tapping into the children's revolution.

Levi Strauss should launch a new brand to serve as the uniform for the Kid's Revolutionary Army. This should be a new brand, not a line extension of the Levi's brand. Kids want their own thing, not a variation of an adult brand.

Carl Williams, for example, launched a street-chic clothing brand in 1989 that has started to make waves. Dubbed "Karl Kani," the brand reaps annual sales of some $60 million.

As a matter of fact, every company should pay far more attention to what is happening at the bottom of the ladder than with what's going on at the top. The best target for a new brand is the younger crowd, who are far more receptive to new brands because they are looking for ways to differentiate their generation. The older you get, the more fixed you are in your ways . . . and your brands.

Many older companies have died out because they were too intent on saving their existing brand with line extensions and other life-support devices instead of launching new brands to appeal to younger customers.

In an ideal situation, every company would have multiple steps, or brands, in a single-focus strategy and then keep feeding in new brands at the bottom while retiring old brands from the top of the ladder.

It's easier to see how this might work in a fast-changing category like perfume. Calvin Klein, for example, launched Obsession, which became a big success. Then they moved on to Escape, another winner. Currently Calvin Klein has a hot product in CK One.

Chanel, on the other hand, is trying to hang on to the Chanel name with Chanel No. 5, Chanel No. 19, and Coco, but their markets are slowly dying along with their customers.

Most companies operate like Chanel, not Calvin Klein. They spend fortunes trying to save old brands rather than investing in new brands. That's why you see so much churning in the marketplace as customers shift from one company to another because the market leaders failed to supply the new brands that younger customers want.

- It wasn't Parker that introduced the new brand of "fat" pen. It was Montblanc.

- It wasn't Coca-Cola that introduced the New Age beverage. It was Snapple.

- It wasn't Seiko that introduced the fashion watch. It was Swatch.

It's hard to find good examples of companies that consistently maintain a multistep focus. In spite of the early success of General Motors, the concept is not well accepted.

What you do find, however, are some companies that own multiple steps on a single-product ladder. Unfortunately, many of these ladders are buried in companies that lack an overall focus. Their tactics might be sound, but their strategies are not.

Take Sara Lee, the cheesecake and panty-hose company. Since 1960, the company (formerly known as Consolidated Foods Corporation) has made more than 150 separate acquisitions.

Among the products acquired were Electrolux vacuum cleaners, Kiwi shoe polish, Hanes hosiery, Jimmy Dean meat products, Champion athletic wear, and Playtex apparel. While many of these were obviously astute purchases, the overall effect was to create a highly unfocused company that can expect to face many problems down the road.

Some of Sara Lee's units have done many things exceptionally well. The company is the world's largest maker of stockings and socks, but it didn't get there by selling only one brand.

Its Hanes unit is the number one department store hosiery brand. With fewer women shopping less frequently at department stores, Hanes looked around for another distribution channel. Which type of store do most women visit at least once a week?

The obvious choice was supermarkets. But supermarkets don't sell panty hose. That's exactly why this distribution choice was such a brilliant move. Eighty percent of success in business is just showing up first. Hanes showed up first in the supermarket channel.

The next decision was the name. Conventional wisdom would have created "Hanes, Too," or some other name that traded off the fact that Hanes was the largest selling hosiery brand. But a multistep approach requires a different and unique name for each step. The choice: L'eggs. (To reinforce the name, the product was packaged in four-inch white plastic eggs.)

A superb choice. Now the new brand had a name that burned the name of the distribution channel into the customer's mind. Where do you buy L'eggs for your legs? The same place you buy eggs.

Today, L'eggs is the number one panty-hose brand in the United States, with 25 percent of the total market. L'eggs accounts for two-thirds of Sara Lee's approximately $1 billion in U.S. hosiery sales.

Hanes and a few minor brands account for the rest. With two brands, Sara Lee dominates the two major panty-hose distribution channels.

Tambrands Inc. is another company that has recently seen the need for a multistep focus. For most of its sixty-year history, the company was focused on a single brand, Tampax, the dominant brand in the tampon field.

Like most companies, Tambrands tried both line extensions of Tampax tampons and diversification into such products as pregnancy testing equipment, makeup, and sanitary pads. Nothing worked very well.

Meanwhile, Tampax's market share drifted down from almost 60 percent of the market to 50 percent. The board was up in arms and kicked out two CEOs in a row, one in 1989 and the other four years later. Finally the company tried the one strategy it should have used years ago: multiple brands.

The issue was paper versus plastic. Tampax is "the real thing," the original paper tampon. Playtex is the newer, plastic tampon. Unfortunately, Tampax is seen as old-fashioned by young women, while Playtex is viewed as hip and modern. "The Playtex Generation" is the general idea.

So Tambrands introduced Satin Touch, a brand with a cardboard applicator that has the look and feel of plastic, although it was flushable and biodegradable like Tampax. Now Tambrands has two steps on the tampon ladder. Tampax in the traditional blue box for the older crowd and Satin Touch in a hot-pink box for the younger crowd.

Another example. Black & Decker is the world's largest power-tool maker, but like Sara Lee it fell into financial difficulty by acquisition, most notably the $2.7 billion acquisition of Emhart Corp. in 1989. Nevertheless, Black & Decker had the good sense to develop a complementary brand to its powerhouse house brand.

Introduced in 1992, DeWalt is the new brand directed at the professional crowd, while the Black & Decker brand remains focused on the amateur, do-it-yourself market.

Previous to the launch of the DeWalt brand, the company had only 10 percent of the heavy-duty tool market. The Big Macgillicuddy in this market was Makita, a Japanese company with almost 50 percent of the professional market.

Known by Black & Decker insiders as the "Acura concept," DeWalt has been a smashing success. In less than three years, DeWalt became a $350 million business, the market leader in professional power tools and the second largest power-tool brand after Black & Decker.

There are many different ways to segment a multiple-step ladder. What matters the most is the consistency of the steps. What you are trying to avoid is an overlap between the steps. (An overlap means you are competing with yourself.) The way to get around this difficulty is to focus the entire ladder on one characteristic of the product line. Some examples:

- Price. This is the most common ladder, best illustrated by the car ladder developed by Alfred Sloan for General Motors. Each brand has a specific price range and there are no overlaps. Other examples include the razor ladder (Trac II, Atra, and Sensor), which Gillette uses to dominate the wet-shaving industry. And the beer ladder (Busch, Budweiser, and Michelob), which Anheuser-Busch uses to dominate the brewing industry.

- Age. Brands and products grow old as well as people. When your existing brand starts getting social security checks, one effective strategy is to introduce a new brand directed at younger people. When Tampax was introduced in 1936, it was used only by young women. Today, of course, Tampax is "your mom's brand." Satin Touch is directed at the younger crowd.

- Cuisine. Darden Restaurants (Red Lobster and Olive Garden) cover seafood and Italian food, two of the most popular types of food. As the company grows, it makes sense to add additional types of cuisine to satisfy different tastes. Adding a "general" casual-food concept or a fast-food concept to the Darden Restaurant mix would cut across the existing chains and undermine their business. Compete with your competitors, not with yourself.

- Distribution. There is intense competition between channels of distribution. Trying to sell competing channels with the same brand can be difficult. What if Hanes had used the Hanes name on their supermarket panty hose? What would have happened to their department store distribution? A separate brand designed for each channel is the ideal solution.

These are only some of the possible attribute ladders on which to build a multistep focus. The possibilities are limited only by your imagination. In the past, successful companies have seized opportunities that were not considered by their competitors. The distribution ladder is one of those recent developments. In the future there will be other opportunities not clearly seen today.

Some successful entrepreneurs miss the opportunity to convert an initial success into a multistep focus. Take Wayne Huizenga, for example.

Only a handful of people have been as successful as Wayne Huizenga, first with Waste Management and then with Blockbuster Entertainment. His pattern for both companies was the same. Develop a concept, take it public, and then expand rapidly by buying out the competition.

Where Huizenga has missed the beat is in the music business. Instead of following the Waste Management and Blockbuster pattern, he extended the Blockbuster Video name into music.

Currently the company has more than five hundred stores under the Blockbuster Music name. Will they match the success of the video chain? Highly unlikely.

What's a Blockbuster? Is it a place where you rent videos or buy music? Instead of setting up a ladder with separate steps, Blockbuster has taken the well-traveled path toward an unfocused company.

Not only is Blockbuster a late entry in music, but the company is also getting into a viciously competitive industry where low price is virtually the only competitive advantage.

Continental Airlines made the same mistake. Here is an airline that cut itself in half in order to appeal to two different markets, the full-service, high-fare market and the no-frills, low-fare market. But it forgot to give its low-price service a different name.

In October 1993, Continental confidently introduced its low-price product, CALite, to be backed by a massive $60 million advertising campaign.

But many potential passengers associated CALite with California and not with Continental. Because of the confusion, the CALite name was soon changed to Continental Lite. Either way, the concept was certain to crash. By the time it was shut down in July 1995, Lite had lost $140 million for Continental.

You can't have a multistep focus with a single name like

Continental. For the strategy to work, Continental would have needed a new name totally divorced from the parent company's name. Would Saturn have succeeded if it had been called "Cadillac Lite"? I think not.

Aside from the name, there's another problem. Should Continental have cut itself in half to come up with a second step in its airline ladder? I think not. Why would an airline with less than 10 percent of the domestic market divide its resources to compete with the likes of American and United. That doesn't make sense.

There's another problem, too. Continental itself lacks a focus. What's a Continental? As one passenger said recently, "I know Continental. They're the airline that went bankrupt twice."

Continental has a good name and a checkered past. On what part of the market should the airline focus? They had a good idea in CALite, but they executed it poorly. They could have gone all the way and made Continental a clone of Southwest Airlines. Continental is already a low-cost airline; its unit cost of eight cents per available seat-mile is one of the lowest in the industry.

Continental could have been the first no-frills airline with a "national" name and a national reputation. "Big airline service. Small airline prices."

American Express also illustrates the futility of splitting your forces in the face of more formidable competitors. While the Amex card continues to lose ground against Visa and MasterCard, the company constantly fiddles with variations of its basic card.

The latest is "American Express Optima True Grace," a credit card with a gimmick. With most credit cards, you pay interest on new purchases immediately if you carry a balance. With the True Grace card, the interest doesn't start until twenty-five days after the close of each monthly account cycle, even if the cardholder carries over the balance.

In essence, the company has both a credit card and a charge card under the American Express name, causing the same kind of confusion as CALite and Continental. While the clock ticks, Amex carves out additional steps on its card ladder when they should be concentrating on turning around their basic card. Dividing your force in the face of a superior enemy is almost always a strategic error.

The force, of course, is in the name and reputation of your brand in the mind. With one name spread over two products, you cut the power of the brand in half. With two names, you have potentially twice the power of one name.

That's why a multistep focus should be the goal of every hard-driving company. Once you reach certain limits, the only way to make further progress is by introducing a second brand.

With a single brand, you can never capture more than about 50 percent of a market. As powerful as these brands are, Marlboro has less than 30 percent of the U.S. cigarette market and McDonald's has less than 35 percent of the U.S. sandwich-chain market.

A few brands, of course, have had much higher market shares than that. Both Kodak and Gatorade, decades ago, had 90 percent of their respective U.S. markets. Today, under pressure from Fuji, Kodak's share of the amateur photographic film business has declined to 70 percent. Under pressure from PowerAde and All Sport, Gatorade's share has declined to 80 percent. You can expect these declines to continue.

In a vacuum it's easy to have 100 percent of a market. Jeep once had all of the sports-utility market. Over time, competitors crop up and ultimately hammer the leader's share down to 50 percent or less.

Instead of wringing their hands and trying to get back lost market share, leaders should consider launching second brands at an appropriate time.

What is the appropriate time? Leaders should not respond to competition; leaders should respond to opportunity. Just because you're losing market share is no reason to launch a second brand. More than likely the second brand will turn into a dud because it's a clone of your competition.

Whether your market share is 90 percent or has declined from 90 to 50 percent, the time to launch a second brand is when you find a new focus.

Tambrands found a cellulose-based material that would have the advantages of Playtex's plastic applicator but would be flushable like Tampax.

That was the new focus for the Satin Touch brand. A copycat version of the Playtex product would have been futile. (As a matter of fact, Tambrands did launch such a product under the Tampax name and it did indeed go nowhere.)

Gillette is another good example of a company that has kept its U.S. market share above 50 percent with the judicious use of new brands. Again, the new brands were introduced only when Gillette had honed them into a product with a clear-cut focus.

First there was Trac II, the first twin-bladed razor. Then there was Atra, the first adjustable razor. And finally Sensor, the first shock-absorbent razor. Three brands, three steps on the wet-shaving ladder, one hefty market share in the neighborhood of 65 percent.

A multistep focus works as well in casinos as it does in razors. Compare The Donald with The Stephen. The Donald has three casino hotels in Atlantic City, all named Trump. There's Trump Taj Mahal, Trump Plaza, and Trump Castle.

There are two kinds of gamblers, those that like The Donald and those that don't. What Trump has done is to take his followers and divide them into three markets. Not a very good approach. No wonder The Donald has been in so much financial difficulty over the years.

The Stephen, on the other hand, has three casino hotels in Las Vegas. But Stephen Wynn has given each property a distinct identity. There's Golden Nugget, the downtown place for serious gamblers. There's The Mirage, with the exploding volcano and the white tigers. And the newest is Treasure Island, with a pirate theme.

Now Wynn is building two more casino hotels in Las Vegas, neither of which will be called Mirage, Too or Golden Nugget Jr. There's Bellagio, a high-end property with an Italian theme, and Monte Carlo (a joint venture with Circus Circus), a value-oriented casino hotel with a Victorian theme.

Wynn also won in Atlantic City with the Golden Nugget, a casino hotel he opened in 1980 and sold to Bally Entertainment seven years later. While Wynn owned the property, the Golden Nugget was arguably the best performing, most profitable casino hotel in town.

Since then things have gone downhill fast. Bally, owner of Bally's Park Place, promptly changed the Golden Nugget's name to (what else?) Bally's Grand.

Of the twelve casino hotels in town, Bally's Grand has consistently ranked near the bottom in revenues. It's the Trump problem revisited. You can't have two powerful, successful brands in the same town with the same name. (In different towns, yes.)

You need multiple steps and multiple names in a single-focus strategy. Otherwise you confuse your customers and divide your potential business in half.

Wynn probably wanted to keep the Golden Nugget name for his eventual return to Atlantic City. If so, Bally should have not have bought the property. Without the name most properties aren't worth very much. What would The Coca-Cola Company be worth without the name "Coca-Cola"? Only a small fraction of its $93 billion market valuation.

Another example of a successful multiple-brand company is Hospitality Franchise Systems (now HFS). The world's number one hotel franchiser, HFS doesn't own or operate any hotels. All it does is franchise more than four thousand lodging properties with 420,000 rooms under the Days Inn, Howard Johnson, Park Inn, Ramada, Super 8, and Villager brands. Revenues in a recent year were $313 million and net profits $53 million, a healthy 17 percent.

What is baffling the analysts is the hotel franchiser's recent agreement to buy the Century 21 real estate sales-brokerage franchise from Metropolitan Life for up to $230 million. HFS's CEO sees untapped synergies between the lodging and real estate markets. (Metropolitan Life couldn't seem to find any synergies between real estate and mortgages or real estate and insurance policies.)

Too bad. HFS had a single focus (hotel franchiser) with multiple steps (six brands). Throwing Century 21 into the system unfocuses the organization.

If the real estate business blows in the right direction, they may do well with the Century 21 chain. But what will happen to their core hotel business? Fear of failure in the new business is not the issue. The real issue is the penalty a company could pay for taking management's eyes off its core business, or focus.

Another hotel franchiser (and operator), Marriott International, is beginning to appreciate the value of separate brands. For years it has misused the Marriott name by putting it on a string of different properties: Marriott Hotels, Marriott Suites, Courtyard by Marriott, and the Marriott Marquis hotels in Manhattan and Atlanta. It developed one low-end brand (Fairfield Inns) and bought another (Residence Inns).

Instead of using its Marriott Marquis name at the high end, the company and a group of investors recently bought 49 percent of Ritz-Carlton with an option to purchase the other 51 percent within a few years.

Ritz-Carlton (along with Four Seasons) are the premier names in the hotel business worldwide. With Ritz-Carlton at the top of the ladder, Marriott in the middle, and Fairfield and Residence at the bottom, the company has a powerful multistep focus for the years ahead.

Many companies try to have it both ways. They invent a new name for the new step on the ladder, but then they link the new name to the house name. "Courtyard by Marriott," for example. Is it or isn't it a Marriott hotel?

Answer: It is and it isn't. Confusion by Marriott.

Arthur Andersen & Co. ($3.5 billion in revenues) is the largest accounting firm in the United States. The biggest of the Big Six. But the market for tax and audit services has not been booming, so during the seventies the company accelerated its computer consulting business.

Today Andersen Consulting ($3.2 billion in revenues) is the world leader in systems integration, hardware configuration, software design, and operator training for clients, including half the *Fortune* 500.

Andersen Consulting is a big success story, but the name is a potential anchor that will someday limit their growth. "But we're too big and too successful to change our name" is the usual response of successful companies like Andersen Consulting. Actually, the bigger you are and the more famous you are, the easier it is to establish a new name. The media will do the job for you.

Back in 1972, Standard Oil Company (New Jersey) was concerned about the confusion between its name and the names of other "standard" companies: Standard Oil Company of California, Standard Oil Company (Indiana), and Standard Oil Company (Ohio). So Jersey Standard changed its name to Exxon Corporation.

Thanks to the rash of news stories, Exxon became a household word overnight. Any major change by a major corporation is guaranteed to generate the media coverage necessary to accomplish the change where it really counts, in the mind of the prospect.

Windows 95, New Coke, Newton, Edsel, Exxon, any major new product or name change (good, bad, or indifferent) that captures the imagination of the media will also be driven into the prospect's mind. Exxon's rash act of 1972, according to *New Yorker* writer John Brooks, "overthrew one of the oldest axioms of business theory, that a successful trademark is sacrosanct, and that to change it is suicide."

Change is not the question. Names become obsolete as well as products and sometimes need changing. The question is, when to change a name? In general, names should be changed only when you can also connect "news" to the name change.

The Exxon name change became a big story because the media focused on the millions of dollars the company was spending to change all those signs at its gasoline stations. A corporate name change, without the gas stations, is not much of a story.

When you are establishing a multistep focus, the names you choose are important, but there are also other considerations to keep in mind. Here are six principles to help you develop an effective multistep focus.

1: Focus on a common product area. Passenger cars, computers, chewing gum, these are some common product areas to build a multistep focus around. A collection of brands covering a variety of products is not a multistep focus.

The power of any strategy is its ability to narrowly target a single market. With a multistep approach, you spread-eagle the market and then take a bite out of each segment.

2: Select a single attribute to segment. Price is the most common. But others include distribution, size, age, calories, sex. By segmenting a single attribute only, you reduce the potential confusion between brands.

3: Set up rigid distinctions between brands. Again, price is the easiest attribute to segment because you can put specific numbers on each brand. The rigid distinctions are necessary because you want to create separate identities for each brand. When prices overlap, it's very difficult to create those identities. Most customers confuse Oldsmobile and Buick because their price ranges are quite similar.

4: Create different, not similar, brand names. Companies usually like to create a family of names that are similar. This is a major mistake because it undermines the rigid distinctions you are trying to establish. Look at some of Chevrolet's current family of model names: Cavalier, Camaro, Corsica, Caprice. Unless you own one, few people can differentiate among these car lines.

5: Launch a new brand only when you can create a new category. New brands should not be launched just to "fill a hole" in the line.

The Edsel, you might remember, was launched to fill the gap between Mercury and Lincoln. Unfortunately for Ford, there was no gap in the marketplace for Edsel to fill.

6: Keep control of the brands at the highest level. If you don't, you'll find that your carefully organized multistep focus will slowly fall apart.

Marketing people love to tinker. If you don't keep the marketing folks in line, they will launch a multitude of line extensions that will destroy your multistep focus before you can say, "Where have you been, Alfred Sloan? We need you back."

DISCIPLINING A DINOSAUR

Few companies have gone through the kind of wrenching changes that have devastated IBM.

In the past few years nearly half its workforce has been dismissed. Not only are the people gone, the buildings are, too. In 1994 alone, IBM sold close to $2 billion worth of real estate.

A decade ago, IBM was one of the most admired, best managed corporations in the world. Today, IBM is a company struggling to find itself. What went wrong at the International Business Machines Corporation?

Icon worship. Whenever IBM introduced a new product, the company automatically put the IBM name on it. What Big Blue overlooked was the fact that the explosive growth of the computer industry was rapidly segmenting the market. A computer was no longer just a computer.

IBM should have used the Sloan strategy. Multiple steps in a single computer focus. IBM, of course, was the mainframe name.

As new market segments developed, IBM should have used a different brand name for each segment, all under the IBM corporate umbrella, much like General Motors serves as the corporate umbrella for Chevrolet, Pontiac, Oldsmobile, Buick, and Cadillac.

The first opportunity to use a second brand was the minicomputer. Introduced by Digital Equipment Corporation, the minicomputer was perceived by IBM to be competitive with the mainframe. Therein lies the classic dilemma for a company like IBM. Do we fight the minicomputer or do we adopt it? IBM, to their regret, chose to fight.

A second brand neatly sidesteps the question. The second brand endorses the minicomputer concept, leaving the mainframe IBM brand free to fight the concept. It's a horse race in which the market decides the winner. With a two-brand strategy, IBM would have had a bet on both horses.

Many companies agonize over similar situations. They waste time by appointing task forces to study the competitive development. Will the new concept take over the market or is it just a flash in the pan?

It doesn't matter. (Who can foretell the future anyway?) A leader should defend its leadership by launching a second brand to protect itself from a serious competitive move that involves a new category of product that could undermine the leader's core brand. It should be a second brand, however, because launching the new concept under the base brand "unfocuses" the base brand.

Left without serious competition, Digital Equipment made rapid progress and soon became a $14 billion company, the second largest computer company in the world. (But DEC was soon to make the same mistake that IBM did.)

The second opportunity to launch a new brand was in August 1981 when IBM introduced the PC. This was perhaps the biggest single mistake in IBM's history. Not the launch of the product, but the failure to give the new product a new name.

The conditions were perfect for a new brand. Its sixteen-bit architecture made the PC the first *business* personal computer. The three leading products on the market (Radio Shack TRS-80, Apple II, and Commodore Pet) were eight-bit machines, widely perceived to be *home* personal computers.

The new category (business personal computers) exploded. And because IBM was first in the new category, IBM's sales exploded, too. Two years later IBM was the leading personal computer brand, with 21 percent of the market.

Furthermore, IBM had built up a head of steam that was awesome to behold. *Time* magazine put IBM on its July 11, 1983, cover with the headline, "The Colossus That Works."

Things aren't always what they seem to be. Nothing unfocuses a Colossus quite so much as a successful product outside its core product area. If the PC had failed, that would have been the end of it and IBM would have continued to be perceived as a powerful

mainframe company. But success is another matter. Now the name
IBM had to carry the burden of being a computer company in the
broadest sense of the word.

You can imagine what was in the minds of IBM's management at
the time. "If it's a computer, we make it, we market it, we write software for it, we maintain it, and we finance it. And if it's a computer
problem, we consult with you about it."

Lots of companies develop software, semiconductors, PCs, networks, and so on. "IBM alone develops all these, and more," CEO
Lou Gerstner said recently. IBM alone? This should give every
IBMer the shivers. What Lou Gerstner is saying is that IBM doesn't
need a focus. That IBM's strength is the fact that it makes everything. "Whatever you need, we got it."

This kind of thinking led to Systems Applications Architecture, a
massive internal effort at IBM driven by convergence philosophy. Five
software layers (user interface, applications, applications enabling,
communications, and systems control) were to be put on top of three
fundamentally incompatible computer systems (mainframe, midrange,
and PC). SAA was conceived as a system to provide "seamless, easy
solutions that tie products together."

The media pushed IBM to think big. According to the *New York
Times,* IBM is poised "to take advantage of the coming convergence
of whole industries, including television, music, publishing, and
computing. . . . IBM's strongest suit in the expected convergence of
cable and telephone networks with computer and television manufacturers may be technology that it has developed to create extremely
high-speed networks."

But technologies don't converge, they divide. And so SAA silently
faded away, another victim of the convergence follies. By 1992
IBM's all-embracing Systems Application Architecture was dead in
the water. It's too bad the death of SAA didn't get the publicity of its
launch. It might have deterred some companies from following the
same path.

One influential publication did mark SAA's passing with this per-
ceptive thought: "The 1985 decision to impose Systems Application
Architecture," wrote *Information Week* in its January 11, 1993,
issue, "is the direct cause of IBM's downfall." (If you can't tie computers together, how are you going to combine entire industries?)

While IBM was trying to tie things together, the market was dividing, a result that could have been expected based on the principle of division. Competitors were creating new computer categories that were going to make IBM's job extremely difficult.

In particular, the 1982 introduction of the UNIX workstation by Sun Microsystems. Sun did for the engineering community what the PC did for the business community: provide a low-cost computer so that each person could have his or her own individual machine.

This was the third opportunity for IBM to launch a new brand. But they didn't.

Without serious opposition from IBM, Sun Microsystems grew rapidly. In the process Sun became a $5 billion company that dominated the UNIX engineering workstation category.

It was the personal computer opportunity, though, that is the most tragic. This is the category that IBM pioneered. This is the category that has grown to dominate the computer business. Even today IBM's $9.5-billion-a-year PC operation is the company's biggest hardware unit.

Size is not synonymous with success. Focus is. IBM is ten times as big as Microsoft, but Microsoft has a focus and IBM does not. Today, IBM's share of the worldwide personal computer market is down to about 10 percent.

Even worse, IBM has lost its number one position in personal computers and will never get it back. The mantle of leadership has fallen on Compaq.

Nor is IBM awash in PC profits. The "seriously messed-up PC division" is what *Business Week* calls the IBM operation and estimates its 1994 operating loss at $1 billion. (That same year Compaq had sales of almost $11 billion and net income of $867 million.)

What went wrong? In the mind of the prospect, IBM was a mainframe company and still is. IBM lost its focus by introducing an IBM personal computer. It should have used a second brand.

It's what Apple Computer did. Apple was a home personal computer that couldn't make the transition to the office. So in 1984 Apple launched a new brand (Macintosh) that became Apple's entry into the office.

Unfortunately, IBM and the clones got there first. Ultimately, Macintosh found a niche with a first of its own, desktop publishing. But nothing can replace being first in the office, not even a better product like the Macintosh.

The name is the anchor that keeps IBM from achieving its PC goals in the face of its more focused competition. But it's probably asking too much for insiders to see the connection.

To see clearly you need distance and objectivity. Insiders invariably see problems in terms of products and operating difficulties. "We had a business which had never functioned correctly," says Rick Thoman, the new head of the IBM Personal Computer Company.

So, should IBM change the name of its Personal Computer Company? Of course not. Timing is everything in life. You can't go home again and you can't go back to the past and change a name. IBM has to play the computer game with the cards it has dealt itself. It can't go back and reshuffle the deck.

Look what happens when it tries. In addition to the name mistake, IBM made two major technical errors when it introduced the PC. It let Microsoft control the operating system, the heart of the software, and it let Intel control the microprocessor chip, the heart of the hardware.

To correct these errors, IBM introduced the OS/2 operating system and the PowerPC chip. So far it has spent some $2 billion on the new operating system (currently called OS/2 Warp) to replace MS-DOS (called Windows 95 in its latest iteration). The PowerPC chip, developed in cooperation with Apple and Motorola, represents an equally sizable investment.

Neither is likely to be successful. Timing is everything. "Executives spend more of their time trying to unmake the past," writes Peter Drucker, "than on anything else."

In a step that further contributes to the unfocusing of IBM, the company recently created a new consumer division to focus on the home computer business, a market that Packard Bell dominates. As a minimum IBM should focus on the business customer, not the home consumer. A narrower focus is an advantage, not a disadvantage.

What else should IBM do? If it can't go back and develop the multistep focus it sorely needs today, what can IBM do instead?

First of all, it should take a hard look at the computer industry. Contrary to convergence gospel, the industry itself has divided into three segments: hardware, software, and chips.

In general, hardware companies have not done well in software or chips. Witness IBM's failure to get OS/2 Warp up to speed. Neither have the software companies done well in hardware or chips. Microsoft has dabbled in hardware with few tangible successes.

The chip companies, on the other hand, have remained chip companies, although many have tried to get into the hardware business. What leads companies like Intel and Motorola down the garden path is the quality axiom, the belief that all they have to do to be successful is to launch a better product.

But the problem is not the product, the problem is the perception in the customer's mind. A chip company doesn't have credibility as a computer manufacturer even though they have all the engineering and manufacturing skills they need. After all, they are already making the guts of the product.

Don't confuse a focus with the facts. A focus exists in the mind of the customer and it drives your business. (You might have all the facts on your side as you watch your business go down the drain.)

In software IBM is twice as big as Microsoft. In 1994, Microsoft had less than $5 billion in software sales, while IBM had $11.3 billion. Roughly half of IBM's business is hardware, the other half is software, services, maintenance, and finance. In spite of this division of revenues, IBM should focus on hardware.

What you focus on, what you sell, and what you make money on can be three different things. The average new-car dealer in the United States makes less than 20 percent of its profits on new cars. Service and used cars account for more than 80 percent of a dealer's profits. Should the dealer focus on service? Or used cars? Of course not. The dealer should focus on new cars.

New cars drive both the dealer's service business and the dealer's used-car business. (You don't have a service business unless you sell new cars. And you don't have a used-car business either without the trade-ins.) The same thing is true at IBM. Its hardware sales drive both its software and service businesses.

IBM should focus on hardware. The software and service businesses follow the hardware. (It should come as no surprise that 80 percent of IBM's software sales are for mainframes and midrange computers.) Whenever IBM has tried to make it in personal computer software, the company has come up a cropper.

Wails the *Wall Street Journal* recently: "It's one of the great mysteries of the computer industry: Why has the world's biggest computer maker—the company that practically created the personal computer market—floundered in PC software? Some of IBM's failures include: Top View, an early windowing system for DOS. DisplayWrite, a character-based word processor, never upgraded to graphical. OfficeVision, a strategy for linking PCs and PC applications to host-based systems. LAN Server, a network operating system."

Nor have Taligent and Kaleida, IBM's highly promoted joint software ventures with Apple, burned up the track. And then, of course, there's OS/2 Warp.

OS/2 continues to win kudos from the trade press. In 1994, *Infoworld* named OS/2 Warp as its "Product of the Year" in the operating system category. In 1995, *PC World* also named it "Product of the Year." Maybe, just maybe, OS/2 Warp is a better product than Windows 95. Does it matter?

The latest scheme is called Workplace OS. This is software that allows the PowerPC system to run multiple operating systems, including Windows and MS-DOS. Maybe, just maybe, Workplace OS is a great piece of software. Does it matter?

IBM has also announced its intentions to be a "serious player" in the interactive multimedia market. It has already launched ten CD-ROMs and has plans for a dozen more. Its highest hopes are on the "Adventures of Hyperman," a CD-ROM and also a Saturday morning CBS cartoon show. We'll see.

The $3.5 billion purchase of Lotus is the latest act in the IBM Software Follies. Forget 1–2–3, which is never going to get back on top. What about the crown jewel, Notes?

Make a note. Lotus will turn out to be an unwise purchase for IBM. It will rank right up there with IBM's acquisition of Rolm or AT&T's acquisition of NCR. It's a question of focus. Whether a computer company buys a telephone company or a telephone company buys a computer company, the results are the same. You wind up with an unfocused mess.

Customers echo the same concern. "Right now, Notes is the absolute focus of attention of Jim Manzi and the Lotus organization," says Charlie Paulk, chief information officer for Andersen Consulting, which has twenty thousand Notes users. But if Notes is swallowed up by IBM, "Does it continue to get that focus?"

It doesn't have the absolute focus of attention of Jim Manzi anymore. He recently resigned from IBM.

The company that should have bought Lotus is Microsoft, although the Justice Department, I'm sure, would not have agreed. IBM should have been concerned that the department didn't protest the Lotus deal. Unless the government objects, it's probably not a good acquisition.

When Lou Gerstner arrived at IBM in 1993, he immediately undertook a whirlwind tour of the company, its people, its facilities, and even its customers. Then he proceeded to fix things. One by one, he reviewed each operation and decided what had to be done.

This is the classic method used by turnaround specialists. Put each operation under a microscope and make a decision about what to do. With the emphasis, of course, on downsizing and cost reduction. In truth, IBM has come down considerably in both size and expenses.

The stock is up and IBM has started to make money again, although not in the same proportion to sales as in the past.

What IBM needs for the long term, however, is not a house cleaning but a focus. IBM used to stand for something (mainframe computers). Today IBM sells everything even remotely related to computers, from laptops at Radio Shack to multiyear consulting contracts with *Fortune* 500 firms.

The Gerstner way is unlikely to uncover an IBM focus. The best he can hope for is a return to marginal profitability. IBM is likely to become another Sears. A lumbering, slow-moving, barely profitable giant without much hope for the future.

Is there a better way? I think so. Here is an outline of a focused approach to the IBM problem.

First of all, forget about focusing on a single line of products or a single class of customers. IBM is too big and too complex for this strategy to work. Also, forget about establishing a series of brands to turn IBM into another General Motors, a General Computers Corporation, if you will. It's too late for this strategy to work.

Also, forget about building every product around a single line of chips, such as the PowerPC (as has been suggested by some consultants and even Lou Gerstner himself). This is an artificial solution that has no long-term future. What happens when the PowerPC chip becomes obsolete? Like the One-Horse Shay, does IBM fall apart all at once?

If you can't find a focus inside the company, look on the outside.

Who is IBM's enemy? Most business analysts would probably agree that Microsoft fills this role very well. One reason IBM poured so much money into OS/2 was the goal of blocking Microsoft's Windows 95 and Windows NT.

The fastest way to find a focus is to find an enemy. Business is competition. When you have isolated the enemy, you have also identified your problem. And a problem well stated is half solved.

When you try to find your focus inside your own company, you tend to get out a big ribbon and wrap up everything in one neat package. Attractive inside the company maybe, but useless in competing with strongly established competitors on the outside. "We're going to be the company that has the capacity to deliver total solutions," says Lou Gerstner, "and a multiproduct, multisector approach to the market."

Does any customer ever call a computer company and say, "I want a multiproduct, multisector, total solution to my problem?" Customers don't think like that; customers don't talk like that.

If Microsoft controls the operating system, Microsoft controls the application software, too. The hardware becomes a commodity, and IBM is in a difficult spot. Microsoft is definitely the enemy.

One of the criticisms of IBM is that they didn't change fast enough. Change may keep a company producing the latest hot product, but change itself isn't necessarily a benefit. Change is often the primary cause of a company's problems. Unless fashion is your focus, chasing the latest fad is a sure formula for failure.

Change, however, is related to the one aspect of IBM's problem that some analysts have overlooked. IBM has been the traditional leader of the computer industry. When changes occurred, IBM has generally been the company to call the tune. "We are going to continue to be an industry leader," says Lou Gerstner, and I think in this respect he is right on.

There's an old truism: "If you want to be the market leader, you have to lead the market." Where is IBM leading the market?

That's the weakness of a multiproduct, multisector approach. "Whatever you want to buy, we got" is not a leadership approach. Leaders should tell customers what to buy because they have a vision of the future. They are leaders.

"Nobody ever got fired for buying from IBM." Why? Because IBM told you what to buy and they were almost never wrong. IBM was the leader.

It's this sense of direction that's missing from IBM's current approach. Where is the industry headed? IBM should set the direction for the industry and then push in that direction. That's what leadership is all about, isn't it?

If Microsoft is the enemy, what's the issue for the computer industry? For what single aspect of the computer industry can IBM set direction?

Forget the desktop. That battle has been lost to Microsoft and Intel. "If you're losing the battle, switch the battlefield."

Forget mainframes. Global mainframe sales peaked in 1989 and have declined by about 50 percent since then.

What's left is the mushy middle, the world of client-server and a possible opportunity for IBM. This is the area that Microsoft is trying to move into with an operating system called Windows NT (for New Technology). Someday, the theory goes, Microsoft will merge Windows 95 with Windows NT and "own" the entire computer industry from top to bottom. At least that's the theory.

Microsoft has made progress. Hewlett-Packard, an important supplier of client-server hardware, already supports both Windows NT and UNIX, the industry's "open" operating system. Digital Equipment has jumped on the NT bandwagon. Even IBM, as part of its "all things for everybody" policy, has included NT on some of its offerings. The only major holdout is Sun Microsystems.

What should IBM focus on? My suggestion would be "open." IBM should draw a line in the sand and say that Windows is a good operating system for the desktop, but that client-server computing needs an operating system that is "industrial strength."

Furthermore, the operating system should not be "proprietary," in control of a single supplier. It should be "open." In other words, the operating system should be UNIX, the computer industry's only open system.

But isn't it too late? Isn't Microsoft and its Windows operating system in one form or another bound to lock up the entire computer industry, from bottom to top?

Who knows? (SAA in its day was also perceived to be inevitable.)

Nobody can predict the future. But based on the principle of division there's hope that the industry will divide with Windows on the desktop and a more robust operating system like UNIX on the client-server or enterprise side.

What happens also depends on what individual companies do. If all the players accept the inevitability of a Windows solution, then that's what will happen. If, on the other hand, a leader arises that can take the industry in a different direction, then that creates another possibility.

"Open" is a powerful concept for a computer leader to own. The computer buyer does not want to go back to the past, where all computer systems were "proprietary." No matter what company you did business with, you wound up locked into a single supplier. It was difficult to change computer vendors without writing off your investment.

Take Macintosh. As marvelous as the Mac is, the product is slowly dying as a general business computer. Nobody got fired for buying IBM, but the *Fortune* 500 purchasing agent who bought Macintoshes doesn't sleep too well at night. Dataquest forecasts that Apple's market share will be sliced in half over the next five years.

"Open" is a powerful word for IBM to own because it allows them to paint the Microsoft enemy as "closed." That also shifts the battlefield from "Which is the better operating system?" to "Which system is open and which system is proprietary?" It's hard to argue that a closed system in theory is better than an open system.

Focusing on "open" would cause problems. First of all, IBM would have to shut down OS/2, its own proprietary system. That's not necessarily bad. It would keep IBM from throwing more good money after bad.

Second, it would mean that IBM would have to deal with the many "flavors" of UNIX. It's a tough problem, but for the open concept to really take off, it needs to focus on one variation that would be used by everyone.

But hey, that's what leaders are for. To set direction and then to convince the followers to follow. You can't be a leader without followers. The UNIX issue is ideal for IBM to demonstrate its leadership. IBM should put its weight behind the "open" movement and push for a single flavor of UNIX.

Leaders should lead. And they should lead in a direction that benefits the majority of the industry, not just the leader. By promoting open systems, IBM would have the support of most of the computer industry, including the media. And once again, customers would buy from IBM because they have confidence in the direction IBM is taking the industry.

That's the theory and that's the word. Powerful ideas are usually utterly simple. "Safety" for Volvo. "Overnight" for Federal Express. "Open" for IBM.

But simple ideas can be awfully difficult to sell. Can you imagine the reaction I would get if I presented this idea to Lou Gerstner and his staff?

"I have the answer to your problem, Mr. Gerstner. I have the word that will turn around your $60 billion company."

"What is that word, Mr. Ries?"

"Open."

"Next consultant, please."

CROSSING THE TRENCH

Kaizen is a Japanese word meaning continuous, incremental improvement. While *kaizen* can work wonders on the manufacturing line, it can be a disaster in the boardroom.

Continuous, incremental improvement is usually translated by managers into the concept of keeping up with the market. "Wherever the market goes, we will go" is the normal expression of this philosophy.

It's a trap. The market never goes anywhere all on its own. Nobody ever said they wanted an alkaline battery when the only batteries on the market were zinc-carbon. Nobody ever asked for light beer, front-wheel-drive automobiles, desktop computers, videocassette recorders, oversized tennis racquets, acetaminophen, ibuprofen, or naproxen sodium when these products weren't on the market.

Not only were they not asked for, these products were almost totally ignored by most prospective customers until the owners of these products found a winning formula. Products lead and sometimes the market follows and sometimes the market doesn't.

When you are following the market, you are following one or more market leaders, and by then it's too late to be the leader yourself. You have lost the opportunity to be a big winner.

Timing is critical. Too early and you're a John the Baptist in the Wilderness. Too late and you're an also-ran. Success is almost always a question of being in the right place with the right product with the right name at the right time.

Success is having the right strategy to "cross the trench."

Years ago, Bayer aspirin was the number one over-the-counter pharmaceutical drug. Bayer and its competitors practiced *kaizen*, although they probably didn't call it that. They made continuous improvements in the product, the packaging, the advertising, the merchandising, the displays.

Anacin practiced *kaizen*. The product contained a combination of ingredients, including aspirin, that gave you "fast, fast, fast relief."

Bufferin practiced *kaizen*. The product had a special coating on the aspirin that made it "stomach friendly" and "twice as fast as aspirin."

So who won the aspirin battle? Bayer, the product that invented the category, or Anacin, the combination of ingredients, or Bufferin, the buffered aspirin?

None of the above. The winning pain reliever is Tylenol, the first acetaminophen.

That's the way business is. In between each generation is a trench. First there was the aspirin generation, dominated by Bayer, then the acetaminophen generation, dominated by Johnson & Johnson with its Tylenol brand. Crossing that trench is the most difficult job in management.

From time to time companies have tried to topple Tylenol. Bristol-Myers tried it with Datril, touted as just as good as Tylenol but at half the price. Tylenol dropped its price and Datril more or less disappeared.

Low price by itself is almost never a good attribute to focus on. Only when the low price is the natural result of some other attribute of the product does low price work as a motivating factor.

At $1,280, the Volkswagen Beetle was hundreds of dollars cheaper than the cheapest American cars in 1956, yet buyers bought the car for its durability and reliability. Its low price was the natural result of its practical, no-nonsense, unchanging styling.

When a product is cheaper than its competition, prospects ask themselves, "Why?" In Volkswagen's case, the answer was obvious. It was small, it was ugly, it was reliable. That's the reason the car was inexpensive. Without a reason to be cheap, prospects think the product must not be any good.

The next trench in the analgesic category is the one between ibuprofen and acetaminophen. Getting on the other side first was

American Home Products with its Advil brand. Advil is slowly, but surely, doing to Tylenol what Tylenol did to Bayer. And there's not much that Johnson & Johnson can do about it, except to fight a tenacious rearguard action.

The next trench is the one between naproxen sodium and ibuprofen. On the other side of the trench is Procter & Gamble with its Aleve brand. Three months after its launch, Aleve had about half the market share of Advil. That's a surprisingly strong showing in the fiercely competitive over-the-counter drug category.

One, two, three, four. Bayer, Johnson & Johnson, American Home Products, Procter & Gamble. You see this same pattern over and over again. One company "owns" the market and then is replaced by a next-generation product from another company. The pattern keeps repeating itself.

Why does the next-generation product almost never come from the previous generation?

It's the trench phenomenon. The leader thinks they can extend their leader product into the next generation. It seldom happens.

Atari was the leader in video games. As a matter of fact, Atari *was* the video game market. Then the company moved, or tried to move, the Atari brand into personal computers. The trench between video games and computers was too much of an obstacle.

Meanwhile narrowly focused Nintendo took over the video game market with a next-generation product (and next-generation name). What Nintendo did to Atari, Sega did to Nintendo, and they did it with a next-generation approach.

The essence of the Sega approach was that its sixteen-bit system was superior to Nintendo's eight-bit system. Many companies are inclined to ignore the powerful implications of a simple strategy like sixteen bits versus eight bits. Since the buyer can't see, feel, or taste the eight extra bits, the manufacturer is tempted to ignore their existence as a mere technical detail. Not true.

The eight extra bits were the tools that helped Sega dig the next-generation trench. "Why get stuck with a Nintendo eight-bit machine when you can buy a Sega sixteen-bit machine?" It's a powerful approach.

Next up is the Sony PlayStation. With its thirty-two-bit technology and CD-ROM storage, the Sony machine is poised to repeat the process. The Sony name is weak because it's a line-extension name and the PlayStation name is generic, but at least it's a "fresh" name in the category, a name not tarnished by an eight- or a sixteen-bit past. The PlayStation should do well.

When Sega and Nintendo jump into the thirty-two-bit category, they will have two strikes against them. They will be late, and they will be burdened with sixteen-bit names. It's going to be difficult for the two current leaders to cross the trench.

Why didn't the 3DO Interactive Multiplayer, a thirty-two-bit video game player, go anywhere? Backed by AT&T, Time Warner, and Matsushita, the company received stacks of favorable press and few sales. One reason is the name, another candidate for "truly terrible name of all time," right alongside the MITS Altair 8800, the world's first personal computer.

Another reason is the price. The launch price of $699 put the 3DO machine in a different category than the under $200 Nintendo and Sega machines. Since reduced to $399, the 3-DO Interactive Multiplayer has not been able to escape its perception as a specialty video game, not a "mainstream" product. You never get a second chance to make a first impression.

The next-generation concept is a template that can be used by almost any company. Leadership in an industry is almost never achieved by a conventional "better and cheaper" strategy. It's almost always achieved by a next-generation approach.

Yet companies continue to pour money down the "better and cheaper" rathole. The conventional approach usually involves two stages, one outside and one inside. (1) The outside stage consists of "benchmarking" the product against the competition to get the quality up. (2) The inside stage consists of "reengineering" the manufacturing process in order to get the costs down. Result: a better and cheaper product than the competition.

Meanwhile, the farsighted competitor is building a strong beachhead on the other side of the trench. Eveready was making better batteries (heavy-duty and extra heavy-duty) on the zinc-carbon side of the trench while Duracell was building a fortress on the alkaline side. Eveready lost its leadership not to a better zinc-carbon battery but to an alkaline battery.

Already you can see a new territory developing on the far side of the alkaline trench. That territory is called "lithium," and so far no company has staked it out with a new brand. Why are the battery companies missing the lithium boat? The opportunities are often self-evident years in advance.

IBM dominated the office typewriter business while Wang was building a powerful stronghold on the word-processing side of the trench, a stronghold that unfortunately didn't last very long. Wang lost its leadership not to a better word processor but to a personal computer.

Didn't Wang also make personal computers? Sure, but you can't cross a trench with the same name. The customer keeps you stranded on the near side of the trench whether you want to be or not.

In the mind Wang was a word processor. Therefore Wang could not become a personal computer. Eveready was a zinc-carbon or flashlight brand, therefore it couldn't become an alkaline brand.

Volkswagen was a small, ugly, reliable car. Therefore, VW couldn't cross the trench into larger, more stylish cars.

Didn't IBM cross the trench into personal computers? Initially, yes, because they were first in the office market and because they were IBM, the eight-hundred-pound gorilla. But you'll notice their leadership hasn't lasted very long.

When you carry your name across a trench, the baggage you have to carry with you is enormous. You might meet with some initial success, but in the long run the lack of focus can be deadly. Again, look at the personal computer market.

AT&T, Digital Equipment, Hewlett-Packard, IBM, Xerox, and other established multibillion-dollar companies have launched personal computer lines. And so who is the world's largest maker of personal computers?

Compaq, the one company that had no baggage to carry across the trench. In other words, Compaq has a personal computer focus, the others do not. So naturally Compaq is in a stronger position to capture the leadership of the category than are the big brands.

This is contrary to conventional thinking. IBM, the bigger, older company, is thought to be a better brand than Compaq. So if Compaq outsells IBM in personal computers, then the difference has to be in either the product, the pricing, or the marketing. Maybe all three. This is the heart of the matter.

What I'm suggesting is that the difference is in the focus. Compaq, the narrowly focused company, has the powerful perception of a specialist. IBM does not. IBM is a generalist. Over the long term, business is not a battle of products, it's a battle of focus, and the narrowly focused company is generally the winner.

This is a circular argument that always comes back to the same issue: What about the product? Surely product quality has something to do with sales success. If Compaq computers couldn't compute, the focus issue would be mute.

Competition is the great equalizer. Walk into a computer store and compare various brands. Do you notice any big differences? Ask questions of the sales representative. Are you left with any big quality differences in the brands?

Competition is intense. Companies copy the best features of their competitors' products on a regular basis. Look at the Macintosh operating system, which was systematically copied by Microsoft, first with Windows, then with Windows 95. Every product development that has customer acceptance ultimately gets copied by the competition.

The only thing competition can't copy is the name. It's against the law. So when products are roughly equal, the only significant difference is the name. And customers think the specialist makes a better product than the generalist.

Then the specialist becomes the largest selling brand in the category, again reinforcing the better product perception. Because, of course, customers believe the largest selling brand is the better quality product.

The way to fight the specialist is to set up a new category of your own and then dig a trench that blocks the generalists and gives you time to dominate the new category before other specialist competition develops.

Sometimes the specialists never do arrive, which allows the category to be dominated by a generalist. When this happens, companies laud the power of line extension, forgetting that in the land of the blind, the one-eyed brand is king.

Look at light beer, which now accounts for 43 percent of total U.S. beer volume. The first major light beer was Miller Lite, introduced nationally in 1975. Then came a raft of other light beers, all line extensions: Schlitz Light, Stroh Light, Coors Light, Michelob Light. It wasn't until 1982 that Anheuser-Busch introduced Bud Light.

Miller Lite had the advantage of being first to cross the trench from regular into light beer. It also had the advantage of a powerful advertising program, widely considered to the most popular beer commercials ever.

Featuring ex-athletes arguing over the merits of Miller Lite, the advertising focused on one of the great tag lines of all time, "Tastes great. Less filling." Its only disadvantage was that it was a line extension. Miller tried to have a barrel on both sides of the beer trench.

So what is the best-selling light beer in America today? The first brand in the category? No. The brand with the most memorable advertising? No. The best-selling light beer in America today is Bud Light by a margin of 10 percent, and that margin is increasing every year. Why? Because Budweiser is the largest selling regular brand of beer.

When beer drinkers cross the trench from regular to light, their first inclination is to buy a brand that is the light-beer specialist. Finding none, they settle for the light version of their regular beer.

Since Budweiser is the largest selling regular beer, Bud Light was certain to become the largest selling light beer . . . in the absence of focused competition.

(The success of Bud Light is a mixed blessing for Anheuser-Busch. Sales of regular Budweiser have been declining every year, which is just what you might expect as a result of the Bud Light line extension.)

IBM is the largest selling mainframe computer brand by a wide margin. If there were no Compaqs, no Apples, no Packard Bells, no focused competition, then IBM would be the largest selling personal computer brand by a wide margin.

If you're the leader and you believe in line extension, then the strategy to follow is to get all your competitors to also make the same mistake. (If they're foolish enough to do so.)

Of the forty largest selling light-beer brands in America, only two are not line extensions. But both use "light" in their names, which is a severe disadvantage since it implies that they are line extensions. In spite of their defects, both have done well.

One is a domestic brand introduced with an absolutely awful name, "Anheuser-Busch Natural Light." Now called "Natural Light," it's the fourth largest selling light beer (after Bud Light, Miller Lite, and Coors Light).

The other is an imported brand, "Amstel Light," which as you might expect has become the largest selling imported light beer.

Crossing the trench clearly requires a second name or brand. Yet many companies stubbornly resist this approach. In some cases they would rather use their poor corporate name than invent a new name with potential. (At least IBM had a great name when they decided to use it on personal computers.)

Take Western Union in the mid-eighties. The telegram was all but dead. The Mailgram was mired in a muddled joint-management arrangement with the U.S. Postal Service. And Telex was just starting its long slide because of competition from facsimile technology.

The 1984 breakup of Ma Bell created an opportunity for Western Union, a company with a past but not much of a future. Western Union had the facilities, the experience, and the people to compete in the long-distance telephone market. It was a booming market, and many companies were going to benefit. (MCI stock bought in 1980 for $1,000 was worth $29,000 a decade later.)

But not Western Union. The corporation confidently launched its long-distance telephone service under the (what else?) Western Union name, but the business went nowhere. By 1988, Western Union had taken a $600 million charge to leave the long-distance phone business.

"We don't want to be in a business where we are a very small player in a large market," said CEO Robert Amman in announcing the write-off. "How can we possibly have the same cost structure as AT&T? There's no way we can compete with AT&T and expect to be profitable."

Size, cost structure, and other tangible factors are the reasons normally given for a company's failure to penetrate a market. Almost nobody says, "We had the wrong name." But the truth is, you can't cross the telephone trench with a telegram name.

Even worse, customers consider the Western Union name to be hopelessly old-fashioned. The one Western Union business that still works is wire transfer of money, an old-fashioned concept in today's cashless economy.

When the parent company (New Valley) went bankrupt, the Western Union money-transfer operation was sold for an astonishing $1.2 billion.

There's a blind spot in management's eyes. "We'd never do that" is the universal response to the Western Union story. "We'd never try to get into the telephone business with a telegram name like Western Union."

Of course, their own name is a different matter. "On the other hand, we have a great company name that can be used on many different products. As a matter of fact, we don't use it on enough products. We could make a lot more money if we line-extended the name."

- Donald Trump thought so, too. He still does.

- IBM thought so. They still do.

- AT&T thought so. They're having second thoughts.

Call it loyalty or self-love, there's a feeling you get in attending corporate meetings in America today. Every major corporation thinks it has a great name, universally respected by millions of customers around the world.

And they probably do. But the way to strengthen a name is by narrowing the focus. When you broaden the focus, you weaken the name.

Take Tektronix, the world's largest maker of oscilloscopes. Here's a company that has been panting to get into the computer business. First with workstations and now with color printers, with little success. Tektronix spent upwards of $150 million to enter the fast-growing computer-aided-engineering business, an operation it got rid of for just $5 million.

Tektronix? To cross the trench from oscilloscopes to computers would require two things: (1) an idea or concept the company can be first in, and (2) a new name.

Yet neither of these two critical elements gets much attention in a typical corporation. The emphasis is generally on developing a better product that presumably sells itself.

Many management consultants have pointed out that rising stars of tomorrow-type businesses are almost never the same as the stars of today's more mundane industries. It's not that today's mainstream companies lack the talent or the ideas. The typical *Fortune* 500 corporation is usually brimming over with new product concepts, too many to pursue efficiently.

Very few of these concepts get airborne, because management refuses to see the trench between today's business and tomorrow's opportunity. Crossing the trench is a chief executive's biggest challenge. Many of them are falling short.

It's easy to misread this issue. You probably know of companies that have used their existing names to cross a trench and achieve leadership in a new industry. They tend to be of two types.

The first type is the company that finds the next-generation territory unoccupied. It's like a military invasion. It's easy to take an undefended beach. Furthermore, if the competition doesn't move in quickly, the invader has time to strengthen its defenses.

Then, if competition also uses a line-extended name, the winner has to be a company that used an existing name to cross the trench.

The second type is the anonymous company. Your company might have been around for decades, yet if few people know your name, it's a new name as far as the next-generation territory is concerned. Anonymity is a resource when planning a next-generation move. It's better to be an unknown company than to be known for the wrong thing.

Marlboro has become the largest selling cigarette in the world by virtue of its cowboys and its "masculine" approach. Yet many strategists are only too happy to point out that at one time, Marlboro was a woman's cigarette. Conclusion: It's easy to move from one territory to another, it's easy to cross a trench.

Well, Marlboro was and it wasn't. It literally was a woman's cigarette, except that few people knew that. It had the advantage of anonymity, so it could easily move to seize the masculine ground.

Would you rather have a well-known name or an unknown name? It all depends upon what you want to do with it.

If you're strongly embedded in the mind with one product or concept (like Xerox in copiers), it's hard to use that well-known name to cross the trench into a new product like computers.

Often a company will use its name as its *only* weapon in a new product area. "If we don't use our well-known name on this new product," the CEO will say, "it can't possibly succeed." Which could be right. The company might not have any other angle to exploit except the name.

Rather than launching a line-extended product that has no chance of success (AT&T computers), the company should go back to the drawing board to see if it can come up with a new angle. And, of course, a new name to match the new angle.

Time creates opportunities. Sometimes you can be successful not because you're better but because you're younger. Pierre Cardin was the big name in men's fashions until Ralph Lauren came along. Now Tommy Hilfiger is in the process of becoming the next big name in the fashion industry.

In four years, Hilfiger's sales jumped nearly sixfold, to $321 million. Net income has been increasing even faster, to $41 million.

Tommy's timing was just right. He wasn't too early and he wasn't too late. As long as enough time has passed, there's always an opportunity for a new company to move in and proclaim themselves to be a next-generation company.

But the easiest way to seize the leadership of an industry is to introduce technological change that insulates your company from the previous leader.

One-hundred-year-old Schwinn used to own the U.S. bicycle market, with as much as 25 percent of the business. Western Union messengers used Schwinns to deliver telegrams. (When I was a kid, if you had a Schwinn, you were the luckiest kid in the world.)

Then in 1974 Gary Fisher built the first off-road bike with a wide gear range, heavy-duty braking, thumb shifters, and motorcycle brake levers. He dubbed his creation the "mountain bike," and Schwinn has never been the same.

A host of mountain-bike manufacturers rode into the market. Each of the three current leaders had an angle. Trek pioneered carbon-fiber frames. Cannondale checked in with aluminum-frame bikes. And Specialized Bicycle Components and its founder Mike Sinyard became synonymous with mountain-bike racing.

By 1992, two-thirds of adult bikes sold were mountain bikes, and Schwinn was bankrupt.

With new management Schwinn is trying to pedal its way back into the bicycle business. With mountain bikes, of course. Analysts say it needs to change perceptions among the cycling cognoscenti if the company wants to make inroads at the high end. "We have an image challenge," says Schwinn's marketing director.

But you can't change strongly held perceptions. Yesterday Schwinn needed a new name to ride across the mountain-bike trench. Today, it's too late; the trench is too deep. Today Schwinn needs a new focus, presumably at the low end or with kids.

Digital Equipment is trying to cross the trench from thirty-two-bit workstations to sixty-four-bit workstations. It has a new chip called Alpha and a new line of workstations called AlphaStations. The AlphaStation 600, for example, is billed as the "fastest workstation in the universe."

Unfortunately, the 600 is not billed as a sixty-four-bit workstation. Like most of the high-technology products on the market today, the thrust is on performance, the better-product approach. Digital claims to outperform Sun, Silicon Graphics, and Hewlett-Packard.

True? Probably, but also irrelevant. The urgent need at Digital is to set up the sixty-four-bit workstation as a "next generation" product. Digital has already lost the thirty-two-bit battle; it has to set up the sixty-four-bit battlefield.

It's what Microsoft has done so brilliantly with Windows 95. Do they claim that Windows 95 is a better operating system than the current Windows product?

Indirectly, yes, but the emphasis is on the next-generation aspect of the new software. This approach creates a feeling of inevitability, and sometimes even grudging acceptance, on the part of the customer.

(A sailing-ship veteran once complained about the ugly, dirty steamboats taking over the transatlantic trade. "True," came the rejoinder, "but this is steamboat time. And when it's steamboat time, you steam.")

Encyclopaedia Britannica is a beautiful, thirty-two-volume sailboat selling for $1,500 at a time when you can get *Encarta,* Microsoft's CD-ROM encyclopedia, for about $55. It's CD-ROM time, and many companies have developed products that contain text, graphics, and photos of an entire set of reference books on a single silicon disk.

The sailboat is slowly sinking in the sunset. Britannica sold 117,000 sets in 1990 and just 51,000 sets in 1994. In the last three years the company lost an estimated $22 million on sales of some $1.6 billion.

Sure, Britannica also has a CD-ROM, but it costs $995 and it doesn't have the multimedia sound and graphics of its competitors.

Sooner or later every company faces the *Encyclopaedia Britannica* problem. Your existing product (encyclopedias) is threatened by a next-generation product (CD-ROMs). What should you do about the situation?

There are four fundamental things you must do to successfully cross the trench: (1) Act early, (2) develop a totally new product, (3) give the new product a new name, and (4) move boldly.

ACT EARLY

If possible, you should be the one to make your own product obsolete, not the competition. "He who hesitates is lost." Companies that are all too willing to go out and compete with their customers nevertheless are hesitant about competing with themselves.

They should remember the old adage: When you compete with yourself, you are fighting a battle you can't lose.

Actually, Britannica was one of the first companies into the CD-ROM encyclopedia field when they launched *Compton's MultiMedia Encyclopedia* in 1989. But they got discouraged and sold out to The Tribune Company in 1993, the same year that Microsoft introduced *Encarta*.

DEVELOP A TOTALLY NEW PRODUCT

Bayer wasn't replaced by an improved form of aspirin. It was replaced by Tylenol acetaminophen.

Schwinn wasn't superseded by an improved street bike. It was superseded by the Trek mountain bike.

Atari wasn't outmoded by an improved four-bit video game. It was outmoded by Nintendo, an eight-bit video game.

GIVE THE NEW PRODUCT A NEW NAME

You can't cross a trench with a name that nails you into your current position. You need a new name to make the transformation.

Bayer tried to introduce Bayer acetaminophen, a product advertised as a "nonaspirin" pain reliever. This is line extension at its worst, and the product went nowhere.

Unless you are both "first and lucky," you can't cross a trench with an existing name. Your name means more than just quality and service and all those other "soft" attributes, it also stands for a specific product or a category.

Bayer means aspirin. IBM means mainframes. Hershey means chocolate. Prudential means insurance. Wrigley means chewing gum.

Most of the companies in the world have a focus they consistently try to undermine by pushing their names into new territories. Fortunately, customers help companies keep their focuses by resisting these encroachments.

MOVE BOLDLY

You can't be timid or halfhearted if you hope to seize the high ground on the other side of the trench.

To launch Aleve, Procter & Gamble spent $100 million the first year, including $60 million in advertising.

To launch Acura, Honda set up a nationwide chain of dealers, totally separate from existing Honda dealerships.

To launch an unknown designer with almost no sales, Tommy Hilfiger Corporation spent $20 million on advertising.

Boldness is in short supply. The motto of many corporations seems to be: Act incrementally.

Military history is illuminating in this respect. Many opportunities have been thrown away by generals who spent too much time planning and probing and not enough time fighting.

"Many assume that half efforts can be effective," wrote Carl von Clausewitz. "A small jump is easier than a large one, but no one wishing to cross a wide ditch would cross half of it first."

Wherever you look, you seldom see big winners playing an incremental game. Take the world of golf. A decade ago the big names were Wilson, MacGregor, and Spalding in woods and Karsten Manufacturing (Ping) in irons.

Each year the big names came out with minor product improvements, much like the annual model changes in the automobile industry.

What drove the leaders into the rough was the arrival of Ely Callaway, a seventy-six-year-old former president of Burlington Industries. Instead of a small change, the Callaway Golf Company introduced the Big Bertha, the first oversize driver, in 1991.

Today Callaway is the largest U.S. manufacturer of golf equipment with recent annual sales of $449 million and profits of $78 million.

What Callaway did in drivers, Cobra Golf did in oversize irons. Today Cobra is the number one brand in high-end irons. Both Cobra and Callaway illustrate the power of a next-generation approach as compared to the incremental approach of just introducing a new, improved product.

Are these new oversize clubs substantially better? It's hard to tell. In the past twenty-five years the average winning score of golf professionals has improved by exactly one stroke per round. What has improved is the perception of Callaway and Cobra, which are widely considered to be "next-generation" golf clubs.

Were Wilson, MacGregor, and Spalding asleep at the switch? The media is quick to criticize: "They didn't change fast enough." But you can't cross the trench into the next generation just by changing the product. You also have to change the name.

It's not that "oversize" was such a radical idea in the sports field. The leaders could have studied the history books and noted the success of Prince Manufacturing Inc.

Back in 1976, Prince launched a tennis racquet with a 57 percent larger head. Scoffers called it the "cheater's" racquet, but it rapidly captured 30 percent of the quality tennis-racquet market. Two of Prince's victims: Wilson and Spalding.

Leaders are cautious. Incremental change is seen as safer. "Why gamble on an oversize club? What will that do to our existing clubs? What if the new product doesn't sell?"

All of these questions keep a leader from making a bold move across the trench. That's why you continue to see a parade of new names like Callaway, Cobra, Compaq, Sega, and Trek move in and create next-generation focuses.

And the parade is likely to continue until leaders adopt similar strategies. Leaders should introduce next-generation products with next-generation names, as Honda did by launching Acura.

This strategy combines boldness with safety. You can launch a new brand without considering its effect on your existing brand. Should the new brand fail, the fallout will not affect the reputation of your existing brand.

Leaders often hesitate to act boldly. The ski industry is the latest example of this truism. Leaders like Salomon, Rossignol, and Atomic have had plenty of advance warning. At Stratton, Vermont, in the early eighties, Jake Burton developed a downhill device he called a "snowboard."

Today, snowboarding is a rapidly growing sport, and Burton Snowboards Inc. is the leader with a third of the market. (While only 10 percent of the ski population use snowboards, they buy 30 percent of the lift tickets.)

And since 80 percent of snowboarders are still under twenty-five, this growth is likely to continue. Snowboarding is a next-generation sport.

So far, most of the established ski companies have been left out in the cold. By the time they get around to introducing a brand (or more likely buying one of the hundred or so snowboard companies), it may be too late.

By getting into the mind first and creating a perception of leadership, companies like Burton Snowboards and Ride Snowboard (the number two company) are going to be too far down the hill to catch.

The roller-skate industry was also blindsided by a next-generation product. Created by an ex-professional hockey player, Rollerblade, the company, and in-line skating, the concept, have taken the industry by storm. And what happened to the traditional manufacturers of roller skates? They got left behind.

Today, the in-line skating sport is dominated by Rollerblade, Inc., with almost half of the $700 million market.

McGraw-Hill is another example of a company that has become infamous for its failure to cross the trench. "The publishing giant, owner of such famous names as *Business Week* magazine and Standard & Poor's Corp.," wrote the *Wall Street Journal,* "has become notorious on Wall Street for lackluster profits, disappointing acquisitions, and frequent reorganizations."

Much of the eighties was spent on an ill-starred plan to lessen McGraw-Hill's emphasis on print publishing by expanding into electronic information. But crossing the trench from print to electronic publishing turned out to be a lot more difficult than McGraw-Hill figured.

Instead of setting up separate electronic operations with separate names, the company did the opposite. It reorganized itself into "market focus groups." There was an "energy" group, a "transportation" group, even a "management" market focus group, among others.

McGraw-Hill would become an "information turbine." Data would come in one end of the turbine, be manipulated, and go out the other as various information products. All kinds of synergies were going to be possible. It never worked as planned, and the company went back to a more traditional organization.

While the information turbine was running out of steam, McGraw-Hill missed a major shift in the direction of its core trade publications. The electronic revolution created an opportunity in magazine publishing that its competitors were only too happy to exploit.

Once the country's foremost trade magazine publisher, McGraw-Hill has fallen far behind. Currently its annual magazine revenues ($420 million) trail those of International Data Group ($910 million) and Ziff-Davis ($820 million). Fast-moving CMP Publications ($320 million) is also rapidly closing the gap.

Turning magazines into electronic vehicles hasn't worked so far. Witness the number of publications that have tried to make it on television, notably *Good Housekeeping* and *USA Today*.

The most expensive failure ever in first-run syndication, *USA Today on TV* lost an estimated $12 to $15 million the first year and was canceled during its second season.

Not that magazine-type shows can't be successful on television. One of TV's perennial winners is *60 Minutes*. It's just that magazine-type names can't be successful on television. What's needed on TV is a separate television identity.

The lesson is clear. You can't be successful by putting things together under a common name or concept like McGraw-Hill tried to do. If you want to cross the trench into the next generation, you have to create a separate, next-generation identity. You need a second focus.

Which brings us back to Eastman Kodak, the Big Kahuna in photographic film. A decade ago, the company had sales of $10.6 billion and net income of $923 million. Today, Kodak has sales of $16.9 billion and net income of $557 million. In other words, sales are up 60 percent and profits are down 40 percent. There are a lot of unhappy campers in Rochester, New York.

In the eighties, Kodak "restructured" five times in the search for greater efficiencies. The company "diversified" big-time into computers, pharmaceuticals, household products, even batteries. Nothing worked. (For decades to come, Kodak will be a monument to the failure of diversification as a corporate strategy.)

George Fisher, the new CEO, found a focus. "Imaging offers Kodak tremendous opportunities for long-term success and growth," he said. "To achieve maximum success, we have concluded that we must commit our entire resource base to imaging opportunities and divest noncore businesses."

Currently more than 80 percent of Kodak's current revenues come from traditional, silver-halide-based photographic products, from film to cameras. The market is there. The world has 450 million camera users, all eager to buy film. At the same time, half of humanity has yet to take a photograph.

Just as Kodak is refocusing on film, the digital generation looms on the horizon. "Digital imaging had better boom," said a headline in the May 1, 1995, issue of *Fortune*, "before Kodak film busts."

Over the past decade Kodak has spent huge sums on digital-imaging research and development. (Some estimates have been as high as $5 billion.) Yet few products have emerged from the laboratories.

One possible reason is that Kodak executives might have been fearful that digital products would cannibalize photography sales.

Again, George Fisher made the right move. He put all Kodak digital products in a new division and hired Carl Gustin, a former Digital Equipment and Apple Computer marketing executive, to head the unit.

Two smart moves and then one dumb one. What name is Kodak using for the new division? Kodak Digital Science. "We need to leverage the Kodak master brand," says Mr. Gustin, "and describe our new digital competencies."

Why is that? What hope does Kodak have to cross the trench into the digital future with a photographic name? Not much. Especially in the face of determined competition. There are hundreds of global companies itching for a piece of the digital action. Casio, Canon, Fujitsu, Sony, Silicon Graphics, and Hewlett-Packard among them.

Strange as it might seem, it's the strength of the Kodak brand that will make it more difficult for Kodak to cross the digital trench.

If you have a powerful perception for one class of product, it becomes almost impossible to extend that perception to a different class. According to the most recent EquiTrend survey, Kodak photographic film is the top-quality brand in the United States. (Disney was second and Mercedes-Benz was third.)

The Photo CD is Kodak's first major digital product. The problem with the Photo CD, which transfers slides or negatives onto a photo CD disc, is that it's a transitional product. Neither fish nor fowl.

A transitional product is like a power-assisted horse and buggy. It doesn't appeal to techies who want the latest thing, nor does it appeal to traditionalists who want to keep what they already have.

Neither the electronic typewriter nor the word processor stayed in good shape as customers moved from the typewriter to the computer. Both Smith Corona and Wang, for example, went bankrupt.

It's obvious that Kodak needs a new, digital name to make the leap across the trench. By itself, of course, the new name isn't enough. What Kodak needs to do is to hang the new name on a revolutionary idea or product. Then let the success of the new product drive the new name into the mind.

Polaroid Corp. is in the same situation as Kodak, except that Polaroid means "instant" photographic film. When Polaroid tried to use its "instant" name to capture a share of the "regular" film market, it met with little success. Trying to take the Polaroid name into the digital market would be almost impossible.

Remember when Kodak tried to compete with Polaroid in instant photography? Polaroid beat Kodak two to one in sales, before beating them one to nothing in a patent-infringement case. If Kodak can't make Kodak mean "instant," how does Kodak expect to make Kodak mean "digital"?

You need a separate identity to cross the trench. Nobody calls a butterfly a "flying caterpillar," because people perceive them to be two separate species. Photography and digital imaging are two separate species. Kodak Digital Science is a flying-caterpillar name.

On the other side of the trench, it's the new name, the new company, that has the advantage.

In spite of the fact that Kodak is the top-quality brand in the United States, the Kodak name is at a disadvantage in the digital arena. This is not to say that other companies will take advantage of the situation.

Maybe they will, maybe they won't. Kodak's competitors might fall into the same line-extension trap. Certainly Fuji Digital Science is not going to be a better approach than Kodak Digital Science.

Take another example. Salads used to come in heads and bunches. Heads of lettuce, bunches of carrots, plus individual peppers, onions, etc. No more. The next-generation salads are precut and sold in special plastic bags that regulate the oxygen/carbon dioxide balance. "Packaged salads" are a booming $650-million-a-year business growing at an annual rate of 80 percent.

The pioneer in packaged salads is Fresh Express, Inc., a small company in Salinas, California. The Goliath in the field, however, is

$3.8 billion Dole Food Co., a shipper of fresh fruits and vegetables and canned fruit.

You might think that Dole, with many more resources, including a field salesforce several times larger than Fresh Express, might have the upper hand in packaged salads. Not so. Dole made the classic mistake of using a pineapple name (Dole) on a vegetable.

Today Goliath (Dole) has 24 percent of the market and David (Fresh Express) has 40 percent of the market. David is also growing faster than Goliath.

It's not the size of a company that matters and, within limits, not the total resources a company has at its command that counts. What matters in the business world today is focus. If you are first on the scene and you have a focus, you are the odds-on favorite to emerge as the leader.

Not always, however. Sometimes the mind of the customer has been invaded by a previous reincarnation of the product. Take the current rush to be first with a next-generation acid indigestion and heartburn product. Johnson & Johnson was first with Pepcid AC, an over-the-counter version of the prescription drug Pepcid.

After one month, Pepcid AC was the leader in the antacid category, with 19 percent of the market compared to the previous leader, Tums, which had a 17 percent share. Three months later SmithKline introduced Tagamet, another next-generation antacid with a prescription drug heritage. Soon to come is Zantac, to be marketed by Warner-Lambert. Who will win the three-horse race?

Zantac. Even though Zantac was the last horse in the race, it's first in prescription sales in a class of drugs called H2 blockers, which actually block the production of stomach acid. Zantac should be able to transfer its prescription leadership into over-the-counter leadership.

The three products didn't start off on an equal footing. Zantac, and to a lesser extent Tagamet, have a greater awareness in the minds of customers than did Pepcid. And that greater awareness will lead to sales leadership. Which one is the best product? Does it matter?

The over-the-counter drug category demonstrates the power of legitimacy or credibility in the selling process. As with most products today, customers can't see any differences between various types of drugs. Nor are they able to evaluate a drug by studying its active ingredients. What does matter is what the medical profession thinks about different drugs. The magic word is "prescription."

Which is why the Aleve package says: "Now in non-prescription strength." Virtually every successful over-the-counter drug started its career behind the prescription desk. It gives a product the advantage of credibility.

Motrin is the prescription version of ibuprofen. Five years after the launch of Advil and Nuprin, over-the-counter Motrin IB was introduced. Five years is a long lead to give any competitor, especially in the fast-moving drug category, yet today Motrin IB is the second largest selling ibuprofen. Motrin is behind Advil, but well ahead of Nuprin.

Another fast-moving category is computer retailing. At first business customers bought their personal computers from retail stores like Businessland and ComputerLand. But the arrival of networks and an avalanche of hardware and software products soon made the purchase and installation of computer networks a complex endeavor.

So there was an opportunity for a next-generation retailer who would buy hardware, peripherals, and software from different suppliers and put them together for a corporation. Then install and test the equipment.

Enter Entex Information Services and Vanstar Inc. Both companies buy, install, and test personal computers as well as service equipment, manage networks, set up and run help desks, train workers, integrate systems of different types, and provide advice. Both have become rapidly growing billion-dollar companies.

What's not so well known is that the two companies arose out of the ashes of Businessland and ComputerLand.

Businessland was sold, merged, and ultimately wound up in a bankruptcy filing. Later a management-led investor group bought the remnants of the information systems unit and renamed them Entex.

ComputerLand sold its franchise operations and changed its name to Vanstar. The name changes have been a key element in both companies' moves from the old-format computer retailing to the new systems sell.

Meanwhile, the traditional computer retailing concept has gone the superstore route, à la Toys "R" Us. The leading contenders are CompUSA and Tandy Corp.'s Computer City. The narrowly focused CompUSA would seem to have an advantage over Tandy, which has spread its resources over a number of different retailing formats.

Sooner or later every company comes face-to-face with the imminent arrival of the next generation. Do you fight the new generation or do you join the revolution? It all depends on your answers to four questions: (1) Are we first? (2) Will the next generation amount to anything? (3) Can we find an appropriate name? (4) Will we be better off standing pat?

ARE WE FIRST?

If you can be first, by all means jump into the pool. Being first does not literally mean being the first company to introduce the next-generation product. It means being the first company to get into the customer's mind.

Whenever there is a movement from one generation to the next, there is a period of flux. Nobody is quite sure who the leader really is. Market shares shift rapidly from one company to another.

When customers finally recognize one company as the leader, the pecking order becomes semipermanent. The time to exert maximum pressure is early in the game. Once the situation becomes fixed in concrete, it's too late.

WILL THE NEXT GENERATION AMOUNT TO ANYTHING?

This is a loaded question. Nobody ever believes the next generation will amount to anything.

Did Bayer believe that acetaminophen would overtake aspirin? Did Schwinn believe that mountain bikes would replace street bikes? Did Digital Equipment believe the personal computer would replace the minicomputer? Did Wilson or Spalding believe the oversize contraption would replace the traditional tennis racquet?

Apparently not, because none of these five companies did anything about the next-generation products until it was way too late. The market never looks bigger on the other side of the trench. Most companies, especially market leaders, always expect the next generation to be a "subset" of the mainstream product they dominate.

Will digital photography replace photographic film? "Digital will grow quickly," says Eastman Kodak's George Fisher, "but it will not replace traditional photography, at least in my career." Mr. Fisher is fifty-five.

Back in 1981, IBM introduced the personal computer. You can

imagine someone at Smith Corona saying, "Personal computers will grow quickly, but they will not replace traditional typewriters, at least in my career." Well, they did.

The safest approach is to think big and assume the next generation will be a big deal.

CAN WE FIND AN APPROPRIATE NAME?

It's absolutely essential to use a new name for a next-generation product, and it's also expensive. It's a whole lot cheaper to assume the next generation is not going to go anywhere.

Companies are often quick to conclude they can't find an appropriate name, so they use an existing one. When a company uses its existing name on a next-generation product, it often is making a statement about the size of the potential business, not about the desirability of a second name. "Why go to all that expense if the business is not going to develop?"

A better way to plan for the next generation is to play it safe. If the business doesn't develop, then all you have lost is money. If the business does develop and you're not prepared with a second name, then you could lose your leadership. Money can be replaced. Once lost, leadership can almost never be regained.

WILL WE BE BETTER OFF STANDING PAT?

If you can't be first and there are a host of competitors out in front of you, then consider the possibility of doing nothing.

Standing pat and reinforcing your traditional focus is one way to remain successful as fads come and go.

Too often companies procrastinate, then join the revolution in a halfhearted way. They become a hybrid company, neither fish nor fowl. They lose their focus. And once their focus is gone, their future is usually gone, too.

FIFTEEN KEYS TO A LONG-TERM FOCUS

Over the years I've found fifteen principles or "keys" that are helpful in developing an effective long-term corporate focus.

Or in recognizing an effective focus when you run across one.

1. A FOCUS IS SIMPLE

When Charles Kettering ran the General Motors Research Laboratory in Dayton, Ohio, he had a plaque put on the wall that said: THIS PROBLEM WHEN SOLVED WILL BE SIMPLE. Nothing is more helpful in recognizing a good corporate focus than asking yourself this question: "Is the proposed focus simple?"

Since a focus has to work in the mind of the customer, it can't be complicated, high-minded, flowery, obtuse, or difficult to understand. It has to be a simple idea, expressed with simple words, and immediately understandable by your customers, your employees, and the media.

A simple focus is unlikely to come out of the overly complex strategic systems in place at many companies. Some computer-aided strategic design programs look like the floor plan of an automobile assembly plant.

You're not building an automobile. You're building a perception in the mind. And it's done with words, not bricks and mortar. Simple words like "safety" and "driving" and "overnight."

When Lloyd Reuss was president of General Motors, he had a vision for reforming the company, which he expressed in a pyramid under the headings Vision, Mission, Values, Objective, Strategies, Initiatives, and Goals.

The Strategies section alone had seven subsections: Quality, People, Cost, Fast, Great, Marketing, and Materials Management. No one could possibly follow a leader as confused as Reuss was. Nor could one find a focus in such a jungle of jargon.

Nor are you likely to find a focus with an overly complicated team approach. One multibillion-dollar service company decided to formulate a corporate strategy with a series of monthly meetings held over a six-month period. Invited to the sessions were key representatives of the operating units and functional heads.

What emerged from the meetings is exactly what you might expect: mush. A focus might be simple, but it's not likely to be formulated in a frying pan into which everyone throws an idea or two. The more people involved in the process, the less likely the group will be able to cook up a powerful focus.

A general doesn't gather the troops, divide them into teams of ten, and ask each team to generate a strategy for the army to consider. But managers often do.

In working with many companies, large and small, foreign and domestic, I find they all have a blind spot when it comes to idea generation. They assume that the critical element in their success or failure is the quality of the ideas generated by their staffs or their outside consultants. So they "divide up into groups" and press for more and better creative suggestions.

Most companies don't need more ideas; they need fewer ideas. Most companies don't need ideas at all, they need a simple focus that may not seem creative, in and of itself, but in the world outside turns out to be very powerful.

When someone at Packard Bell said, "Let's focus on the *home* personal computer market," I'm sure the group didn't jump up and down and say, "What a great creative idea!"

What most companies lack is not ideas at all but judgment. In 1937, Chester Carlson patented a dry-copying process he called "electrophotography" and then spent seven years trying to sell it to corporate giants like General Electric, RCA, IBM, and Remington Rand.

Finally, he sold it to Battelle Memorial Institute, a nonprofit research organization in Columbus, Ohio. It took three more years to find a company to develop the machine. Haloid Company, later Xerox Corporation, took a chance and made history in the process.

Good ideas are everywhere. Good judgment is a relatively scarce commodity. In 1949, when the Beetle arrived on our shores, how many automobile dealers rushed to get a Volkswagen franchise? Very, very few.

In January 1975, when *Popular Electronics* carried a picture of the first personal computer on its cover, how many people rushed to Albuquerque, New Mexico, to interview Ed Roberts, the inventor of the MITS Altair 8800?

There weren't very many, but one who did was Paul Allen. (You probably know the name of his partner at the time, Bill Gates.)

A good focus will be simple, but recognizing a good focus is not so simple. It takes judgment, which is in incredible short supply in the world today.

2. A FOCUS IS MEMORABLE

You can't make yourself or your company successful. Only your customers can do that for you. Since a focus has to work in the mind of the customer, it has to be memorable. If your customers can't remember what you stand for, what good does it do to take that stand?

What's memorable and what's not? One of the most important ingredients of a memorable idea is uniqueness at the time you first make the claim. What you say about yourself has to be different from what other companies are saying.

When Volvo said they made "safe" cars, no one else was saying quite the same thing. Now that every car company is saying they make safe cars, the only car company with a memorable focus is Volvo.

A memorable focus also has an element of shock. If you can use an unexpected or negative word, you're much better off. If James Carville had said, "It's the economy," the media probably would have ignored the message. "It's the economy, stupid," got their attention.

If Subaru had said "inexpensive," prospective car buyers would have ignored the message. "Inexpensive and built to stay that way" got their attention.

Sometimes the entire focus can be expressed in a memorable way by using only the negative. "I have nothing to offer," said Winston Churchill in his first statement as prime minister in the House of Commons, "but blood, toil, tears, and sweat."

Some companies claim their mission statement is their focus. The trouble is, mission statements aren't very memorable. Perhaps the most famous mission statement of all time is the 308-word "Credo" of Johnson & Johnson.

Here are the first twenty-five words of the Credo: "We believe our first responsibility is to the doctors, nurses and patients, to mothers and fathers and all others who use our products and services." The other 283 words are equally unmemorable.

Try asking a Johnson & Johnson employee what the Credo is. The employee is likely to say, "It means we should do the right thing." Well, of course.

A focus should be as memorable as an anthem, a banner, a battle cry. Some of the more memorable slogans have come from wars like the Spanish-American War, "Remember the Maine," and World War I, "The war to end war."

One way to make a focus memorable is to be audacious. People respond to challenges that are unreasonable, even outrageous.

When John F. Kennedy said, "I believe this nation should commit itself to achieving the goal, before this decade is out, of landing a man on the moon and returning him safely to earth," people instantly responded, yes, we should and we can.

If Kennedy had said, "We're going to try to put a man on the moon, hopefully sometime in the next decade or so," no one would have paid much attention to his commitment.

Employees are willing to make sacrifices in order to accomplish great goals, but they have to know what those goals are. They have to have a target to shoot for. Just exerting employees to "try harder" is not enough.

When the CEO raises the corporate flag and says, "I am your leader," the employees ask, "Where are we going?"

It can be exceedingly profitable for a corporate leader to tell them where they are going in a unique and memorable way.

3. A FOCUS IS POWERFUL

The more often a word or concept is repeated, the more powerful it becomes. By establishing a focus for your corporation, you create an environment in which the focus gets repeated over and over again. In the process, the focus increases its power.

The same thing is true of publicity. When an idea generates a lot of favorable media attention, it carries its own sense of "inevitability." When customers expect you to be successful, they act in ways that make you successful.

Notice how the "hot" product, the "hot" restaurant, the "hot" music group cannot seem to fail. This is what momentum is all about. It is the creation of the belief in the mind of the customer that your company or brand is going to be a big success.

Presto, it is a big success.

The first time the customer heard that Snapple was made with "all natural ingredients," I'm sure the customer yawned. After twenty-three years of repeating the "natural" mantra, Snapple achieved an aura of the only thing for today's younger generation to drink.

(The 1995 purchase of Snapple by Quaker Oats for the outrageous price of $1.7 billion unfocused both companies. What is a New Age natural beverage like Snapple doing in an old-fashioned food company anyway?)

Some managers equate size with power. Is a large company more powerful than a small one? Not necessarily. A highly focused company is more powerful than a less focused company. When Snapple was an independent company, it was more powerful than it is as a division of an unfocused Quaker Oats.

What provides an organization with its power is its degree of focus and its share of market. Size is only important if it contributes to an increase in market share. That's why mergers can either increase a company's focus or decrease it. A merger of similar companies tends to increase the combined company's focus. A merger of dissimilar companies results in a larger, less focused combination.

Power gives a company the ability to "control" an industry, taking it in a direction that will only increase the company's power and domination.

A focus is also powerful because it attracts exactly the right employees who can help reinforce a company's strength. The opposite is true for an unfocused company. In order to keep its software dreams alive, IBM paid $3.5 billion to buy Lotus Development Corp. If you're a software expert, are you more likely to want to work for IBM/Lotus or for Microsoft?

The best people want to work with the best people at the best company. Microsoft has managed to attract the best and the brightest software experts in the industry.

When IBM acquired Lotus, there was much speculation that many of Lotus's top people would leave because they didn't want to work for a hardware company. Like Snapple, Lotus has lost some of its power due to the acquisition. It has become unfocused.

A focus is also powerful because it drives employees to embrace the company's core business and values. When the home crowd at a basketball game chants "Dee . . . Fense" in unison, you can feel the single-minded determination in the stands and on the court.

When everyone in a company is repeating a single focus, it concentrates and enhances their performance in achieving a single goal. Repetition alone is a powerful motivating force. "Fo . . . Cus."

Yet distractions abound. A company with 20 percent of one market is constantly looking around for opportunities to get 1 or 2 percent of a half-dozen other markets. All in the name of diversification or line extension or extending the equity of the brand. What they forget is that diversification comes with a price. It unfocuses the company and leads to loss of power.

Better to look for ways to increase the share of the business you are already in rather than constantly looking over your shoulder for new fields to conquer. That way you also increase your power.

Ocean Spray has 78 percent of the U.S. cranberry market. That's power. Furthermore, the marketing cooperative constantly looks for new ways to increase the market for cranberries, introducing such products as Cranapple, Cran-Grape, and Cran-Raspberry juices.

Wouldn't it be easier to increase the share of a business you know than to try to get a share of a business you don't know? If you're a lawyer, should you try to increase the size of your legal business or should you hire a few accountants and open an accounting practice on the side?

Familiarity breeds respect. Companies that know their own industry inside out often feel that they can't make any more progress in the business they're already in. The competition is just too smart and too tough.

Unfamiliarity breeds contempt. On the other hand, they confidently wade into a business they don't know, secure in the knowledge that the competition is dumb and easy to overcome.

Why, then, are some companies that lack a focus powerful? Even some conglomerates are relatively powerful, most notably Asea Brown Boveri (ABB) in Switzerland, Hanson in the United Kingdom, and General Electric in the United States. Maybe the concept of focus is not the essence of successful management.

Maybe. But management theorists should consider the difference between a science like physics and the art of management. One exception is enough to disprove a theory of physics, but management is different.

Management is not a science; it's an art. There are no universal laws, true in every sense. There are only general principles to discover, which may or may not be applicable to a specific situation.

Still, the success of a handful of conglomerates should cause concern among those who believe, as I do, in the power of a focus. Maybe there are special circumstances to consider.

One that is instantly obvious is the question of age. Most of the successful conglomerates are relatively old. ABB is 112 years old. GE is 117 years old.

As a result, most of the successful conglomerates operate in mature businesses. ABB is primarily a manufacturer of power-generation and electrical equipment. And because the businesses are mature, the conglomerates have few competitors. And their competitors are often other conglomerates.

(How many companies have been formed recently to manufacture products like turbine generators, diesel-electric locomotives, or power transformers?)

When two conglomerates compete with each other, the winner is unlikely to be a highly focused company. The winner is bound to be a conglomerate.

In looking for leadership secrets, some management theorists study what leaders do *after* they become leaders. They note that leaders often diversify into other businesses looking for synergy. Ergo, the secret of success is to become a conglomerate like General Electric.

Rich people wear Patek Philippe watches and drive Rolls-Royce automobiles. But you won't find the road to riches by buying the right watch or driving the right car.

What you need to do is to study what leaders did *before* they became leaders, not what they did after they became leaders. In

1890, The Edison Electric Light Company (the forerunner of GE) was a very successful $10 million company. It was Thomas Edison's invention of the light bulb that sparked General Electric's initial success.

4. A FOCUS IS REVOLUTIONARY

If you're thinking of developing a focus for your company, keep in mind that you're going to meet with tremendous resistance. A focus is a simple, easy-to-understand concept that is going to be difficult to sell to your associates. A focus goes against the grain of conventional thinking.

Managers have been taught to aim for growth, to expand their product lines, to get into new areas, to take advantage of synergy. Conventional thinking is totally oriented toward growth. Bigger is better. Growth can do no wrong.

The fact that these expansionist theories don't usually work has not stopped their adoption. If you believe that something *should* work and it doesn't, then the fault lies in the execution, not the theory. It should work, goes the theory, therefore we have to find a way to make it work.

If you believe that growth is good, then you will resist any attempt to focus a corporation. The truth is, focus does restrict growth outside a selected area, much like pruning a plant forces it to grow only in a specific direction. If you want to focus a corporation, you have to be prepared to break a few GAMPs.

A GAMP is a Generally Accepted Management Practice. At the heart of GAMP thinking is the demand for growth. Not just growth in sales, but growth in profits, growth in return on investment. When viewed from a growth platform, any attempt to focus a company is considered reactionary.

To make an omelette, you have to break a few eggs. To focus a corporation, you have to break a few GAMPs.

Growth is the primary GAMP philosophy, and the numbers are the tools of the trade. All across America companies believe in the virtues of growth and are run by the numbers. If a given decision results in better numbers (i.e., growth), then that decision is a good decision. If a given decision produces poorer numbers, then that decision is a poor decision.

(Any company that continually produces better numbers is a company headed for problems. ITT, you might remember, had a string of fifty-eight consecutive increases in quarterly earnings before the string was ended in 1974.)

Some CEOs actually like running a company by the numbers. It removes them from the responsibility of making strategic decisions. All they have to do is look at the numbers and replace the division heads who fail to measure up. These companies are usually strong believers in decentralization, which is why a decentralized company is usually a defocused company, too.

With growth as the philosophy and the numbers as the arbitrator of that philosophy, the average American company faces a dim future. A company run by the numbers is a company being run into the ground.

Not that numbers are unnecessary in running a business. They are necessary. From time to time you have to check the numbers to see where you are. The numbers serve as a reality check to see if your strategy is on target.

In focusing a company, you start out by cutting back. In the short term, the numbers might reflect this pruning process. Sometimes you have to take one step backward in order to take two steps forward. Instead of asking whether a given decision will improve the numbers, ask whether the decision will improve a company's focus.

If it improves your focus by narrowing your product lines, it will ultimately improve your numbers by increasing your market share, the ultimate arbitrator of your power.

The price of your stock is also not the measure of your future success. It's nice to have a healthy stock price to reward executives and finance strategic acquisitions, but your ultimate goal should be the health of your business. A healthy business is a narrowly focused business with a dominant market share. Such a business produces healthy profits and is almost impervious to competition.

Business is like mathematics. And higher business is like higher mathematics. When you move up to higher mathematics, you don't deal in specifics, you deal in concepts. (There are almost no numbers in differential calculus, for example.)

The same is true for business. On a higher, or strategic, level business is a battle of concepts, not specifics. You have to be able to see the outline of the forest and not be too concerned about counting the number of trees.

5. A FOCUS NEEDS AN ENEMY

Unrestricted growth in many different directions robs a company of an essential element for its long-term success: a viable enemy. Business is competition. Any product or service sold by your company is a product or service not sold by somebody else. It is not enough just to remain profitable. For you to be truly successful, others must fail.

A diversified company with many products and services quickly loses sight of its enemy. In truth, it has so many enemies that it cannot keep an eye on any one. Which is why a diversified company is repeatedly defeated by surprise attacks by its unseen enemies.

If you've ever worked for a conglomerate, you probably have noticed how internally focused they are. A conglomerate's executives rarely attend industry meetings, for example. (What industry are they a part of?) Their time is spent mostly on internal meetings, trying to straighten out who does what to whom.

This is one of the essential problems with alliances. A major company like IBM has hundreds of alliances. So who is the enemy? Any potential enemy will probably turn out to be one of IBM's allies. This is confusing to both employees and customers.

When MCI was focused on AT&T, it made steady progress, reaching 20 percent of the long-distance telephone market. But progress has stalled recently as MCI has gotten involved in a raft of new businesses, including a $2 billion joint venture with News Corp. to develop an on-line computer service and other information products.

In 1994, MCI lost market share to AT&T for the first time in a decade.

MCI also is getting into the data services business with the purchase of SHL Systemhouse for $1 billion. And the music business with the launch of Project Diamond, which allows consumers to buy CDs over phone lines.

Who is MCI's enemy? It's Sam Goody, EDS, IBM, America Online, and AT&T, to name a few. Instead of a long-distance phone company, MCI is turning itself into a diversified conglomerate selling everything from consulting services to music CDs.

Is MCI worried? They don't seem to be. "There's nobody in the world who doesn't believe that MCI, with its marketing and sales strength, can't pick off 15 percent of any market," says CEO Bert Roberts. "We could pick off that much of the shoe market and we don't even make shoes."

Well, there is one. Me.

MCI has lost its enemy. A focused company, on the other hand, always knows who the enemy is and what they are doing. It can develop specific plans to deal with the enemy. If necessary it can rapidly mount counterattacks. (If the enemy is an unfocused, diversified company, all the better.)

Coca-Cola's enemy is PepsiCo, Inc. But who is General Electric's enemy? A conglomerate has no enemy and no external focus. As a result, it spends an inordinate amount of time inside the company trying to keep a multitude of divisions and departments organized.

6. A FOCUS IS THE FUTURE

It bears repeating that the primary job of a corporate leader is not to manage the corporation but to find the future. Not just the future in general but the specific future for the corporation under his or her care. A focus is the future in the sense that it makes a prediction about where the future lies and then takes specific steps to make that future happen.

When Volvo selected "safety" as its focus, it was not only predicting where the automobile industry was headed but by its own actions it made that future possible. Today, not just Volvo but the entire automotive industry is focused on safety. (Without followers, there cannot be leaders.)

When Silicon Graphics latched onto "3-D computing" as its focus, there was no market for 3-D computing. Today, thanks to the efforts of industry leader Silicon Graphics, the market is booming.

The Defense Department has been running 3-D video war games in lieu of on-the-ground maneuvers. Many other industries are taking advantage of 3-D's ability to create lifelike simulations. Medicine, oil exploration, product design, and architecture are just some of the industries making extensive use of the process. And, of course, video games, motion pictures, and advertising use 3-D effects.

As 3-D has grown so has Silicon Graphics. Since 1991, the company has more than tripled its revenues to a current $2.2 billion a year.

There's a paradox here. Some consultants suggest that CEOs should spend three-quarters of their time looking, planning, and preparing for the future. Hello, think tanks and Caribbean retreats. Welcome to dreamland, blue-sky thinking, and the brave new world of tomorrow that never seems to arrive.

What CEOs should do is find the future in today's activities. What single product, service, or idea is your best hope for the future? That becomes your focus. It's as simple as that and as difficult.

For most companies, finding products, services, or ideas that have bright futures is not difficult. What is difficult is selecting the one concept to focus on. Most companies don't want to sacrifice. They'd rather have a handful of horses in the race to the future. It sounds right, but it doesn't work.

Let's say Silicon Graphics decided not to bet the future on 3-D. They might have also introduced a line of business workstations, engineering workstations, even office personal computers. So where would Silicon Graphics be today? Just another also-ran in the workstation market.

Again, it's a question of the short term versus the long term. In the short term, the extended line would probably have produced better results for Silicon Graphics. In the long term, the 3-D focus undoubtedly produced better results.

History repeats itself. One of the most significant repetitions, from the point of view of planning for the future, is the "next-generation" phenomenon. Aspirin gets replaced by acetaminophen, which gets replaced by ibuprofen. The eight-bit home computer gets replaced by the sixteen-bit office computer, which gets replaced by the thirty-two-bit computer. Is there any doubt the next generation will be the sixty-four-bit computer?

Some industries are so wrapped up with extending their own technologies into other areas they don't see the threat from the next generation. The cable television industry is so busy figuring out how to get in the telephone business and the video-on-demand business that they don't seem to see the threat from direct satellite systems like DirecTV.

7. A FOCUS IS INTERNAL AS MUCH AS EXTERNAL

While this book has primarily discussed strategies for developing an external focus, the focus needs to be turned around and applied internally as well. When you have a focus, you know what people to hire, what research to conduct, what products to introduce.

In a world where knowledge is rapidly expanding, a focus may be of particular help in the research and development area. No one company can hope to stay on top of technical developments in many different fields. An external focus can help direct a company's internal research and development as well as its management and marketing efforts.

An unfocused company tries to achieve balance. Each of several fully functional, independent operating divisions is treated as the equal of all the others. A company will often shift products, factories, and other operations in order to achieve "equality" or balance between its divisions.

Let's not let any of our employees feel that he or she is not on the front line. Management want everyone to have a stake in the company's success.

Texas Instruments invented the integrated circuit in 1958, yet the company has been a major disappointment for most of the decades since. Instead of focusing on semiconductors, TI tried to leverage its chip leadership into consumer electronics, personal computers, laptop computers, minicomputers, and software.

Most of its efforts have come to naught. The digital watch was a fiasco. The minicomputer business was folded. The home computer business was shut down with $600 million in write-offs. Currently, Texas Instruments is limping along in the notebook computer business.

What's driving the company, of course, is the chip business and the $700 million a year in royalties TI's semiconductor patents generate. What if TI had focused on semiconductors?

Compare Texas Instruments with Intel, a company focused on microprocessors. In the past decade Intel has been growing about 20 percent a year, TI about 5 percent. In the past decade Intel had $45 billion in sales and $8 billion in net income. TI had $68 billion in sales and less than $2 billion in net income.

A focused company puts its best people and most of its resources into the products or services that represent the future. While it may have to deal with products or services from its past, the focused company makes no bones about the fact that these are not in its future plans.

Focusing a company literally means moving from yesterday's products to tomorrow's products. In the short term there will be a need to handle yesterday's products in an efficient way. That should not, however, distract management from putting most of their attention on tomorrow's focus.

If nothing ever changed, a decentralized company would be more efficient and effective than a centralized company. There's no question that decentralization contributes to motivation and a sense of responsibility on the part of both the operating unit's management and employees. But how does a decentralized company develop a focus?

It doesn't. Decentralization removes top management's ability to point the company in one specific direction. And then to change that direction when conditions in the marketplace change. Decentralization is efficient, but inflexible.

Better to run an inefficient but centralized company with a powerful market-oriented focus. Employees would rather work for a winner than a loser, no matter how much motivation the loser's management provides.

Digital Equipment is the latest company to fall victim to decentralization's allure. Under a massive restructuring plan, the company has been reorganized into semiautonomous business units that will be able to set their own advertising, pricing, and marketing strategies. While Digital is decentralizing, it is watching its lead in sixty-four-bit workstations disappear.

Almost by definition, a decentralized company cannot have a focus or a corporate strategy. It can only serve as a center for accumulating financial results and disseminating them to investors and analysts. What the decentralized company misses the most is the opportunity to jump on and dominate the next-generation concept.

Take 3M, everybody's favorite decentralized company. While the company continues to churn out a host of "coatings" products (sixty-six thousand at last count), there seems to be a shortage of revolutionary new products that could carry the company to new levels of success. The last big winner was Post-it notes, a product introduced in 1980.

Sales at Minnesota Mining and Manufacturing are up 33 percent since 1988, but profits have been relatively flat.

Without a focus, 3M could easily miss a big idea hidden in its laboratories. In 1950, for example, 3M invented Thermofax copying and became the market leader in copy machines.

Why didn't 3M sponsor Chester Carlson's experiments in electrophotography? It would seem to be a natural. Maybe 3M figured that copy machines and paper were just one category out of thousands of products and they didn't want to put all their research eggs into one product basket.

Haloid, on the other hand, decided to focus on copy machines, a decision that resulted in the introduction of the 914 copier and the emergence of Xerox Corporation, which today is a larger company than 3M. While Xerox has had its own focusing problems, the success of the company in the copier business is a testament to what can be achieved with a narrow focus.

A corporation today is sitting on top of an expanding mountain of knowledge. Spreading the research dollars to cover all the technical angles is stretching the tent awfully thin.

Having a focus automatically concentrates those dollars into one area where they might produce results. It doesn't do much good to discover a marvelous new technology that your company doesn't have the resources, the people, or the perceptions to exploit.

Pundits fault Xerox for its failure to exploit its Palo Alto Research Center's personal computer discoveries. Perhaps the real mistake was pouring dollars into researching the wrong product.

How was Xerox going to organize itself into becoming a personal computer powerhouse? Where were the people and the resources going to come from? Perhaps it could have been done, but in doing so, Xerox would have needed a new focus.

Perhaps the research dollars should have been put into the laser printer, a product more in keeping with Xerox's copier background. Specifically, the company might have been better off putting their computer research dollars into a desktop version of the 9700, a mainframe laser printer introduced in 1977.

In retrospect it seems clear that Xerox threw away an early lead in laser printers and let Hewlett-Packard move in and dominate the category.

8. A FOCUS IS WHAT THE COUNTRY NEEDS

What's good for a company is also good for a country. Commentators complain every time an industry decides to pull up stakes and move to a foreign country. The latest is the television set, a product no longer made in America.

Why should everything we buy be manufactured in the United States? Wouldn't it make sense for countries to specialize? Wouldn't it make sense for each country to make only those products it had an affinity for?

This is exactly what a focus does for a company. It drives people and resources in the one product area where the company is most competitive.

Countries shouldn't fight the focusing process. Let competition dictate which countries make which products and services. Let's end all trade barriers, which only protect the inefficient producer and do nothing for the customer and, in the long run, nothing for the employee either.

There are great benefits when communities, cities, states, and countries find a focus. The United States dominates the world in products like commercial airplanes and computers. Japan does the same in automobiles and electronics. Germany in engineered products, France in wine and perfume, Switzerland in banking and watches, Italy in design and clothing, Russia in vodka and caviar.

When a country has a focus, it creates a powerful perception in the minds of customers around the world. Customers prefer American airplanes, Japanese automobiles, German engineered products, French wine, Swiss watches, Italian designs, Russian vodka. Are watches better because they are made in Switzerland? Does it matter? The real power of the focus lies in the mind of the customer.

A focus is self-reinforcing. People and services tend to gravitate to those places that have a focus.

Take Silicon Valley in northern California. As the area became famous for the emerging electronics industry, it attracted an infrastructure that helps maintain the Valley's leadership. Venture capitalists, lawyers, accountants, contract manufacturers, and other electronic specialists flocked to the area.

Take Branson, Missouri, which bills itself as the "music show capital of the world." Within a few miles of each other are over forty theaters featuring name entertainers like Bobby Vinton, Tony Orlando, Andy Williams, Glen Campbell, Anita Bryant, and the Osmonds.

Where one music theater might be hard-pressed to make ends

meet, forty music theaters are well and prospering. It's the power of a focus.

The same is true on one block of Forty-seventh Street in Manhattan between Fifth and Sixth Avenues. This is the heart of the diamond district in New York City. On this one block are 357 retail jewelry stores. Again the diamond district serves as a magnet for jewelry designers, engravers, repairers, polishers, platters, consultants, and other suppliers to the jewelry industry. That's the power of a focus.

You'll find similar areas in every city in the country. Used-car dealers, for example, instead of being spread out in every section of a city are often clustered along "automotive row." Where one dealer might have trouble surviving, a handful of dealers are prospering. That's the power of a focus.

Cities have done the same thing. With its central location and good weather, Memphis bills itself as "America's distribution center." Federal Express has its hub here. (The international airport is socked in by weather an average of only eight hours a year.) Trucks roll in and out of Memphis twenty-four hours a day because a large number of companies have located warehouses in America's distribution center.

What Memphis has done for trucks, Omaha is doing for the telephone. So many catalog companies, credit card servicing centers, and hotel reservation services are consolidating their 800-number operations in Omaha that the city is easily "America's toll-free capital." It is also the base of operations for three of the nation's five largest telemarketers.

The twin cities of Spartanburg and Greenville, South Carolina, have become a hub for foreign companies that want to set up U.S. manufacturing operations.

The fastest growing metropolitan area in the country is Las Vegas, Nevada. That's the power of a focus.

Yet both countries and communities keep looking for a balance of industries. What they should be trying to do is to "unbalance" their economies by establishing a focus.

For years New York City has bemoaned the loss of manufacturing jobs. With its inflated real estate and high taxes, should New York be a mecca for manufacturing? I think not. Better to establish a focus as the communications and financial capital of the world.

These are eight of the things a focus is. There are seven other things a focus is not. They include the following.

9. A FOCUS IS NOT A PRODUCT

The 914 copier was the most profitable single product ever produced by any American company. Yet Xerox was not focused on copiers. Xerox was focused on the "plain-paper" attribute of the 914 copier. Plain paper was the flag that led Xerox to its business success.

In the same way, Volvo is not focused on automobiles. Volvo is focused on "safety." BMW is focused not on automobiles but on "driving machines." Mercedes-Benz is focused on expensive, prestige motorcars.

Why doesn't a product focus work? The answer to this question lies in the nature of competition. If you had a monopoly, a product focus would be immensely profitable. You could design your product to appeal to all markets. But competition removes that opportunity.

Whatever position your product occupies in the mind, the competition does the opposite. If you make expensive products, the competition introduces cheap products. If you make cheap products, the competition introduces expensive models.

Big/small, light/dark, high-fashion/grunge, amateur/professional, there is no such thing as one type of product bought by everybody. There is always an opportunity to segment the market.

If the dominant leader tries to be "all things for everybody," the result is a loss of focus. What the leader must do is decide which aspect of the market to focus on. Then support that decision with pricing, packaging, and distribution that reinforces that focus.

If you're not willing to walk away from a segment of your business, then you don't have a focus.

10. A FOCUS IS NOT AN UMBRELLA

Some companies think they have a found a focus when they have established a uniform theme to hang on all their products. According to chief executive Robert Allen, "AT&T is fundamentally a networking company. We bring people, information, and services together, all in the name of time-based competitive advantage."

That might surprise most of AT&T's customers who consider the company to be fundamentally a supplier of long-distance telephone service.

Unisys has been spending a lot of money in an attempt to become an "information management" company. Yet most customers probably consider Unisys to be a computer company. What is an information management company? Is that a library?

What AT&T and Unisys have found is an umbrella. They believe in the idea that a company can find a focus or a vision by inventing a grandiose concept that can cover all of a company's products and services.

In their desire to find the "big idea" to cover everything, corporate executives often move one level up the abstraction ladder. Sure, "information management" covers everything, but it doesn't mean anything.

A powerful focus, by its nature, doesn't cover everything. A focus is a point of attack that may encompass only a small percentage of a company's products or services. A focus should cover only that aspect of your business that represents the future.

At any point in time, a company has three kinds of products: (1) yesterday's products, which are candidates for disposal; (2) today's products, which are producing the bulk of the company's profits; and (3) tomorrow's products, which are the company's future. A focus is the bridge that takes the company from today to tomorrow.

What you focus on, what you sell, and what you make money on might be three different things. Lotus was focused on groupware, but most of their sales were spreadsheets and personal computer software. They only made money, however, on Lotus 1-2-3, their pioneering spreadsheet product.

In one sense of the word, every company is unfocused. (In the same sense that every closet is unfocused.) This has to be true because of the changing nature of life itself. Nothing stays still long enough for a company to be perfectly focused.

The objective of a focus should be to lead the company in a coherent direction. It could be called leadership by idea rather than leadership by force of personality.

11. A FOCUS DOES NOT APPEAL TO EVERYBODY

No one product or service can appeal to everybody. There are always people who want to be different, who want to choose something that the majority does not want. This is true in clothing, in hair styles, in lifestyles, in products, in services.

The attempt to appeal to everybody is the biggest single mistake a business can make. Better to stake out your own ground and write off everyone else.

Take the presidential elections in the United States. Starting in 1824, when the popular vote had a direct influence on the electoral vote, no presidential candidate ever received more than 61.1 percent of the national vote.

Not Abraham Lincoln (55.1 percent) or Franklin Roosevelt (60.8 percent), two of the most popular presidents of all time.

In forty-three national elections, the presidential candidate who received the highest percentage of the popular vote was Lyndon Johnson in 1964. One reason Johnson did so well was that his opponent in the election was Barry Goldwater, one of the weakest candidates in recent years.

What's true of presidents is also true of products. Very rarely does a single manufacturer capture more than 50 percent of a market. And you're more likely to achieve a large share of a market when you have a narrow focus.

When you attempt to have a broad focus, you wind up with a small share of the market. What politician, for example, would try to appeal to everyone? Yet companies routinely try to do this.

What about the perceived need to increase sales? How does a company grow except by broadening its appeal?

One way is to go global. There's hardly a product or service successfully sold in the United States that doesn't have a potential market overseas. It's much better to be narrowly focused globally than broadly focused domestically.

In a world of big thinkers, it's sometimes hard to sell a narrow-minded approach. Why can't we appeal to everybody? (Obviously you can, but it doesn't work.)

A little reductio-ad-absurdum thinking will also demonstrate the ultimate absurdity of trying to appeal to everyone. There are 150,000 businesses in America with over a hundred employees. What if every business tried to get into every market? And, within each market, tried to appeal to everyone? No one would be very strong anywhere.

12. A FOCUS IS NOT HARD TO FIND

A large organization with more than twenty thousand employees decided to search for a focus. As the first step, a committee with more than a dozen members was appointed with instructions to report back to the chief executive after they had developed the new strategy.

A focus is not hard to find, but it was certain to get lost in the crowd. A committee by definition can't find a simple idea. A committee can only build something complex. (The larger the committee, the longer it takes and the more complex the report.)

When found, a focus will be simple. If you're looking for a simple idea, you can't have a complex search procedure.

(In our consulting work we are often asked about the details of the process used to generate a focusing strategy. The process is not very complicated. "We think about the problem and then we tell you what you should do.")

A good way to generate an effective focusing strategy is to put two people in a room and ask them to come up with an answer to the problem. Two people are ideal: one to think, the other to evaluate.

Naturally the thinking and evaluating roles will switch back and forth.

13. A FOCUS IS NOT INSTANTLY SUCCESSFUL

In the short term, narrowing the focus will cost you business. Fewer people will want to buy your product or service. Or you might lose sales by dropping products or services. A powerful focus is almost never effective in the short term.

If this were not true, then every company would be enormously successful. All you would need to do is to try a number of different approaches. If it works, keep doing it; if it doesn't work, try something else. Sooner or later your company would have established a powerful upward momentum.

It's not true. What tends to work in the short term doesn't tend to work in the long term. A company run by chasing success is a company ultimately headed for failure. You need to have the courage to make a focusing decision and then wait for the market to react to your move. It won't happen overnight.

Ford Motor Company tried a safety approach for one year and then abandoned the concept. "Safety doesn't sell" became a watchword in Detroit. Volvo, on the other hand, used exactly the same focus as Ford. The difference is, Volvo didn't abandon the safety ship after the first year. They kept at it, for thirty years in a row.

You have to have patience. It takes a long time to turn a battleship around in a river.

14. A FOCUS IS NOT A STRATEGY

General Motors had a strategy. They wanted to become a full-line transportation company. Hence the acquisition of Hughes Aircraft.

A strategy, as defined by most companies, doesn't put much restraint on their activities. At GM, for example, anything that flies, rolls, or slides would fit into a transportation strategy.

IBM has a computer strategy. Anything involving computers (hardware, software, networks, communication) fits into IBM's strategy, including the acquisition of a software company like Lotus Development Corp. A strategy assumes a company can obtain 100 percent of a market. Since this is impossible, any strategy is doomed to failure.

A focus implies a "narrowing" of the business with the intent to dominate a segment. There's power when you can "own" a market. There's no power when you are a bit player.

15. A FOCUS IS NOT FOREVER

Sooner or later even the most powerful focus becomes obsolete. That's when a company must refocus itself.

On the other hand, a focus is not a fashion that ought be changed every few years. The time frame is more like decades rather than years. Then, too, it depends on the industry. Rapidly changing high-technology industries will wear out a focus much faster than low-technology industries will.

Digital Equipment had a focus, "minicomputers," which made the company the second largest computer company in the world. But the market turned to personal computers. Digital couldn't find a way to cross the trench.

IBM had a focus, "mainframes," which made the company the most powerful and admired corporation in the world. But the market divided. IBM's answer to the segmenting of the computer market was to be all things to everybody. It didn't work.

Eastman Kodak had a focus, "photography," which allowed the company to dominate the photography business worldwide. But today the world is turning electronic, and Kodak needs to find a way across the trench.

Federal Express had a focus, "overnight delivery," which revolutionized the air cargo business and made founder Fred Smith a wealthy man. But today the air cargo business has gone global and Federal Express needs a new focus.

What about your company? Are you still living with yesterday's strategies? The future belongs to those companies that develop a powerful focus today.

Focus. The future of your company depends on it.

INDEX